Europe and the Environment

Europa Law Publishing, Groningen 2004

Europe and the Environment

Legal Essays in Honour of Ludwig Krämer

Edited by Marco Onida

Europa Law Publishing is a publishing company specializing in European Union Law.
For further information please contact Europa Law Publishing via email: info@europalawpublishing.com or visit our website at: www.europalawpublishing.com.

Typeset in Scala and Scala Sans, Graphic design by G2K Designers, Groningen/Amsterdam

NUR 828; ISBN 90-76871-23-x

British Library Cataloguing-in-Publication Data
A catalogue record for this book is available from the British Library

Preface

A Community policy on environment was not in the mind of the founders of the European Communities. But it did not take long before the need emerged to take action at Community level in order to protect the environment. In October 1972, the first summit conference of the Heads of State and Government of the – for the first time – enlarged Community took the view that economic expansion is not an end in itself and that it should, among other things, result in an improvement in the quality of life as well as in standards of living. *"As befits the genius of Europe"*, it was stated, *"particular attention will be given to intangible values and to protecting the environment, so that progress may really be put at the service of mankind"*.

Shortly afterwards, in April 1973, the Commission forwarded to the Council its proposal for a Draft Council Resolution on a Community environmental programme. After a period of rich legislative activity – but during which the Community's environmental role had still not received full explicit recognition – a chapter on environment was finally inserted in the Treaty by the Single European Act in 1987. The objective of preserving, protecting and improving the quality of the environment was made explicit among the actions of the Community. At this time, a principle was also introduced in the Treaty that environmental protection needs must form part of the other Community policies.

Some years later, with the Maastricht Treaty, this integration clause was moved to Article 6, in the chapter dedicated to the basic principles of the European Community. Today, almost fifty years from the foundation of the European Communities, rules on environmental protection in the Member States to a large extent find their origin in Community measures. Since the foundation of the EC, significant improvements have been made in the state of the environment. Much remains to be done, and, despite the arguments which are inevitable in advancing any ambitious environmental policy, it is essential that measures that are environmentally sustainable in the long-term continue to be promoted and developed.

Ludwig Krämer has personally witnessed the above developments. He now leaves the Commission, after some thirty years dedicated to environmental issues. During this time, with his distinguished and learned publications, Ludwig Krämer has added substantially to knowledge of EC environmental law beyond the European institutions. He has contributed greatly to the development of EC environmental law, as is confirmed by his colleagues, who have decided to express their gratitude on the occasion of his retirement by producing this *liber amicorum*.

Communication, in all its meanings, is one of the pillars on which good governance is based. I therefore welcome this book and I trust that this collection of essays "from the inside" will make interested citizens feel closer to the European Commission.

Brussels, 9 July 2004

Romano Prodi, President of the European Commission

Table of Contents

CHAPTER 5 **Prevention and Control of Industrial Emissions; An Overview of EC Rules and Their Specific Impact on Emissions**
Alexandre Paquot

CHAPTER 6 **Environmental Protection by Product Policy; Focus on Dangerous Substances**
Marco Onida

CHAPTER I

Access to Justice in Environmental Matters

A Fundamental Democratic Right

Birgit Dette[1]

1 Introduction[2]

'A milestone in strengthening democracy in environmental policy-making'[3] – that is how on October 24, 2003 the European Commission presented several legislative proposals in order to pave the way for the ratification of the *UNECE Convention on Access to Information, Public Participation in Decision-making and Access to Justice in Environmental Matters* (Aarhus Convention). The 'proposal package' consists of three different legislative instruments that will empower citizens and associations to 'assume responsibility for the environment' after its entry into force planned for January 2005: *Proposal for a Council Decision on the conclusion, on behalf of the European Community, of the Aarhus Convention,*[4] *Proposal for a Regulation of the European Parliament and of the Council on the application of the Aarhus Convention to EC institutions and bodies,*[5] *Proposal for a Directive of the European Parliament and of the Council on access to justice in environmental matters.*[6]

Long before the signing of the Aarhus Convention the discussion on the democratisation of environmental rights and on access to justice had started on European level thanks to Ludwig Krämer. In numerous publications and on many occasions Ludwig Krämer heightened the importance of public participation and access to justice for the enforcement of environmental law.[7] It is truly characteristic of Ludwig Krämer's work that he has engaged in environmental law not only in theory but also in practical terms. This is true for a number of environmental areas including access to justice. It is therefore not surprising that the 'proposal package' was elaborated under Ludwig Krämer's guidance.

Against the background of the 'proposal package' the following article will discuss the importance of access to justice in environmental matters (hereinafter referred to as *ajem*)[8] in our democratic society (2), outline the present legal situation of *ajem* at international level, at EC level and at Member State level (3).

---

1 Official of the Ministry of Environment, Rural Development and Consumer Protection of the Land of Hesse/Germany; former national expert at the Environment Directorate-General of the European Commission. The opinions contained in this article are strictly personal.

2 The present article is based on developments until end of January 2004.

3 *Environment Daily* Issue 1540, Tuesday 28 October 2003.

4 COM (2003) 625 final.

5 COM (2003) 622 final.

6 COM (2003) 624 final.

7 Krämer (2003c) 271; (2002e) 257; (2002b) 283; (2000b) 265; (2002f); (2000a) 144; (1999b) 1; (1997b); (1996a) 1; (1995); (1991) 129.

8 For the purpose of this article 'access to justice in environmental matters' is referred to as *ajem. Ajem* is to be understood as access to judicial as well as non-judicial proceedings before an independent and impartial body established by law. 'Legal standing' or *'locus standi'* describes the ability of any natural or legal person to bring a case to a review body or a court.

From that starting point the article will reflect upon recent developments and changes initiated at EC level by the 'proposal package' (4) and finally come to conclusions as regards adequate access to justice in the interests of environmental protection (5).

2 The democratic society as origin of access to justice in environmental matters

A democratic society, whether national or European, needs the participation of its citizens. Established democratic rights, such as the right to vote, form the basis of such participation. However, democracy needs and provides for further forms of participation such as participation in administrative procedures or access to justice. The right of citizens to review the exercise of public power is ultimately the foundation of both the principle of democracy and popular sovereignity.[9] Access to justice therefore is an essential instrument in a democratic society for the citizens to effectively confront violations of law and ensure its enforcement. This is even truer when breaches of environmental law are at stake, since the environment can not defend itself and needs an interest defender in order to challenge impairments of environmental law in court.[10] *Ajem* therefore means giving the environment a voice not only when private interests are at stake but also independently of individual interests when the environment itself is harmed or due to be harmed.

A healthy environment – often referred to as 'our common heritage' – has crucial importance for the well-being of present as well as future generations, but also for the flora and fauna as such. In view of its importance on the one hand and the democratic right of access to justice on the other hand, it seems obvious that members of the public should have the right to defend in court the environment as one of the most precious assets of humankind. Allowing citizens or non-governmental organisations to defend the public interest in a healthy environment would reflect the ongoing democratisation of modern pluralistic political systems.[11] There is no doubt that whenever an individual right of a citizen is violated, be it a civil or a public right, citizens can institute proceedings in order to defend their individual rights and ensure the implementation of law. Until now, the concept of a healthy environment in general is not linked to a corresponding direct individual right to a healthy environment that can be enforced in court.[12] Thus, the environment still has no legal defender of its interests. Therefore, often, breaches of environmental law are not adequately

---

9 Ragnemalm (2000) 19.

10 Krämer (1999b) 9.

11 Rehbinder & Loperena (2001) 286.

12 Krämer (1999b) 5; Ebbesson (2002) 22.

prosecuted. This results in shortcomings in the enforcement of environmental law at local, national, European as well as international level that have been pointed out for years.[13] The Commission acknowledged these shortcomings and repeatedly stressed the importance of public involvement in the enforcement of environmental law.[14] As a consequence, the EU Council[15] and Parliament[16] have suggested and called for the Commission to take legislative initiative for a directive on *ajem*.

The recently issued 'proposal package' is based on the idea of giving certain members of the public *ajem* in specific cases without them having to show the impairment of an individual right or interest. Once adopted, these legislative instruments will contribute to the enforcement of environmental law and thus to a better environmental protection.

3 Access to justice in environmental matters at international, European and national level

3.1 Present situation at international level – the Aarhus Convention

A new dimension of *ajem* took its starting point on the occasion of the 4th pan-European conference of Ministers for the Environment on June 25, 1998, when 35 states as well as the EC signed in the Danish City of Aarhus the Convention on Access to Information, Public Participation in Decision-making and Access to Justice in Environmental Matters.[17] As stated by the United Nations General-Secretary Kofi-Annan this Convention is 'the most ambitious venture in environmental democracy undertaken under the auspices of the United Nations'.[18]

---

[13] European Commission, Implementing Community environmental law – Communication to the Council and the European Parliament, COM (96) 500 final; First annual survey on the implementation and enforcement of Community environmental law SEC (1999) 592; Second annual survey on the implementation of Community environmental law SEC (2000) 1219; European Court of Auditors Special report No 3/92 concerning the environment, OJ 1992 C 245/1; Lübbe-Wolff (1996) 1; Wegener (1998) 1. Scheuing (1999) 475.

[14] See 5th EAP COM (92) 23 final/84; 6th EAP COM (2001) 31 final/14; Implementing Community environmental law – Communication to the Council and the European Parliament, COM (96) 500 final/14; European Commission White Paper on European Governance OJ 2001 C 287/1.

[15] Council Resolution of 7.10.1997 on the Drafting, Implementation and Enforcement of Community Environmental Law OJ 1997 C 321/1.

[16] Resolution on a communication of the Commission on implementing Community environmental law, OJ 1997 C 167/92.

[17] See for the text of the Convention http://www.unece.org/env/pp/.

[18] UN-ECE, Implementation Guide of the Aarhus Convention, Foreword, see www.unece.org/env/pp/acig.htm.

So far, 27 States have ratified the Aarhus Convention.[19] Eastern States in particular opted for ratification in order to strengthen their democratic and constitutional orders. Seven out of ten of the Accession Countries have already ratified the Convention.[20] The EU and its Member States, however, are still reluctant to ratify.[21] Even after signing, they are afraid of directly granting rights to individuals in environmental matters.

The Aarhus Convention gives the public different rights that are divided into three 'pillars'.[22] The first pillar grants the right of access to environmental information, the second pillar bestows the right to participate in decision-making processes and the third pillar aims to ensure access to justice for the public. This is the first international convention to recognise that the protection of nature and environment can only be achieved through involvement of all stakeholders.[23] Whereas most multilateral environmental agreements cover obligations that Parties have to each other,[24] the Aarhus Convention covers obligations the Parties have to the public.[25] In addition, the Convention establishes international minimum standards in order to ensure application of these rights in practice. The Convention thereby goes far beyond existing international instruments for the protection of the environment. It is consequently not only a milestone in strengthening democratic and constitutional principles in environmental matters, but will hopefully also have impact on the democratisation of other fields of law.

The access to justice pillar of the Aarhus Convention has two major objectives: Firstly, it ensures the consistent and effective implementation of the Convention's access to information rights, Article 9(1) and public participation rights, Article 9(2).[26] Secondly – and this is the major innovation – it contains in Article 9(3) a provision on the enforcement of law relating to the environment in general.[27] Article 9(3) reads as follows: *'Each Party shall ensure that, where they meet the criteria, if any, laid down in its national law, members of the public have*

---

[19] By 17 February 2004, 40 states and the EC had signed and 27 of these had ratified the Convention, important exceptions being the U.S. and Russia – see http://www.unece.org/env/pp/ratification.htm.

[20] Cyprus, Estonia, Hungary, Latvia, Lithuania, Malta and Poland – see http://www.unece.org/env/pp/ratification.htm.

[21] So far, only six out of fifteen have ratified the Convention – Belgium, Denmark, France, Italy, Norway and Portugal – see http://www.unece.org/env/pp/ratification.htm.

[22] Article 1 of the Aarhus Convention refers to the term 'right'. Although this term is not further used in other Articles of the Convention, the objective, structure and context of the Convention are rights-oriented; see J. Ebbesson (2002) 12.

[23] UN-ECE see note 17 above.

[24] Rehbinder & Loperena (2001) 283.

[25] See *supra* footnote 23.

[26] Articles without further specification refer to the Aarhus Convention.

[27] Zschiesche (2002) 2; Brady (1998) 72.

access to administrative or judicial procedures to challenge acts and omissions by private persons or public authorities, which contravene provisions of its national law relating to the environment'.

The great importance of Article 9(3) is that it enables members of the public, including individuals and environmental organisations, to invoke the power of law when environmental law has been violated. By that, it aims to overcome the fact that the environment has no legal interest defender.

The difficult negotiations on Article 9(3) and the discussion on its scope[28] show the importance of this provision. The wording as it now stands became more vague during the last negotiation rounds. It was weakened by making reference to national law.[29] The discussion on the interpretation of Article 9(3) has been clarified by the recent 'proposal package' issued by the European Commission.[30] The proposal package is based on the fact that Article 9(3) creates obligations on the Parties and that a different interpretation would not be not in line with the spirit of the Aarhus Convention and therefore would undermine its general obligation to give the public a wide access to justice.[31] This interpretation by the European Commission is an important step forward to make operational the access to justice provisions of the Convention.

Further provisions of the Convention deserve consideration. According to Article 9(4) 'review procedures shall provide adequate and effective remedies, including injunctive relief as appropriate, and be fair, equitable, timely and not prohibitively expensive'. Article 9(5) requires the Parties 'to ensure, that information is provided to the public on access to administrative and judicial review procedures and to consider the establishment of appropriate assistance mechanisms to remove or reduce financial and other barriers to access to justice'. These provisions are of practical importance for an effective *ajem* and compliance with these provisions will prove demanding for the Parties.

3.2 Present situation in the European Union

In the EU legal framework *ajem* encompasses different dimensions, such as standing before the European Court of Justice (hereafter: the ECJ) with regard to EC acts and omissions (EC level) and standing rights in the Member States before national courts with regard to national acts and omissions (Member State level).

---

28 Task force on access to justice – see http://www.unece.org/env/pp/a.to.j.htm; Dross (2004).

29 Zschiesche (2000) 28.

30 The reference to national criteria has been discussed controversially with view to the obligations created by that provision. Interpretations differ from the standpoint that the Parties would have a considerable discretion to define limiting criteria for standing and would de facto have no real obligations to improve standing to the standpoint that an action popularis should be introduced. See *e.g.* Lee and Abbot (2003) 105; Epiney (2003) 179.

31 Ebbesson (2002) 24.

3.2.1 The EC level

The EC Treaty contains no specific provisions on *ajem*. There is no special environmental court. *Ajem* therefore follows the general provisions on access to the European Court of Justice under the EC Treaty. The ability of members of the public, including environmental associations, to initiate proceedings in environmental matters is limited by the scope of Article 230(4) EC[32] which provides that any natural or legal person – which would include an environmental organisation – may only institute proceedings directly against a Community institution if the person is the addressee of the institution's decision or if the decision is of direct and individual concern to the person.[33] In almost no environmental decisions taken by Community institutions are citizens or environmental organisations the addressee of the decision. Thus they have to prove that they are directly and individually concerned by a decision by resorting to the second alternative provided by Article 230(4) EC. As will be shown, this proves almost impossible in environmental matters due to ECJ adjudication on standing.

In a series of decisions the ECJ has held that persons are to be considered 'individually concerned' by a decision if it 'affects them by reason of certain attributes which are peculiar to them or by reason of circumstances in which they are differentiated from all other persons and by virtue of these factors distinguishes them individually just as in the case of the person addressed'.[34] This ECJ adjudication has been criticised[35] because it requires the identifica-

---

[32] So far in environmental matters no case has been submitted to the ECJ under Article 232(3) EC. The present discussion will therefore focus on Article 230(4) EC.
On restrictions upon members of the public to bring an action to the ECJ under other provisions of the EC Treaty, such as Article 234 EC or Article 226 EC, see Krämer (2003) 278 and (1996) 3, 9 and 16; Hanf (2003) 275; Usher (2003) 586; Ragolle (2003) 90; Somsen (2000) 311; see also footnote 39, para 47 and footnote 41, para 49.

[33] For the context of this paper, cases concerning the review of decisions by the European Institutions are of interest and will be further discussed. See on the different categories of cases brought to the European judiciary, such as cases concerning the legality of environmental directives and regulations or cases concerning decisions by the European Institutions; Krämer, (1996a) 6; Godt (2000) 79; Ebbesson (2002) 75.

[34] Case 25/62 *Plaumann* v. *Commission* [1963] ECR, p. 95; Case T-2/93, *Air France* v. *Commission* [1994] ECR II-323; Case T-465/93 *Consorzio Gruppo di Azione Locale 'Murgia Messapica'* v. *Commission* [1994] ECR II-361; Case T-585/93 *Stichting Greenpeace Council* v. *Commission* [1995] ECR II-2205; Case C-321/95 P *Stichting Greenpeace Council* v. *Commission* [1998] ECR I-1651; see for further adjudication in environmental cases Krämer (2002f) 464 and (1996a) 5.

[35] Hanf (2003) 274; Krämer (2002f) 465 and (1996a) 16; Ebbesson (2002) 80; Schwarze (2002) 1309; Arnull, (2001) 7; Schikhof (1998) 279; Allkemper (1995) 1; Peel http://www.globalpolicy.org/ngos/role/globdem/globgov/2001/peel-wto.htm./2.

tion of a 'closed class' of affected individuals in order to invoke the criterion of 'direct and individual concern' and allow access to the ECJ. It was set out in the 1960s with a view to individual interests of producers and before environmental matters became a concern in the European Union. Although it was not intended to be applied to environmental interests it has been since then and is still applied in cases where public interests such as the protection of the environment are at stake.[36]

Where an interest such as the environment is concerned, the problem with this definition is obvious. By its very nature the environment concerns the many rather than the few, and only in extremely rare circumstances would an environmental problem affect an individual in a manner that singles him out from all other individuals.[37] In fact, under the Court's interpretation the more people are harmed by a violation, the less they have access to the court. The limited scope as regards standing of the general public was made clear in a case brought by *Greenpeace* to the ECJ, where the environmental organisation was not allowed to bring the substance of the Commission's alleged infringements to the Court's attention because *Greenpeace* was not considered to be affected by the violation in a manner that distinguished it from all other persons.[38]

However recently there was some hope that a shift of thinking could take place. In its ruling in *Jégo-Quéré* v. *Commission*[39] the Court of First Instance (CFI) significantly enhanced the possibilities for a direct action against Community acts of a general legislative nature. Conscious of the need to ensure effective protection of the legal rights of private parties it redefined the notion of 'individually concerned' by departing from the 'closed-class' interpretation and regarding a person as individually concerned 'if the measure affects his legal position in a manner which is both definite and immediate, by restricting his rights or imposing obligations on him'.[40] It was in fact Advocate General Jacobs who first called for a broader interpretation of Article 230(4) EC in his Opinion in the case of *Unión de Pequeños Agricultores* v. *Council*[41] and who encouraged the revolutionary judgement of the CFI in *José-Quéré*.[42] However the CFI and Advocate

[36] Gale (1997) 134.

[37] WWF, EEB, FoEE, et al., Greening the Treaty II – Institutional Reform, Citizens' Rights and Sustainable Development – Proposals for the 2000 Intergovernmental Conference; Stotz in Rengeling (2003), Vol.I, 45.C.III/99.

[38] T-585/93 *Stichting Greenpeace Council* v. *Commission* [1995] ECR II-2205; C-321/95 *Stichting Greenpeace Council* v. *Commission* [1998] ECR I-1651; Krämer (2002f) 457.

[39] Case T-177/01 [2002] ECR II-2365.

[40] *Idem*, para 51.

[41] Opinion in Case C-50/00 P [2002] ECR I-6677; [2002] 3 C.M.L.R. 1 delivered on March 21,2002, para 103.

[42] See for further details of the recent development of European adjudication *e.g.* Ragolle (2003) 101; Usher, 575; Köngeter (2003) 130; Hanf (2003) 276.

General Jacobs were overruled by the ECJ which in its judgement in the case of *Unión de Pequeños Agricultores* v. *Council* reconfirmed the established case-law.[43]

In sum, the ECJ has not interpreted the requirements for access to justice in such a way that collective interests such as the environment can be well defended and that no enforcement gap exists at EC level.[44] Additionally, the current interpretation of Article 230(4) EC is considered not to be in line with Article 9(3). It also does not correspond to the Community's political commitment to broaden *ajem* by signing the Aarhus Convention.

There was some hope that access to justice would gain a new dimension through the Draft Treaty establishing a Constitution for Europe, presented on 18 July 2003 by the European Convention. However, the Draft Treaty basically takes up in its Article III-270(4) the provisions of Article 230(4) EC on access to justice for natural or legal persons. Thus, on the basis of the Draft Treaty, there will be no fundamental shift towards better *ajem*.[45]

3.2.2 The Member State level

Due to the different legal history and legal culture, the various legal systems of Member States evolved during many decades and currently exhibit considerable differences.[46] These differences concern *e.g.* legal standing, the type of review proceedings, namely whether they focus on administrative or judicial review and whether they include civil or penal law actions, as well as the duration of such proceedings.[47] Differences can also be found as regards the scope of review or the costs of instituting actions, such as court fees, attorney rates, expert testimony or financial securities, which may be prohibitively expensive and thereby create a barrier to the use of standing rights. It would go

---

[43] Case C-50/00 P [2002] ECR I-6677; [2002] 3 C.M.L.R. 1.

[44] Krämer (2002f) 465 and (1996) 16.

[45] In contrast to Article 230(4) EC, the wording of Article III-270(4) of the Draft Treaty establishing a Constitution for Europe gives the possibility for natural or legal persons to 'institute proceedings against an act addressed to that person or which is of direct and individual concern to him or her, and against a regulatory act which is of direct concern to him or her and does not entail implementing measures'. According to Article 32(1) of the Draft Treaty 'a European regulation shall be a non-legislative act of general application for the implementation of legislative acts and of certain specific provisions of the Constitution'. With view to this definition of 'regulation' the additional value of Article III-270(4) of the Draft Treaty will be limited – see Köngeter (2003) 130.

[46] See for the legal situation in the Member States different studies undertaken in recent years: de Sadeleer, Roller, Dross (2003) 1– see http://europa.eu.int/comm/environment/aarhus/pdf/accesstojustice_final.pdf; Ebbesson (2002) 1; Epiney, Sollberger (2002) 1; Kroiss (2001) 87; Verschureen et al. (2000) 1; Prieur (1998) 1; Deimann, Dyssli (1995) 1; Führ, Omond, Gebers, Roller (1992) 1; Winkelmann (1992) 1; Führ, Roller (1991) 1.

[47] There are only few appeal procedures at Member State level specifically relating to the environment, for example in Austria and Denmark, see *supra* footnote 46.

beyond this article to describe the details of all 15 different Member State systems. However, one of the most controversial aspects and also one of the major hurdles as regards *ajem* – legal standing – shall be outlined as it is considered substantial for the ongoing developments as regards *ajem* in the context of implementing Article 9(3) of the Aarhus Convention.

Member State approaches differ as a result of the general requirements to guarantee standing under the respective legal order. They range from an extensive approach where standing is broadly recognised by way of an *'actio popularis'*, to a very restrictive approach allowing standing only in cases where the impairment of an individual legally granted right can be shown. In an intermediate approach, standing can be attained by demonstrating a sufficient interest in the case.[48]

Member States allowing for an *actio popularis* in environmental matters have thereby acknowledged the possibility to institute an administrative or a judicial proceeding in the interest of the environment without having to show a private interest or the impairment of a private right, because the protection of the environment is thought to be of private interest per se. This approach is followed in Portugal and in a differentiated form also in the Netherlands, in Greece and in Ireland.[49] Looking at the accession countries, Poland has a broad access to justice in environmental matters coming close to standing in the form of an *actio popularis*.[50]

The opposite of this broad approach are legal systems which limit legal standing for individuals or environmental organisations to cases where they can demonstrate the impairment of an individually granted legal right. These systems are focussed on the protection of individual rights and not on the protection of collective interests such as the protection of the environment. Environmental interest groups in general cannot show a private interest in the case, because in general it is not their private property or financial assets that have been harmed, but the environment as such. This restrictive approach is followed in Germany,[51] in a lesser form in Italy and to some extent in Denmark.[52]

Finally, other Member States[53] have chosen an intermediate approach, granting standing to individuals and environmental organisations where they can show a sufficient interest in the case.[54] Standing in these Member States

---

48 De Sadeleer, Roller, Dross (2003) 28.

49 See *supra* footnote 46.

50 Jendroska (2002) 1.

51 This restrictive approach was loosened by introducing the possibility for environmental associations to institute under certain conditions proceedings in environmental matters, see Rehbinder in Ebbesson (2002) 248 and 250; Kroiss, (2001) 90; Ormond in Führ, Roller (1991). 77; Dross (2004).

52 However, in practice these systems are coming close to the intermediate approach, see Epiney & Sollberger (2002) 300.

53 Such as France, Belgium, Spain, UK, Sweden, *supra* footnote 46.

54 Ebbesson (2002) 25; Dross (2004).

depends to a large extent on the interpretation of the sufficient interest by the judiciary.[55]

Most Member State systems make some specific provisions for environmental organisations as regards standing, because such organisations are acting in the public interest.[56] However, the opportunities for environmental associations to involve themselves in legal procedures differ considerably between EU Member States.[57] In most jurisdictions criteria for standing of environmental organisations draw on the general principles of the respective jurisdiction, with some additional requirements, such as acting on a non-profit basis or making reference to the organisation's structure or statutes. These requirements often need to be demonstrated through some kind of registration of the organisation.[58]

A well known argument by Member States against broader *ajem* is a supposed overload of the court systems. However, even in Member States which provide for broad legal standing as a matter of legal principle, an overburdening of the courts or other independent and impartial bodies has not been found.[59] This has been demonstrated by a recent study based on empirical data.[60] Experience shows that non-governmental organisations make careful use of their right of access to justice, as any proceeding is costly and time-consuming.[61] The actual number of actions brought by non-governmental organisations is thus rather limited. The absolute number of cases in environmental matters in relation to the overall number of administrative proceedings is negligible.[62] Once a non-governmental organisation decides to institute a proceeding this is generally based on sound reasoning. Therefore, in comparison to other litigation, their complaints and court actions are over-proportionally successful[63] and thereby contribute to a better enforcement of environmental law.[64] The experience gained in practice with legal standing for environmental non-governmental organisations shows that this instrument can enhance respect for and implementation of environmental law. It thus helps administrations to fulfil their obligations of practical application and enforcement of environmental law.[65]

---

55 Epiney & Sollberger (2002) 100.

56 Whether or not the different Member States are in line with Article 9(3) of the Aarhus Convention has to be assessed on a case by case basis and goes beyond the scope of this article.

57 Ebbesson (2002) 29.

58 *E.g.* France, Italy, Luxemburg, Germany, Sweden; Ebbesson (2002) 30 and 33.

59 De Sadeleer, Roller, Dross (2003) 10; Busson (2001) 59.

60 De Sadeleer, Roller, Dross (2003) 10.

61 *Idem* p. 40.; see in general for the role of Environmental NGOs: Newell & Grant (2000) 225.

62 *Idem*, p. 9 and 42.

63 *Idem*, p. 12 and 42.

64 See references in footnote 46; Blume, Schmidt, Zschiesche (2001) 1; BUWAL (2000); Epiney (1999) 485.

65 *Idem*.

However, due to the different approaches there are so far no uniform standards as regards *ajem* throughout the Member States. This produces a disparate level of enforcement of environmental law, which shall be remedied by the recent proposal for a Directive on access to justice in environmental matters.[66]

4 Recent developments at European level – the 'proposal package'

The genesis of the 'proposal package' started long before the signing of the Aarhus Convention. Thanks to Ludwig Krämer, discussions within the Environment Directorate-General of the European Commission on *ajem* became more concrete in the early nineties. In 1992, under Ludwig Krämer's direction, a study on Access to Justice including a draft proposal for an EC Directive on *ajem* was carried out.[67] In the same year, preparation for a proposal on *ajem* was on the Working Programme of the Commission. Building upon this groundwork, a first preliminary draft proposal for a Directive on access to justice was elaborated within the Environment DG in September 1992. At the beginning of 1993 the Commission decided to establish a working group on access to justice in order to launch a communication on that theme. However, the Commission never carried these initiatives through, so that until the late nineties there was no further progress.

After the EC had signed the Aarhus Convention on June 25, 1998, access to justice again came on the agenda of European environmental policy. By signing the Aarhus Convention, the EU acknowledged its objectives in the international arena and politically obliged itself to implement it. Due to this signature and in order not to loose its credibility, the European Union is now under a strong commitment: Not only to go ahead with the implementation of *ajem* at Member State level but also with regard to its own institutions. The 'proposal package' presented recently is an important step to fulfil this two-fold obligation in implementing the Aarhus Convention.

4.1 Proposal for a Regulation implementing the Aarhus Convention with respect to the EC institutions

With respect to the Community's own institutions, implementation of the Aarhus Convention will be realized through the *proposed Regulation on applying the Provisions of the Aarhus Convention to the EC Institutions.*[68] This

---

[66] See 4.2.1.

[67] Führ, Ormond, Gebers, Roller (1992); Öko-Institut (1994) 261.

[68] Proposal for a Regulation of the European Parliament and of the Council on the application of the provisions of the Aarhus Convention on Access to Information, Public Participation in Decision making and Access to Justice in Environmental Matters to EC Institutions and Bodies, COM (2003) 622 final.

proposal for a Regulation covers all three pillars of the Aarhus Convention as had been pointed out by the working document issued by DG Environment in September 2002.[69]

As mentioned before,[70] due to ECJ adjudication on Article 230(4) second alternative of the EC Treaty, environmentally committed citizens and environmental associations wanting to institute proceedings in the interest of the environment generally cannot prove that they are 'individually and directly concerned'. As a consequence they generally do not have legal standing before the ECJ.

As long as an amendment of the EC Treaty or a broad interpretation of 'directly and individually concerned' under Article 230(4) EC is not in sight,[71] the EC has to look for other options to implement the obligations of Article 9(3) with respect to its own institutions. In its proposal for a Regulation the European Commission basically had to tackle three aspects: *how* could standing be realised, *who* shall have standing and *what* could be challenged.

In order to overcome the procedural barrier of the present concept of standing, it was worth looking not only at Article 230(4) second alternative but also at its first alternative.[72] According to Article 230(4) first alternative of the EC Treaty the addressee of a Community decision may institute proceedings in the ECJ. So far, citizens and environmental organisations are generally not the addressees of environmental decisions taken by European institutions.[73] However, the proposal for a Regulation, shows from a legal point of view a solution to grant standing to the ECJ according to Article 230(4) first alternative of the EC Treaty: Under Article 9 of the proposal for the Regulation qualified entities are entitled to lodge a request for reconsideration of the procedural and substantial legality of Community acts or omissions with the respective institution responsible for those activities (request for internal review). The respective Community

---

69 Aarhus Convention and Community institutions Consultation of interested parties on a working document on the application to Community institutions of the Aarhus Convention – see http://europa.eu.int/comm/environment/consultations_en.htm. The first and second part of the proposed Regulation implement the first and the second pillar of the Aarhus Convention on information and participation rights. For the purpose of this article the further discussion will focus on the third part of the proposed Regulation implementing Article 9(3) on access to justice.

70 See 3.2.1.

71 *Idem.*

72 Article 230(4) EC stipulates: 'Any natural or legal person may, under the same conditions, institute proceedings against a decision addressed to that person or against a decision which, although in the form of a regulation or a decision addressed to another person, is of direct and individual concern to the former'.

73 *E.g.* Decisions under Regulation (EC) 1164/1994 establishing a Cohesion Fund, OJ L 130/1 and Council Regulation (EC) 1264/1999 amending Regulation (EC) 1164/1994, OJ L 161/57; Decision of the Commission under Regulation (EC) 1980/2000 (eco-label scheme – OJ L 237/1;) Decision of the Commission under Directive (EEC) 91/689 (hazardous waste – OJ L 377/20).

institution or body will have to accept or reject the request. Such decision will be addressed to the qualified entity that has lodged the request for action, thus allowing for review in the European Court of Justice under Article 230(4) first alternative of the EC Treaty. Regulation (EC) 1049/2001 of the European Parliament and of the Council of 30 May 2001 regarding public access to European Parliament, Council and Commission documents[74] follows the same concept. Thus, the present proposal is based on an established and proven precursor in European legislation.

Further aspects when implementing Article 9(3) are 'who' shall have standing and 'what' can be challenged. Standing under Article 12 and 13 of the proposed Regulation is limited to recognised qualified entities, meaning environmental non-profit organisations acting on Community level with a certain organisational and institutional structure. The limitation to qualified entities is considered in line with Article 9(3), as this provision gives the Parties the possibility to lay down criteria for members of the public to be granted legal standing.[75] An overload of the ECJ is not to be expected due to the same reasons pointed out with regard to the Member States.[76] It is also to be expected that the preliminary procedure will have a 'filtering' function, which as a consequence could relieve the ECJ.

The definition of Community acts and omissions[77] that can be reviewed is by its very nature difficult to undertake. Generally speaking one can approach such a definition by a closed list enumerating certain acts and omissions – which bears the risk of exclusion and of non-flexibility to new developments – or one can avoid such effects and define the subject matter in general terms. It is to be welcomed that the proposal for the Regulation takes the second approach and stipulates that according to Article 1 h) of the proposal for a regulation administrative act, means any administrative measure taken under environmental law by a Community institution or body having legally binding and external effect. According to Article 1 i) of the proposal for the Regulation the same applies to administrative omissions.

The definition of 'environmental law' under Article 1 g) of the proposal for the Regulation uses a non-exclusive list ('such as...'). This ensures that all fields of environmental law are included. In addition, it covers any legislation that has as its objective the protection of the environment, even if the protection of the environment is not the major or only objective of the respective legislation.

'Community institutions or bodies' are defined in Article 1 c) as 'any public institution, body, office or agency established by or on the basis of the Treaty establishing the European Community and performing public functions except

74 OJ 2001 L 145/43.

75 COM (2003) 622 final/16.

76 See 3.2.2.

77 For reasons of consistency the proposal for the Regulation and the proposal for the Directive use the same legal terms which are based on Article 9(3) of the Aarhus Convention.

when and to the extent to which it acts in a judicial or legislative capacity'. This definition will have to be interpreted in conformity with Article 230 EC. According to Article 230(1) EC the ECJ is limited to review acts of the European Parliament, the Council, the Commission and the European Central Bank. As a consequence, the preliminary review procedure applies to all Community institutions and bodies covered by the proposed Regulation, whereas access to justice to the ECJ based on the above described preliminary review procedure would be limited to the institutions enumerated in Article 230(1) EC. However, the possibilities of review under the proposed Directive are a step forward to a broader access to justice at European level.

The notion of 'acting in a legal capacity' in Article 1 c) of the proposed Regulation leaves room for interpretation. From the wording itself it is not obvious whether *e.g.* implementation measures taken by way of delegated legislation by the Commission through Comitology procedure are considered to be acting in a legal or an executive capacity.[78] From a procedural point of view, these measures are taken by the executive and not the legislator. However, looking at the result, these measures are implementing or adapting technical annexes of European legislation. The explanatory memorandum to the proposed Regulation points out that 'as bodies or institutions acting in a legislative capacity are not covered by the definition of Community institutions and bodies, related administrative action is not covered either'.[79] This position tends to exclude measures or decisions of delegated legislation as being a related administrative action to a legislative process. However, project-related decisions taken by European institutions, such as decisions on the funding of projects, would be covered by the wording of the proposed Regulation what represents an important improvement from an environmental perspective.

Furthermore, it must be noted that the European Commission opted for a review of the procedural as well as the substantial legality of Community administrative acts or omissions, thus respecting the scope of review asked for by the Aarhus Convention. In sum, the proposed Regulation must therefore be considered a step forward to acknowledge broader *ajem* as regards the Community's own institutions. At the same time, the EU recognises its commitments according to the White Paper on Good Governance[80] and its obligations resulting from its signing of the Aarhus Convention. Once adopted, the proposed Regulation will – together with the proposed Directive on access to justice[81] – enable the EC to ratify the Aarhus Convention as foreseen by Article 1 of the *Proposal for a Council Decision on the conclusion, on behalf of the European Community, of the Aarhus Convention.*[82]

---

78 See for further details on the Committee procedures: Onida (2003) 187; Roller (2001) 1.

79 COM (2003) 622 final/10.

80 European Commission White Paper on European Governance, OJ 2001 C 287/1.

81 See 4.2.1.

82 COM (2003) 625 final.

4.2 Initiatives with regard to the Member State level

4.2.1 Proposal for a Directive on access to justice in environmental matters[83]

Presenting the proposal for the Directive on access to justice in environmental matters together with the above explained proposal for Regulation[84] shows the intention of the European Commission to align the two instruments. The main content of the proposed Directive relates to the same aspects as already discussed for the proposed Regulation, additionally taking into account the different legal cultures of the Member States. Here again, the main questions are: *who* shall have standing, *what* can be reviewed and *how* shall the procedure be structured?

The objective of the proposal is to create a framework of minimum requirements for *ajem* within the Member States and by that to implement Article 9(3) of the Aarhus Convention, to provide for a better enforcement and practical application of Community environmental law as well as to ensure a high level of environmental protection.[85] With a view to the principle of subsidiarity the obligations of the European Community by signing the Aarhus Convention and its obligations according to Article 174 EC justify by themselves a legally binding instrument.[86] The legal basis of the Proposal is Article 175(1) EC thus allowing Member States, if they so wish, to go beyond the criteria set out in the Proposal, *e.g.* to provide for an *actio popularis* in environmental matters.

The main focus of the proposed Directive is to provide for access to justice in the Member States when public authorities fail to apply laws relating to the environment, be it by an act or an omission.[87] To this end, qualified entities that are recognised according to Article 9 of the proposed Directive have access to request the authority to reconsider its activities (request for internal review), without having to show the impairment of an interest or an individual right (Article 5 of the proposed Directive). Where such a request is not dealt with by the respective authority in a timely or sufficient manner, the applicant can institute proceedings according to Article 7 of the proposed Directive before a court or another independent and impartial body.

Law relating to the environment is defined in Article 2(1g) of the proposed Directive in a most comprehensive way, including all possible fields of environmental law and not only enumerating a closed list of EU environmental legislation. Such a definition will ensure that all fields of the environment that need

83 COM (2003) 624 final.

84 See above 4.2.1.

85 See *supra* footnote 83, p. 1 and 2.

86 *Idem*, p. 4.

87 Criminal proceedings have not been included in the proposed Directive, in order to avoid any interference with Article 34(2b) EU.

environmental protection are covered and that the objective of the proposed Directive – to contribute to a better enforcement of environmental law – can be achieved.

As to the standing right, the proposed Directive allows for legal standing for the public concerned, meaning citizens who can show the impairment of an interest or an individual right. Additionally, standing is given to qualified entities.[88] These are according to Article 8 of the proposed Directive national, regional or local associations, organisations or groups, acting on a non-profit base for the protection of the environment and having a certain organisational and institutional structure. Defining such criteria can not be considered a restriction per se but is to be seen as a useful precision of Article 9(3) of the Aarhus Convention. This creates legal certainty as regards the obligations under Article 9(3) of the Aarhus Convention. A supposed overload of the courts by allowing standing to qualified entities has been proven wrong empirically[89] and thereby an argument sometimes brought forward against the Directive has been invalidated.

The definition of public authorities in Article 2.1(a) of the proposed Directive does not – in contrast to the Aarhus Convention in its Article 2.2(c) – include natural or legal persons having public responsibilities or functions or providing public services in relation to the environment under a public authority. A possible reason for that differentiation could be that Article 2.2(c) of the Aarhus Convention was formulated with a view to Council Directive 90/313/EEC[90] on the freedom of access to environmental information[91] and not with a view to *ajem*.

A possibility of review against the private sector has been introduced by Article 3 of the proposed Directive. The working documents had not foreseen such a possibility. Article 3 of the proposed Directive refers to the wording of Article 9(3) of the Aarhus Convention by making reference to criteria laid down in national law and thus leaving a great margin of discretion to the Member States. In connection with Article 10 of the proposed Directive proceedings in environmental matters between private persons would have to meet the conditions set out in Article 10, meaning that 'Member States shall provide for adequate and

---

[88] During the preparation process the notion of 'qualified entity' underwent changes in scope. Whereas in the working documents it also included citizen groupings this approach was finally not further followed. Although there were good reasons for including such groupings because they are generally well informed about the situation on the spot in practical terms, this will not have the effect of an enforcement gap for two reasons. Very often members of citizen groupings can demonstrate the impairment of an individual interest or right. Moreover, under the proposed Directive infringements of environmental law could be taken up by a local NGO or a national environmental NGO.

[89] De Sadeleer, Roller, Dross (2003) 10.

[90] OJ 1990 L 158/56.

[91] See *supra* footnote 23, p. 33.

effective proceedings that are objective, equitable, expeditious and not prohibitively expensive'.

In sum, the approach of the proposed Directive shows due regard to the Aarhus Convention and gives the somewhat ambiguous wording of Article 9(3) of the Aarhus Convention concrete shape. Furthermore, it takes into account and is based on existing administrative and judicial proceedings in Member States. From that point of view, acceptance by Member States of a future Directive on *ajem* seams closer then ever.

4.2.2 Further Directives containing provisions on access to justice in environmental matters

Other recent proposals for Directives or meanwhile adopted Directives also contain provisions on *ajem*[92] which aim to contribute to paving the way for the ratification of the Aarhus Convention: Directive 2003/4/EC[93] on public access to environmental information, Directive 2003/35/EC[94] providing for public participation in respect of the drawing-up of certain plans and programmes relating to the environment and amending with regard to public participation and access to justice Council Directives 85/337/EEC[95] and 96/61/EC[96] and Proposal for a Directive on Environmental Liability with regard to the Prevention and Remedying of Environmental Damage.[97]

Directive 2003/4/EC implements the first pillar of the Aarhus Convention on information rights and guarantees that the right of access to information can be reviewed before a court of law or other body established by law in which the acts or omissions of the public authority concerned can be reviewed (see Article 9(1) of the Aarhus Convention).

With respect to the second pillar of the Aarhus Convention on public participation in decision-making Directive 2003/35/EC provides in Article 3(7) for the EIA Directive and in Article 4(4) for the IPPC Directive that, in accordance with the relevant national legal system, the public concerned as well as non-govern mental organisations[98] have access to a review procedure before a court of law

92 These proposals for Directives were all elaborated under the direction of Ludwig Krämer.

93 OJ 2003 L 41/26.

94 OJ 2003 L 156/17.

95 OJ 1985 L 175/40 (the EIA Directive – environmental impact assessment).

96 OJ 1996 L 257/26 (the IPPC Directive – integrated pollution prevention and control).

97 COM (2002) 17 final.

98 As regards non-governmental organisations Article 3(7) and 4(4) stipulate the following: 'To this end, the interest of any non-governmental organisation meeting the requirements referred to in Article 1(2) shall be deemed sufficient for the purpose of subparagraph (a) of this Article. Such organisations shall also be deemed to have rights capable of being impaired for the purpose of subparagraph (b) of this Article'.

or another independent and impartial body established by law to challenge the substantive or procedural legality of decisions, acts or omissions subject to the public participation provisions of this Directive (see Article 9(2) of the Aarhus Convention). According to Article 2.3 of Directive 2003/35/EC Member States shall identify the public entitled to participate, including relevant non-governmental organisations meeting any requirements imposed under national law, such as those promoting environmental protection. Although it would have been desirable not to let Member States determine at what stages of the EIA and IPPC procedures the decisions, acts or omissions may be challenged, Member States will have to give under Directive 2003/35/EC environmental organisations *ajem* in relation to project-related decisions.[99]

A further example of introducing provisions on access to justice is the legislative process relating to the current proposal for a Directive on Environmental Liability with regard to the Prevention and Remedying of Environmental Damage.[100] According to this proposal qualified entities, which have beforehand lodged a request for action with the respective authority, shall have access to justice to a court or another independent and impartial body.

5 Conclusion

Environmental law suffers more than any other field of law from shortcomings in its enforcement at local, national, European as well as international level. In order to secure effective enforcement it is essential to look beyond individuals affected directly by infringements of environmental law. The overriding importance of the protection of our environment presents a clear need for standing rights in the interest of the environment. However, until now access to justice in environmental matters is restricted – in terms of access to both the ECJ and national review bodies or courts. The ECJ still upholds its restrictive interpretation of 'individually and directly concerned' under Article 230(4) EC. In most Member States there is a trend towards relaxing the criteria for standing in environmental matters, but this trend is slow and heterogeneous. The signing of the Aarhus Convention initiated a shift in thinking in June 1998. This Convention acknowledges for the first time on an international level the need for broader access to justice in environmental matters. Under the Aarhus Convention, members of the public, including environmental organisations, must be given legal standing for proceedings in environmental matters. Better access to such proceedings will have a number of positive effects on the implementation, application and enforcement of environmental law. By signing the Aarhus Convention, the EC is under an obligation to implement access to justice in environmental matters as regards its own institutions as well as with

99 See for further details Mathiesen (2003) 37.

100 COM (2002) 17 final.

respect to Member States. The 'proposal package' issued by the European Commission in October 2003 gives cause for confidence that the overdue change as regards access to justice in environmental matters will prevail, both with respect to Member States but also with respect to EC institutions, paving the way for ratification of the Aarhus Convention and enhancing environmental protection. Ludwig Krämer devoted his entire career to promoting environmental protection – his work has been instrumental in setting the stage for current developments.

CHAPTER 2

Commission Infringement Procedure in Environmental Cases

Sibylle Grohs[1]

1 Introduction

Under Article 211 EC, the Commission is required to ensure that the provisions of the Treaty and measures taken under it are applied. If the Commission is of the opinion that a Member State has infringed a requirement of Community law, it has powers under Article 226 EC[2] to refer that Member State to the European Court of Justice.

The Commission has wide discretion in deciding whether or not to instigate infringement procedures and individuals cannot at present question how the Commission exercises that discretion.[3] The Commission may therefore decide to close a case despite a finding that an infringement of Community law has occurred. The Commission is however required to ensure that its discretion is exercised reasonably. Where the infringement has been brought to the Commission's attention as a result of a complaint by a member of the public the reasons for such a decision must be fully explained.[4]

2 The formal infringement procedure

Over the years, the Commission has significantly developed the pre-litigation phase of the procedure building upon the requirements set out in Article 226 EC. Whilst Article 226 refers only to the reasoned opinion stage of the pre-litigation procedure, the Commission introduced a preceding stage in the form of the letter of formal notice. Each stage of the process requires a formal decision of the Commission and whilst the letter of formal notice is seen as a relatively informal first investigation stage of the process, it has been recognised as formally setting the scope of the future procedure beyond which that latter procedure cannot stray.[5]

---

1 Environment Directorate-General, European Commission. The opinions contained in the present article are strictly personal and do not engage the Commission. This Article is based on policy developments as at the end of March 2004.

2 Article 141 is the corresponding article in the Euratom Treaty.

3 See Case 247/87 *Star Fruit* v. *Commission* [1989] ECR 291. Furthermore Case C-422/92 *Commission* v. *Germany* [1995] ECR I-1097.

4 The Commission was criticised by the European Ombudsman in his decision on complaint 995/98/OV concerning the Macedonian Metro Joint Venture where the Commission appeared to inform the complainant that the file was to be closed, as there had been no infringement of Community law. The Ombudsman however found that this was not the reason for the Commission's decision to close the case. Whilst the Commission has discretion not to pursue a case despite an infringement of Community law having occurred, the exercise of this discretion must be clearly explained. See European Ombudsman's Annual Report for 2001, p. 116-119. Available on http://www.euro-ombudsman.eu.int.

5 See Case C-52/90 *Commission* v. *Denmark* [1992] ECR I-2187. Also C-337/89 *Commission* v. *United Kingdom* [1992] ECR I-6103.

The letter of formal notice will normally give the Member State two months within which to reply. If that reply does not satisfy the Commission, it can issue a reasoned opinion. Whilst a letter of formal notice may be issued in cases where the Commission suspects an infringement, the reasoned opinion is normally not issued unless the Commission is more strongly of the opinion that an infringement has occurred. The time limit for the Member State to take action to comply with the reasoned opinion is normally two months. If the Member State is still judged to have infringed Community law after this stage, the Commission may decide to refer the matter to the European Court of Justice.

Since 1996, the Commission has press released its decisions to issue reasoned opinions and to refer a Member State to the European Court of Justice, whilst adopting a more low key approach to letters of formal notice in the hope that this may better facilitate a settlement.

In many cases, this formal part of the procedure may be preceded by what is termed a 'pre-226 letter'. This is mostly reserved for cases where the Commission requires clarification with regard to allegations that have been made, particularly in the context of cases where there are allegations by complainants that Community law has been badly applied in a specific case. Before 1996, it had almost become a practice in the Commission to send such a letter before opening formal proceedings with the issuing of a letter of formal notice. However, after an internal reassessment of the infringement procedure, it was decided that this added unnecessary delay to the procedure and that reliance on such letters should be reduced. Furthermore, emphasis was put on the speeding up of investigations with particular emphasis being placed on the need for cases either to be closed or for formal infringement proceedings to be instigated within one year of a case being opened.[6] It can take many years for a case to proceed from its initial registration as a complaint to the first judgement of the Court. Between 2000 and 2001, the average time span between the dispatch of the letter of formal notice and judgement was 59 months.[7] This excludes the investigations that may have preceded the launching of the actual infringement proceedings, which would probably add about 12 further months to that total. In those 6 to 7 years much polluted water may have passed under the bridge and the environment in question may well have already been destroyed or degraded. Whilst the Commission can apply to the European Court of Justice for interim measures under Article 243 EC this power only appears to be available where a case is pending before the Court or the application for interim measures is part of that application. An application was made to the European Court of Justice in the *Leybucht Case*,[8] but was rejected as the Court found that the Commission

6 Improvement of the Commission's Working Methods in Relation to Infringement Proceedings SEC (1998) 1733 of 15 October 1998.

7 See Krämer (2002b) 485.

8 Case C-57/89 *Commission* v. *Germany* [1989] ECR 2849.

had failed to show that there was sufficient urgency in its application. Since that time, the Commission has not made further such applications.

3 Types of cases investigated

The Commission places cases under investigation into three groups. The cases will involve:

- a failure by a Member State to formally adopt and communicate implementing legislation to the Commission once the implementation deadline in a Directive has passed ('Non-communication cases');
- a Member State's failure to have correctly transposed Community legislation into national law ('Non-conformity cases'); and/or
- a Member State's failure to have correctly applied Community law in a given case ('Bad application cases').

3.1 Sources of infringement cases

Non-communication cases will generally be launched by the Commission at its own initiative. Cases dealing with the failure to correctly transpose a Directive may come to the attention of the Commission in a number of ways, either as the result of investigations by the Commission itself or through complaints from the public.

Bad application cases will normally be brought to the attention of the Commission as a result of direct complainants or through petitions to the European Parliament. Complainants and petitioners are often private individuals, environmental NGOs and sometimes trade organisations where the application of environmental legislation touches their business interests.[9] Although much is made of the role of environmental NGOs as watchdogs[10], individual citizens and not the major environmental NGOs make up the majority of complaints. It might be that the Commission's investigation process is too slow and unpredictable to fit into the campaign planning of many of the larger NGOs. For private individuals on the other hand, the Commission's investigation powers might be their only chance to see an issue being addressed given that the investigation procedure is free and the alternative of court action nationally may be prohibitively expensive.

Sometimes a complainant may address a complaint to the Commission and at the same time raise the matter as a petition before the Petitions Committee of the European Parliament.[11] The Petitions Committee does not generally take

9 Trade organisations have in the past registered numerous complaints about the application of Community waste legislation.

10 See generally Newell & Grant (2000).

11 See Articles 21 and 194 EC setting out the rights of citizens to petition the European Parliament.

direct contact with the Member State concerned, but tasks the Commission with investigating the petition on its behalf. Where a complainant only raises a matter as a petition there are disadvantages as the matter is investigated as if it were a complaint but without the Commission procedure on complaints applying. As a result, the petitioner is not kept informed about progress or decisions to close an investigation directly by the Commission and communication on progress is delayed by having to be relayed between the services of the Commission and Parliament. In certain cases however the Petitions Committee may investigate a matter itself and send a delegation to visit the Member State concerned to discuss the matter.[12] In such cases, there is an advantage for the complainant to have also petitioned the European Parliament as it can raise far wider political questions whereas the Commission's investigations are limited to assessing infringements of Community law.

When the Commission receives a complaint from a member of the public an initial assessment is made as to whether or not the information provided shows that a provision of Community law may have been breached. If this is the case, the complaint letter will be forwarded to the Secretariat-General of the Commission for formal registration as a complaint. A complaint file is opened and it is allocated a formal reference number. The complaint is informed of the registration and the procedure that applies to the investigation of his or her complaint. Complainants are given the option of having their complaint handled in confidence or may opt to waive the right and have their identity revealed. If no further information is received from the complainant in this regard, the Commission will treat the complaint as confidential.

Once registered, the complaint file is forwarded to the department responsible for its investigation within the Commission. The Environment Directorate-General has a specific unit that coordinates the investigation of complaints concerning the implementation of Community environmental law. Allegations concerning the bad application of Community legislation on radiation protection are handled by the Directorate-General for Transport and Energy.

3.2 Non-communication cases

Priority is given to following up non-communication cases. Where the Member State has failed to communicate any implementing legislation, the case is fast tracked through the initial letter of formal notice stage by the Secretariat-General of the Commission as soon as the deadline for transposition has passed. These cases are the easiest for the Commission to follow up as it

[12] For example, in January 2003 a delegation of MEPs from the Petitions Committee visited a cattle incinerator in Glasgow which was the subject matter of petition 1104/2001. Unlike the Commission during its 'package' meetings (see *infra*) where meetings are generally limited to meeting state level officials in the Member State's capital, the Petitions Committee delegation met and spoke with a wide range of local officials in Glasgow. They also visited the incinerator in question and spoke with local residents.

is simply a matter of whether or not implementing legislation has been communicated by the transposition deadline set in the Directive. All efforts are made to ensure that for each Directive in question the infringement procedures against those Member States who have failed to communicate implementing legislation by the deadline are followed up in parallel. Unlike for other cases, the launching of proceedings for non-communication is press released at the earliest letter of formal notice stage. This is on the basis that there is no need for confidential discussions between the Commission and the Member State as the legislation has either been adopted or it has not. Details of progress on transposition are published on a regular basis.[13]

3.3 Non-conformity cases

Priority is also given to those cases where the transposition has been found to be faulty in some way. The theory is that if the Commission can ensure both the timely and correct transposition of its secondary legislation, the number of instances of bad application may be reduced.

Unfortunately, the actual transposition checking of environmental legislation often suffers under the weight of other cases that need to be handled. As a result, the Environment Directorate-General of the Commission has now started to launch regular transposition checking studies to underpin its transposition assessments. With many Member States the transposition of environmental legislation takes place at the regional level and there may therefore be numerous texts for one Directive. The United Kingdom, for example, may communicate separate texts for England, Wales, Scotland, Northern Ireland and Gibraltar. Germany, Spain, Italy and Austria will provide separate texts for each region or Land. These studies, which in the past have been launched on a more *ad hoc* basis, are publicly available on request.[14]

3.4 Bad application cases

In terms of numbers of cases registered with the Commission, bad application cases make up the largest group. Bad application cases however make up the lowest percentage of cases that reach the European Court of Justice. This is in some ways not so surprising. With non-communication cases there

---

13 See the Annual Survey on the implementation and enforcement of Community environmental law at http://europa.eu.int/comm/environment/law/as01htm.

14 See Decision of the European Ombudsman on complaints 271/2000/(IJH)JMA and 277/2000/(IJH)JMA against the European Commission of 31 May 2001 regarding a complaint by the UK environmental NGO Friends of the Earth that they had been refused full access to two transposition studies carried out for the Environment Directorate-General of the Commission. The Commission had argued that the operative conclusions of the reports concerned were confidential. This was criticised by the Ombudsman in his Decision and the reports in question were subsequently made available in full.

is not much argument to be had between the Commission and the Member State. The relevant implementing legislation has either been adopted and communicated or not. These cases can therefore be swiftly processed to reach the European Court of Justice. Incorrect transposition cases are often more complex and may require direct discussion between the Commission and the Member State. However, most of those discussions will revolve around the meaning of legal texts rather than involving a dispute about facts. As such, they are usually relatively easy to resolve or progress through the infringements procedure.

Cases concerning the bad application of a Directive in a given case are by contrast the most difficult cases for the Commission to process. Most bad application cases are brought to the attention of the Commission by members of the public either in a private capacity or by environmental non-governmental organisations (NGOs) or trade organisations. When the case is initially registered, the complainant is asked to provide as much evidence as possible to substantiate the allegations made. Where the complaint concerns a particularly technical matter the clarifications and evidence required by the Commission can often be beyond the capacity of the complainant to provide. This can lead to frustration. Many complainants expect the Commission's investigations to be speedier and more probing. However, without inspectors and a very limited budget to launch its own studies into a matter, heavy reliance is placed on the complainant providing sufficient evidence to build a *prima facie* case.

3.4.1 Types of bad application case investigated

The bad application cases investigated cover the whole range of environmental legislation. However, a large percentage of complaints concern the alleged bad application of the Directives on nature protection[15], wild birds[16] and environmental impact assessment.[17] This is probably not surprising given that members of the public are often most concerned by development projects that affect their local area. The Directives on nature protection, wild birds and environmental impact assessment provide standards that the public can relate to and understand, at least in broad terms. For the Commission, complaints concerning these Directives are often the most difficult to assess in particular where the bad application alleged involves questioning a technical or factual judgement call of a Member State. The Commission cannot become the final forum for appeal for all national decisions that impact on a Community protected nature or bird area. Furthermore, it is impossible for the Commission to provide a quality control service for all environmental impact assessments that are carried out. However, the Commission may decide to step in where a pattern

[15] Council Directive 92/43/EEC, OJ 1992 L 206/7.

[16] Council Directive 79/409/EEC, OJ L 103/1.

[17] Council Directive 85/337/EEC, OJ 1985 L 175/40 as amended by Council Directive 97/11/EC, OJ 1997 L 73/5.

of behaviour becomes apparent which hinders the correct application of these Directives or where an individual breach is particularly blatant.

By contrast, few complaints are registered with regard to Community legislation on chemicals, noise or air quality. This is probably because Community legislation on chemicals and noise is aimed at providing product norms and thus is less aimed at involving members of the public. Furthermore, for air quality Community law provides few clearly enforceable standards.[18]

Where a complaint has resulted in infringement action, this may in itself add fuel for further complaints being made to the Commission. The practice is now to press release decisions of the Commission to issue Reasoned Opinions and to refer a case to the European Court of Justice. It is often noted, in particular with cases concerning Community legislation on nature protection, wild birds and environmental impact assessment that where a case was press released and resulted in wide coverage, further similar complaints may arrive shortly afterwards.

3.4.2 Procedure for investigating bad application cases

Where the facts are sufficiently proved, a letter of formal notice may be sent. However, in many cases sufficient questions remain for the Commission to first pursue the matter through more informal channels either by writing a 'pre-226 letter' to the Member States' Permanent Representative to the European Union in Brussels or by discussing it in a meeting with officials of the Member State concerned.

A pre-226 inquiry letter will normally give the Member State two months within which to reply. The letter is sent to the Permanent Representative in Brussels who is then responsible for forwarding it to the right national authority back home. In many cases, the national coordinating authority will be either the Environment Ministry and/or the Foreign Ministry. The reply itself may then have to be sought from a local or regional authority where the bad application in question is alleged to have occurred. That reply will in turn have to be relayed back through the various national channels to the Permanent Representation in Brussels and on to the Commission. The whole process is very cumbersome and time consuming especially when the reply then leaves matters unclear requiring further requests for clarification or when there is no reply at all. As a result, these formal contacts might be followed up informally simply to avoid further delay where the matter on which clarification is sought is straightforward.

Alternatively, the complaints may be discussed between Commission and Member State officials at so called 'package' meetings. These tend to take place in the Member State once a year. The aim is to allow for direct discussion so that questions can be resolved more quickly. In practice, questions usually remain

---

18 See critique in Krämer (2003a) 273.

for further investigation, not least, as it is not possible to have all the national, regional and local representatives present to answer questions. However, such direct meetings generally provide more immediate results than investigations by pre-226 letter.

3.5 Reaching decisions on whether or not to pursue a case with formal proceedings

The results of these investigations are then assessed. At this stage a decision is made as to whether to proceed with an infringement case and launch a letter of formal notice or whether to close the case. In many cases, complaints can be resolved as a result of these inquiries either because it becomes clear that the matter in question does not in fact raise questions of Community law or because the matter is resolved by the national authorities. If it is decided that the matter should be pursued through formal infringement proceedings, the Commission must keep in mind that it bears the burden of proof when bringing a case before the European Court of Justice. It must carefully weigh whether sufficient evidence exists for the matter to be proceeded with. Furthermore, the Commission has discretion as to whether or not to bring a case before the Court. Even where sufficient evidence exists that a breach has occurred, the case will not necessarily result in infringement action being launched. Where, for example, the Member State has recognised that things have gone wrong and has undertaken to ensure that no repetition occurs, the Commission might decide against launching formal proceedings. However, in reaching a decision on whether or not to proceed with infringement proceedings in such a case the Commission must also keep in mind that Member States have a duty under Article 10 EC to nullify the unlawful consequences of a breach of Community law.[19] In the case of a development being authorised without consideration being given to the need for an environmental impact assessment the Commission could request the Court to order that the unlawful authorisation be revoked.

The Commission has to carefully weigh the advantage of pursuing such a case, as the aim of its action under Article 226 EC is not to step into the shoes of the complainant, but to ensure that such cases do not reoccur and that where possible environmental damage is averted or repaired. Where an unlawfully authorised development had already been built, the value for the Commission of starting an infringement action may be limited if the Member State concerned has given an undertaking to ensure that such breaches do not reoccur. For the complainant the interest in continuing legal action may however remain as he or she might be able to claim compensation if the illegality of the Member State's action is proved.[20] If it is decided not to pursue a case, the Commission must

---

[19] See Case C-201/02 *R* v. *Secretary of State for Transport, Local Government and the Regions* ex parte *Delena Wells*, not yet reported, at paragraph 64.

[20] *Ibid* paragraph 69.

be careful to fully explain its reasoning to the complainant.[21] It may be useful to explain more expansively to complainants the aims of the Commission in pursuing action under Article 226 EC when a complaint is registered. Many complainants are given a false sense of hope when their complaint is registered that swift action will be taken to stop whichever action is in their opinion contravening Community law.[22] However, an application to the European Court of Justice may not always be best suited to such individual cases, especially when this involves detailed disagreements about scientific or local fact based evidence and where the aim of the complainant is to obtain compensation.[23]

3.6 Statistics on complaints handled by the Environment Directorate-General

The Environment Directorate-General of the Commission has a particularly heavy caseload when it comes to handling complaints from the public. It currently handles about 40% of the complaints formally registered with the Commission.[24] Over the last four years, the infringements unit of the Environment Directorate-General has handled over 500 new complaint cases each year.[25] On top of this there are the so called 'own initiative cases' which are cases opened by the Environment Directorate-General, often as a result of a petition to the European Parliament, a parliamentary question or as a result of its own investigations. These new cases add to the existing caseload of older complaint files still under investigation and infringement cases at their various stages in the litigation process. There are currently 16 desk officers in the infringement unit handling this caseload for the existing 15 Member States.[26] More desk officers are being recruited to handle the new cases that will follow on from enlargement.[27]

---

[21] As explained at footnote 4 above, the Ombudsman has indicated that in his opinion the Commission can close a case for political reasons, but must clearly explain these and not hide behind false legal arguments.

[22] See criticisms in Kunzlik (1997) 47 and Williams (1995) 359.

[23] See Somsen (2003) pp. 421-426.

[24] See page 6 of the 20th Annual Report on Monitoring the Application of Community Law (2002) of 21.11.2003 COM (2003) 669 Final accessible on the Commission website at http://europa.eu.int/comm/secretariat_general/sgb/droit_com/index_en.htm#infringements.

[25] In 2002, the environment sector received 549 complaints – see Annex I, fig 1.4.2 of the 20th Annual Report (*ibid*).

[26] Staffing levels of the unit responsible for handling complaints and infringement investigations within the Environment Directorate-General were a matter of some discussion before the Environment Committee of the European Parliament – at the Question and Answer session of the Committee on 2 October 2003 at http://www.europarl.rp.ec.comparl.envi/implemtation/implementation-sessions.htm.

[27] In the past criticisms have been made in that too many desk officers investigating implementation cases were seconded national experts rather than Commission officials. See Williams (1995) 364. Macrory

A criticism made is that this volume of complaints results in the Environment Directorate-General often playing a largely reactive role rather than spending its time on developing more strategic cases.[28] To an extent, this criticism remains true today.

4 Procedural rules

The Commission has made public its internal rules on the handling of complaints in the context of infringement proceedings in its Communication to the European Parliament and the European Ombudsman on relations with the complainant in respect of infringements of Community law.[29]

The rules are set out in the Annex to this Communication. In paragraph 7 the Commission undertakes to inform complainants in writing after each Commission infringement decision of the steps taken in response to their complaint. Paragraph 8 sets out that as a general rule the Commission will arrive at a decision to issue a letter of formal notice opening formal proceedings or close the case within one year of its registration. Where this time limit is not complied with, the Commission may inform the complainant in writing.[30]

Paragraph 9 outlines that the Commission shall decide on how to progress each case at its own discretion. The complainant will be kept informed in writing of the decision taken in each case and of any subsequent Commission decision on this matter. Under the current procedure applied by the Commission each decision to close and each formal step in the infringement procedure (*i.e.* the letter of formal notice, reasoned opinion and the decision to refer the case to the European Court of Justice) requires a decision of the Commissioners as a college. Furthermore, any case that is more that one year old and still under investigation at the pre-infringement stage requires a formal decision of the Commission College to continue investigations.

In order to close a case, the general rule is that the Commission department intending to propose closure will give the complainant prior notice of

---

(1992) 364 quotes from evidence of L. Krämer before the House of Lords Select Committee of the European Communities (Sub Committee F) 13 Oct. 1991 that there were 10 desk officers investigating environmental infringements in 1991, six of whom were on secondment. This criticism is no longer applicable to the current staff of the infringements unit in the Environment Directorate-General.

28 See Macrory (1992) 363.

29 COM (2002) 141 at OJ C 244 10/10/2002 pp 5-8. These rules are separate to the European Code of Good Administration, which applies to the general handling of contacts with the public by the European Institutions. See http://www.euro-ombudsman.eu.int.

30 There is some ambiguity in this last provision as the English version of the text indicates that the Commission *will* inform complainants where the one-year time limit has not been respected, whereas the other linguistic versions of the text indicate that the Commission *may* do so.

this intention in a letter setting out the grounds for the closure proposal.[31] The complainant should be given four weeks within which to submit comments on this proposal. Where the complainant fails to reply, cannot be reached or where his comments do not persuade the Commission department in question, the case may be proposed formally for closure. The closure of the case requires a decision of the Commission College and the complainant is informed of that decision once taken. Commission decisions on infringements are published within one week of their adoption on the Internet site of the Secretariat-General of the Commission.[32]

5 European Ombudsman

Where a complainant considers that, in handling his complaint, the Commission has been guilty of maladministration, he may refer the matter to the European Ombudsman under Articles 21 and 195 EC.[33] The European Ombudsman has been operational in pushing the Commission to adopt more formal and publicly available guidance on how complaints are handled giving complainants basic administrative rights. In the past, the Commission has rightly come in for criticism by the Ombudsman for failing to give complainants clear and timely reasons for closing their cases and for failing to give complainants an opportunity to comment on proposals to close their case. The European Ombudsman launched an own initiative inquiry into the Commission's administrative procedures for dealing with complaints the results of which criticised the Commission's then failure to provide complainants with such administrative safeguards.[34] As a result, the Commission amended its procedure by informing the public of new rules of procedure available in a note appended to the standard complaint form.[35] Further critical remarks of the Commission's handling of complaints were made by the European Ombudsman as a result of his investigation of complaint 995/98/OV concerning the Macedonian Metro Joint Venture.[36] It was in part to answer these criticisms that the Commission adopted its Communication of 2002.[37]

---

[31] See paragraph 10 of the Annex to Communication COM (2002) 141.

[32] See http://europa.eu.int/comm/secretariat_general/sgb/droit_com/index_en.htm.

[33] See also paragraph 14 of the Annex to Communication COM (2002) 141.

[34] 303/97/PD reported in the European Ombudsman's Annual Report for 1997, p. 270-274.

[35] Entitled 'Failure by a Member State to comply with Community law: standard form for complaints to be submitted to the European Commission (OJ 1999 C 119/5).

[36] See footnote 4 above.

[37] COM (2002) 141.

6 Priority setting

Discussions have been ongoing for sometime inside the Commission to establish ways of prioritising cases.[38] In its White Paper on European Governance[39], the Commission announced that it would be applying priority criteria in its follow up of alleged infringements and that these would reflect the seriousness of the allegation made. The criteria listed fall into three groups:

- infringements that undermine the foundations of the rule of law;
- infringements that undermine the smooth functioning of the Community legal system; and
- infringements that consist in the failure to transpose or to correctly transpose Directives into national law.

The first mentioned category covers breaches that undermine the primacy and uniform application of Community law *e.g.* where a complainant had no redress procedures under national law or the national courts refuse to recognise the primacy of Community law in a given case. This category also applies where violations of human rights or one of the fundamental freedoms enshrined in substantive Community law are alleged to have occurred. With regard to environmental cases this would include allegations that there are serious threats to human health at stake as a result of damage to the environment. Also in this category are allegations of a violation of Community law in relation to a project receiving financial support from the Community budget. In such cases, the Commission will be obliged to suspend financial assistance to the project concerned.

The second category covers cross border infringements where this aspect of the alleged infringement makes it more difficult for citizens to assert their rights. It would also cover cases where there is evidence of systematic incorrect application of Community legislation detected by a series of separate complaints.

The third category has been discussed above and has already been a priority in the past.

The aim of this priority setting process is that an infringement that meets these criteria can be processed quickly and proceedings commenced immediately. Details on how this priority setting is to be applied in practice are set out in the Commission's Communication Better Monitoring of the Application of Community Law.[40] According to this Communication, cases of a lower priority will still be handled, but on the basis of a 'complementary mechanism' which includes discussions with Member States at package meetings or through other discussion fora.

---

[38] For more extensive discussion of reforms of procedure see Hattan (2003) 276-280.

[39] COM (2001) 428 final.

[40] Commission Communication of 13 December 2002, COM (2002) 725.

Whilst the setting of priorities is helpful, it is not yet clear how the Commission will apply this new policy in practice. Some criticisms have already been made that the details of how the priorities are to be set are too vague.[41] Furthermore, in the environmental sector where there is the largest number of cases, it is not clear that this workload can be reduced by the new policy. The lower priority cases will still need to be handled in accordance with the Commission's rules of good practice for complaints the observance of which are policed by the European Ombudsman. The complaint will still need to be investigated to assess whether a breach of Community law has occurred and the complainant will need to be provided with an explanation of the investigations undertaken together with their conclusion where possible within one year of the registration of the complaint.

Furthermore, individual complaints may initially appear to concern a one off case of bad application. However, further similar complaints may be made which over time show that what initially appeared to be a one off case is in fact part of an underlying pattern of bad application in that Member State. As a result the initially lower priority case becomes a priority case when taken together with similar cases that appear.

7 Conclusion

Various policies have been adopted and are currently being prepared to find ways to improve the implementation and application of Community environmental law. A Recommendation has been adopted to reinforce environmental inspections at the national level.[42] Furthermore, the Commission is preparing measures to improve access to justice for environmental cases at the national level in line with the Arhus Convention[43] as well as the establishment of a national complaint mechanism and arbitration scheme to tackle practical application problems closer to their source.[44]

At the Commission level, annual reports, regular press releases and the publication of Commission decisions on the Internet also help to inform the public about the progress of infringement cases. Furthermore, serious attempts have been made to clarify and publicise the Commission's own investigation procedure for complaints. In part, these changes have come about through internal pressure resulting from an ever-increasing caseload but they are also the result of nudges from the European Ombudsman. The European Parliament

41 See Muñoz (2003) 6.

42 Recommendation 2001/331/EC of the European Parliament and the Council on Minimum Criteria for Environmental Inspections, OJ 2001 L 118/41.

43 UN/ECE Convention on Access to Information, Public Participation in Decision-Making and Access to Justice in Environmental Matters.

44 Announced in the 20th Annual Report at p. 35.

has also taken an increasingly active interest in the environmental enforcement work of the Commission, with its Environment Committee requiring Commission officials to attend regular sessions to answer questions on the progress of cases under investigation.[45]

Much work however remains. There is considerable public concern about the protection of the environment and the enforcement of environmental legislation.[46] Given that the Environment Directorate-General of the Commission has been serving a potential client base of almost 380 million people for 15 Member States, the recorded level of complaints concerning the environment registered per year is relatively low. This is likely to remain the same after enlargement.

Despite various improvements in the working practices of the Commission, the investigation process is still painfully slow at times and the investigatory tools available for environmental cases remain limited both in terms of powers and staff numbers.[47] Whilst many Member States recognise the need for the Commission to remain the guardian of the Treaty and to investigate transgressions, this recognition does not necessarily translate into political pressure to improve enforcement powers at the Community level. Member States have been keen to stamp on any ideas that might involve the appointment of independent inspectors for the environment whether in the context of the IMPEL network, which is an informal network of national environmental inspectors funded by the Commission, or the Environment Agency.[48] It is often sexier to be preparing new legislation than to concentrate on the unglamorous behind the scenes work of implementation and enforcement.

In the absence of increased resources and investigation powers, practical action can however still be taken to improve upon the current practices. In the writer's personal opinion, much would be gained and little lost if the infringement process was further opened up to the public's gaze. In most cases, the text of Reasoned Opinion's and the Member States response could be made publicly available. The same level of transparency could be afforded to the pleadings before the European Court of Justice. The resulting debate could be illuminating to both sides and would avoid many of the conspiracy theories than tend to appear where decisions are kept secret. Furthermore, it could assist national

---

45 A summary of the regular question and answer sessions of the Environment Committee on environmental enforcement can be found at http://www.europarl.eu.int/comparl/envi/implementation.

46 In *The Environment? What Europeans think – 2002*, a European Commission publication published in 2003 setting out the principal results of Eurobarometer polls conducted in 2002, 40% of citizens in the survey indicated that they thought better enforcement of existing environmental legislation would make it possible to most effectively solve environmental problems.

47 The Environment Directorate-General has no inspection powers or inspectors, unlike the areas of competition, fisheries, customs or regional policy.

48 See Jackson (2000) 7.

courts, which may be grappling with similar issues to see what the opinion of the Commission is in a similar or even the same matter.

Furthermore, clearer explanations can be provided to complainants as to the types of cases that the Commission is likely to pursue, possibly avoiding false hopes being raised that the Commission is able or willing to intervene in a given case.

CHAPTER 3

Protection of the Environment through Criminal Law

Destiny of the Various European Union's Initiatives

Françoise Comte[1]

1 Introduction

Community environmental law has existed for around 25 years. Today there are over 200 Directives and Regulations in force.[2] However there are numerous cases where there is a failure to properly comply with Community environmental law (see under § 2). The extent of environmental crime clearly shows that something has to be done in order to stop this ever-growing, lucrative, illicit business (see under § 3). Some initiatives at European level have been taken by recurring to criminal law in order to have a better implementation of environmental law (see under § 4). In particular, the Council, in January 2003, decided to adopt a Framework Decision on the protection of the environment through criminal law. It adopted this instrument against the will of the Commission which had proposed instead a proposal for a Directive on the same object. This will be the subject of § 5 to see what will be or could be the destiny of these instruments. Finally, in criminal matters, the accident of the *Prestige* made the European Institutions adopt new proposals in order to tackle the specific problem of ship-source pollution (see under § 6). It will be interesting to see what would/could become of these proposals (see under § 6.6).

2 Need to better ensure effective implementation of Community environmental law

Every year the European Commission's Directorate-General for the Environment receives a big number of complaints.[3] In 2001, it received 600 complaints. At the end of 2001, 301 infringement cases were pending against Member States. In 2001 the Commission referred 71 cases to the Court and sent Member States 197 reasoned opinions under Articles 226 and 228 of the EC Treaty. These represent over a third of the total number of complaints and infringement cases that the Commission handles each year. They concern every piece of environmental legislation and all Member States.[4]

These trends have been confirmed by the most recent annual survey on the implementation and enforcement of Community environmental law.[5] During 2002, 555 new complaints were registered by the Commission. These

[1] Administrator at the European Commission, DG Environment. The opinions expressed are entirely personal to the author and do not represent the European Commission.

[2] This number includes modifications of Directives and Regulations.

[3] See the article of Sibylle Grohs in this book.

[4] See *Third annual survey on the implementation and enforcement of Community environmental law (January 2000 to December 2001)*, Commission staff working paper, SEC (2002) 1041, 1.10.2002.

[5] See *Fourth Annual Survey on the implementation and enforcement of Community environmental law (2002)*, Commission staff working paper, SEC (2003) 804, 7.7.2002.

complaints, again, accounted for over one third of all infringements cases investigated by the Commission. The Commission brought 65 cases against Member States before the Court and issued 137 reasoned opinions (on the basis of Article 226 EC).

The Commission, in the context of its role as 'Guardian of the Treaty' announces regularly twice a year, numerous new legal actions against Member States.[6] The Commission takes legal action under Articles 226 and 228 EC for breaches of Community environmental law. For example, the Commission announced in July 2003[7] that proceedings were being brought against 10 Member States concerning water laws, 8 Member States concerning the Wild Birds and Habitats Directives, 15 Member States concerning air pollution law and 8 Member States concerning the Environmental Impact Assessment Directive. In January 2004, the Commission announced that legal action was taken against 8 Member States for non-compliance with EU laws on water quality. Proceedings were also brought against Spain and France in relation, respectively, to Directive 96/82[8] ('Seveso II') and Directive 98/8 ('Biocides Directive').[9] This underlines the need to better ensure effective implementation of Community environmental law into national law.

3 Extent of environmental crime: Two examples

It is very difficult to give reliable figures for evaluating the extent of environmental crime, for the simple reason that it is difficult to evaluate activities and businesses which are, by definition, prohibited and clandestine. However, two examples where environmental crime is particularly active – trade in endangered wildlife species and in the waste sector- are examined below.

Illegal trade in endangered species is estimated, in terms of profits, as being second in importance only to drug trafficking as a global smuggling activity. It is estimated to be worth between €2.1-3.7 bn.[10] One study[11] confirms this evalu-

6 *See e. g. ENDS Environment Daily* – Issue 1488, 24.7. 2003 and *ENDS Environment Daily* – Issue 1586, 13.1.2004. For current statistics on infringements in general see: *http://europa.eu.int/comm/secretariat_general/sgb/droit_com/index_en.htm#infractions.*

7 See Commission's Press Release IP/03/1107-1109-1069-1070, IP/04/5-29-39, published on the Internet at: http://www.europa.eu.int (RAPID database).

8 Directive 96/82/EC on the control of major-accident hazards involving dangerous substances, OJ 1997 L 10/13.

9 Directive 98/8/EC concerning the placing of biocidal products on the market, OJ 1998 L 123/1.

10 National Wildlife Crime Intelligence Unit (UK), information quoted in Poppe (2003) 16. Although the study does not stipulate for which period these figures apply, it may be deduced from the context that this is a per year evaluation.

11 Cook, Roberts & Lowther (2002), information quoted in Poppe (2003) 16.

ation by saying that '*What is clear, however, is that the financial cost of global illegal wildlife trade runs into billions of dollars and the environmental costs are immeasurable*'. Wildlife trade covers many different types of animals and plants, including, for example, live or dead animals as collectors' items, products used for Traditional East Asian Medicine (TEAMs), skins and furs, food (including caviar) and timber. Trade flows are orientated from South to North, going mainly from the less developed to more developed countries. Western Europe is important as a market for trade in endangered species and as an intermediate destination.[12] It is also estimated that most of the live animals traded illegally are transported in very bad conditions.[13] For example, some 80% of wild birds, destined for illegal trade, died on the way to their destination during transportation from Africa to Europe in the late 1980s.[14]

Illegal trade in and disposal of waste and hazardous waste is even more difficult to evaluate. The third environmental assessment report of the European Environment Agency in 2003[15] underlined: '*the lack of sound, reliable, comparable and available data*'. However, it is certain that environmental crime in waste is lucrative and generates very high profits. Some studies emphasise the enormous differential in costs between southern and northern countries for the treatment and disposal of hazardous waste. For instance, it is estimated that, in the late 1980s, '*the average cost of disposal of one ton of hazardous waste in an OECD country was between US$ 100 and $2000 while in Africa, it was between US$2.50 and $50*'.[16] The figures on illegal traffic in waste in Italy give an idea of the extent of the illegal activities in waste in that country. The Italian Parliamentary Commission, created in order to study illegal activity in waste in Italy, estimates that 35% of the 108 million tons of waste produced each year in that country are disposed of incorrectly or illegally and that this generates an estimated turnover of about €7 billion and a tax loss of at least €1 billion.[17]

---

12 Switching Channels – Wildlife trade routes into Europe and the UK, a WWF/TRAFFIC report, December 2002, pp. 6-7.

13 This is not true for legally traded animals, where there are strict controls.

14 Hayman & Brack (2002) 12.

15 European Environment Agency : Europe's environment : the third assessment, Copenhagen, 2003, p. 159.

16 Hayman & Brack (2002) 13.

17 Poppe (2003) 24.

4 Recourse to criminal law in order to have a better implementation of environmental law

4.1 Convention of the Council of Europe on the Protection of the Environment through Criminal Law

In 1998, the Council of Europe adopted the Convention on the Protection of the Environment through Criminal Law[18] ('The Convention'). This Convention is aimed at improving the protection of the environment at European level by using criminal law in order to deter and prevent conduct that is harmful to the environment. The Convention only addresses those activities which are most harmful to the environment, because criminal law is a solution of last resort. This Convention is the first international treaty to criminalise acts causing or likely to cause environmental damage and as such constitutes a significant step towards effective protection of the environment.

The Convention was signed on 16 November 1998. It will enter into force following the deposit of its third ratification. This number of ratifications has not yet been reached.[19]

4.2 The 'Danish initiative': 'Initiative with a view to adopting a Council Framework Decision on combating serious environmental crime'

In February 2000, Denmark presented to the Council an 'initiative[20] with a view to adopting a Council Framework Decision on combating serious environmental crime' (commonly referred to as the 'Danish initiative'). It included some elements of the Council of Europe Convention and was based on Article 31 and Article 34(2)(b) EU. These articles belong to Title VI of the EU Treaty 'Provisions on police and judicial cooperation in criminal matters' and form part of the so-called 'third pillar' of the EU Treaty. The Council had announced that the Framework Decision would be adopted during the session of 15 March 2001.

4.3 The Commission proposal for a Directive on the protection of the environment through criminal law

Ludwig Krämer had been nominated head of the newly created 'Environmental governance' Unit in Directorate-General Environment at the beginning of February 2001. The file 'Environmental Crime' fell within the

---

18 See http://conventions.coe.int/Treaty/fr/CadreListeTraites.htm (ETS 172).

19 For comments on the Convention, see for example Selin (2001) 10(1).

20 The 'Danish initiative': Initiative of the Kingdom of Denmark with a view to adopting a Council Framework Decision on combating serious environmental crime, OJ 2000 C 39/4.

responsibilities of this new unit. This file had not been the subject of much favourable attention until then.

Ludwig Krämer prepared a draft for a Directive on protection of the environment through criminal law, considering that the matter was extremely urgent, as the Council was going to adopt the Framework Decision based on third pillar of the EU Treaty on 15 March 2001. The objective was clearly to allow the Commission to send its own proposal based on the first pillar to the Council before that meeting.

On 13 March 2001 the Commission adopted the proposal for a Directive on the protection of the environment through criminal law.[21] The text was presented to the Council during the session of 15 March and the Council decided not to adopt the Framework Decision in view of this very new element. Ludwig Krämer had won his bet.[22]

This proposal is, from a conceptual point of view, entirely foreign whereas the two abovementioned instruments (the Convention and the original proposal for a Framework Decision) share common foundations. The Commission's proposal is based on Article 175(1) EC. This legal basis belongs to the first pillar of the EU Treaty, and is commonly known under the name of the 'Community method'. The Commission's position over a Community competence in criminal matters is set out in the Commission staff working paper entitled *'Establishment of an acquis on criminal sanctions against environmental offences'.*[23]

Community competence is defined as follows: *'As concerns criminal sanctions the Community cannot purport to act in the criminal area in isolation – as there is no substantive Community competence in relation to criminal matters per se. However, to the extent that this is necessary for the achievement of Community objectives, the Community can oblige Member States to provide for criminal sanctions'.*

Article 174 EC defines general Community competence in environmental matters. Insofar as there is a failure to properly comply with Community environmental law, the Community legislator must require Member States to adopt effective, proportionate and dissuasive penalties, including, where necessary, criminal penalties. This is the purpose of the proposal for a Directive on the protection of the environment through criminal law. The criminal competence of the Community legislator therefore appears as being complementary to the general Community competence as defined in the EC Treaty.

This reasoning is a general one and applies to all Community law. The sector of the environment serves as a legal laboratory,[24] as the rule was adopted by the

---

[21] COM (2001) 139, OJ 2001 C 180/238.

[22] See *Environment Daily* 19/03/2001 ' *Ministers angered by new EU eco-crime plan* ': 'EU justice ministers are furious with the European Commission over its proposal last week of a new Directive on environmental eco-crime (...)'.

[23] SEC (2001) 227, 7.2.2001.

[24] As often in environmental matters, see for example the developments concerning the Convention on Access to Information, Public Participation in Decision-making and Access to Justice in Environmen-

Commission for the first time in a proposal for a Directive concerning Community environmental law. It could however be applied in any matter where the Community has a general competence under the EC Treaty.[25]

4.3.1 Main points of the proposal

The proposal for a Directive establishes a number of basic principles that will allow Member States to adapt their criminal law whilst taking account of national traditions.

The central provision of the proposal for a Directive is Article 3, which requires Member States to ensure that certain activities are criminal offences *'when committed intentionally or with serious negligence, as far as they breach the rules of Community law protecting the environment set out in the Annex and/or rules adopted by the Member States in order to comply with such Community law.'*

The Annex contains a selective list of 51 Directives and Regulations covering the main types of environmental damage. It includes requirements that if breached could cause substantial damage.

In accordance with the subsidiarity principle, the proposal for a Directive limits itself to obliging Member States to impose criminal penalties for breaches of Community environmental law. It leaves Member States considerable freedom to decide what type of criminal penalties they wish to impose, provided they are effective, proportionate and dissuasive, and in accordance with the jurisprudence of the Court on penalties.[26] Member States are also free to adopt or maintain measures more stringent than those provided for in the proposal for a Directive. Moreover, questions of criminal investigations, prosecutions or procedure, including decisions as to whether all offences must be prosecuted

---

tal Matters (Aarhus Convention), which is, as stated by the United Nations Secretary-General Kofi Annan, *'the most ambitious venture in environmental democracy undertaken under the auspices of the United Nations'.*

[25] The Commission made other proposals on the same line of reasoning. See for example the Proposal for a Directive on the criminal-law protection of the Community's financial interests, COM (2001) 272, OJ 2001 C 240 E/125 or the Proposal for a Directive on the coordination of procedures for the award of public supply contracts, public service contracts and public works contracts, COM (2000) 275, OJ 2001 C 29 E/11; More recently, see also Proposal for a Regulation on official feed and food controls, COM (2003) 52. See also below in this article the comments about the proposal for a Directive of the European Parliament and of the Council on ship-source pollution and on the introduction of sanctions, including criminal sanctions, for pollution offences, COM (2003) 92, 05.3.2003.

[26] Examples of Court rulings on Article 10 EC: Case 68/88 *Commission* v. *Hellenic Republic* [1989] ECR 2965; Case C-326/88, *Hansen* [1989] ECR I-2911; Case C 2/88 *J. J. Zwartveld and others* [1990] ECR I-4405; Case C-186/98 *Maria Amélia Nunes and Evangelina de Matos* [1999] ECR I-4883; Case C-333/99 *Commission* v. *France* [2001] ECR I-1025.

and whether criminal penalties may not be imposed in minor or less significant cases, remain matters for the judicial authorities in Member States.

In short, the proposal for a Directive does not require Member States to change their existing criminal law systems but only, where necessary, to supplement them.[27] [28]

4.4 The Council's draft Framework Decision on the Protection of the environment through criminal law

Following the adoption of the Commission proposal for a Directive, the 'Danish initiative' (see § 4.2) evolved, in part because the Commission applied pressure on the Council to agree to examine the first pillar proposal for a Directive. The Council, however, never wished to participate in the co-decision first pillar procedure over the proposal for a Directive. The Commission repeatedly invited it to do so, but the Council consistently refused to examine it. It only agreed to take account of the text as regards its most important provision – Article 3, which requires Member States to impose criminal penalties for breaches of Community environmental law – and to incorporate it in Article 2 of the draft Framework Decision. The Council effectively cut out the substance from the proposal for a Directive and transplanted it to its own draft Framework Decision.

5 Destiny of the initiatives taken at European Union level

5.1 Adoption of the Framework Decision on the Protection of the environment through criminal law

Finally, the Council adopted the Framework Decision on the protection of the environment through criminal law on 27 January, 2003.[29] As already explained, the text of the Framework Decision was amended to correspond more closely to the proposal for a Directive. Its third pillar legal basis is now Articles 29, 31(e) and 34(2)(b) EU.

---

27 For example, Member States that have an administrative criminal law system will not be required to adopt another scheme for criminal justice, but only, where necessary, to supplement it.

28 For other views on the proposal for a Directive, see Buruma & Somsen (2001) 795-797; See also Schrader (2001) 16-17.

29 Council Framework Decision 2003/80/JHA of 27.1.2003 on the protection of the environment through criminal law, OJ 2003 L 29/55.

5.2 Commission's recourse to the Court of Justice challenging the Framework Decision

Very early on, the Commission had announced its intention to challenge the legality of the Framework Decision before the Court if the Council went ahead and adopted it.[30] When the Council adopted the Framework Decision, on 27 January 2003, the Commission made, on the same day, a declaration, annexed to the Framework Decision, in which it reiterated its opposition to the legal basis of the adopted Framework Decision and announced that it reserved all the rights conferred on it by the Treaty.[31]

The action by the Commission was placed before the Court on 15 April 2003.[32] The Commission claims that the Court should declare that the Council Framework Decision is unlawful and annul it. The action is based on Article 35(6) EU. This is the first time that such an action has been brought before the Court on this legal basis.[33] Article 35(6) EU provides the legal basis for the Court to review the legality, amongst other things, of Framework Decisions.[34] Article 35(6) EU is the parallel provision in the EU Treaty to Article 230 EC. Article 35(6) EU is, however, more restrictive than Article 230 EC: the action is only open to Member States and the Commission.

---

30 Letter from Members of the Commission M. Wallström and A Vitorino to the Council Presidency, 24.7.2001.

31 This declaration has not been published in the Official Journal of the European Union, as an annex to the Framework Decision. It appears however in the monthly statement of the acts adopted by the Council. Within its transparency policy, the Council publishes every month a 'statement of the acts adopted by the Council', which is accessible to the public. The monthly statement of January 2003 refers to this Commission's declaration, concerning the opposition of the Commission to the legal basis of the Framework Decision.

32 Case C-176/03 *Commission* v. *Council*, 2003 OJ C 135/21. See also Commission's Press Release IP/03/461, published on the Internet at: http://www.europa.eu.int (RAPID database).

33 The Commission brought an action in legality before the Court under Article 173 EC (renumbered now in Article 230 EC) for annulment of a Joint Action on airport transit arrangements adopted by the Council on the basis of Article K.3 of the Treaty of European Union. At that time, no specific legal basis in the EU Treaty existed in order to found such an action. The Court ruled that where an action is brought before the Court seeking a declaration that, in light of its objective, an act adopted by the Council on the basis of Article K.3(2)(b) of the Treaty on European Union falls within the scope of Article 100c EC, so that it should have been based on that provision, the Court has jurisdiction to review the content of the act in the light of Article 100c EC in order to ascertain whether the Act affects the powers of the Community under that provision. See Case C-170/96 *Commission* v. *Council* [1996] ECR I-2763.

34 The Amsterdam Treaty modified the provisions provided for by Title VI of the Treaty on the EU about police and judicial cooperation in criminal matters and extended the competence of Court within this title.

The summary of the pleas in law indicates that the Commission unreservedly supports the objectives of the Framework Decision but disputes the legal basis adopted in order to provide for the measures in question. The Commission considers that its proposed Directive, if adopted, would secure a better protection of the environment through criminal law than the Framework Decision. The legal character of the Commission's action before the Court therefore focuses on a legal quarrel about the correct basis upon which the act may be adopted. This does not make it easy for European citizens to understand what could be considered as a mere spat between lawyers.

The main arguments, summarised in the Official Journal, refer first of all to the rule that the choice of legal basis for a measure must, according to settled case-law, rest on objective factors which are amenable to judicial review. Those factors in particular include the aim and the content of the measure.[35] In the present case, both the aim and the content of the Framework Decision belong to Community competence as defined for environmental policy in Article 174 to 176 EC. To the extent that it is necessary for the achievement of Community objectives, the Community legislator can oblige Member States to provide for criminal sanctions in their national legal order. Article 47 EU provides for the primacy of the EC Treaty. It is therefore legally impossible to adopt an act on the basis of the EU Treaty if a Community competence exists. Moreover, the Commission refers in its pleas in law to examples as interpreted from the case-law of the Court concerning Article 10 EC (obligation of reasonable co-operation between the Member States and the Community institutions) and to certain Community instruments which themselves define the type of sanctions to be adopted by the Member States.[36]

The Commission has made its challenge on the exclusive basis of the third pillar, ex Article 35(6) EU, probably because this application is the first of its kind. Article 35(6) appears to be the natural third pillar basis for an action in legality against a Framework Decision. It is, however, submitted that the application could also have been founded on Article 230 EC. Considering that the main purpose of the application essentially allows the Court to determine the dividing line between Community competence (first pillar) and inter-governmental competence (third pillar), it could have also been founded on the legal basis for instituting proceedings under the EC Treaty – namely, Article 230 EC.

---

35 See for example, Case C-271/94 *Parliament* v. *Council*, [1996] ECR I-1689, para. 14 and Case C-42/97 *Parliament* v. *Council* [1999] ECR I-869, para. 36.

36 See for instance Council Regulation 2847/93/EEC establishing a control system applicable to the common fisheries policy, OJ 1993 L 261/1.

5.3 Consequences of the Commission's action before the Court of Justice

The Commission's application before the Court has no suspensive effect. The Member States therefore still have to transpose the Framework Decision into their national legal order within two years from its date of adoption.[37] Under third pillar provisions, such a transposition is not subject to the Commission's control,[38] in contrast with the position under the first pillar. A third pillar measure is also not subject to the same intensity of judicial review by the Court.[39] In this respect, a Framework Decision, as regards its effects in the national legal order, can be compared to an international convention.

If transposed into Member States' national legal orders, the Framework Decision may have perverse effects on the effective implementation of environmental legislation.

EU Member States' environmental legislation is essentially of Community origin. The Framework Decision imposes new conditions for implementation of environmental legislation, namely that the act in question is: *'unlawful'*, causes *'serious injury to any person'* and/or *'substantial damage.'* However, certain Community environmental laws provide for absolute prohibitions. In other words, in these cases there is no requirement that conduct be qualified as unlawful in order to be prohibited, or that serious injury to any person or substantial damage must occur.

The adoption of the Framework Decision therefore leads to an important amendment of a substantial part of Community environmental law (by a 'third pillar' text): the application of all the Directives and Regulations listed in the Annex to the proposal for a Directive will, henceforth, be subject to new conditions. This breaches the principle that the instrument which amends an act must be of the same nature as the act itself.

It is difficult to predict the time-frame[40] within which the Court will rule in this case. Even if the Court confirms the position advanced by the Commission and the Parliament, it should be noted that no legal rule appears to oblige the Council to either discuss a first pillar proposal or to proceed with such a measure under the co-decision procedure. The only apparent legal route to possibly force such consideration by the Council would be an action for a failure to act

---

37 See Article 10(1) of the Framework Decision.

38 Article 226 EC.

39 Article 234 EC.

40 See Krämer (2002b) 483. The average duration of procedures in environmental matters before the Court on the basis of Article 226 EC amounted to 21 months over the period 2000-2001. For procedures under Article 234 EC, the average duration was 24 months. The data for procedures according to Article 230 EC (23 months) are not reliable as the Court had to decide in only one case. However in average, in environment cases, the procedure can be normally expected to come to an end within two years.

(under Article 232 EC), for a violation of Article 175 EC – because it is the correct legal basis for the adoption of the Directive.[41]

It may also be considered that, if the Court takes a very long time in order to rule on this case, the solution may be only of historical importance if, in the meantime, a new European Constitution provides for new rules over the division of competencies in criminal matters between Member States and the Community legislator.

6 New European Union initiatives in criminal matters after the accident of the Prestige

6.1 The *Prestige* tanker accident

On 13 November 2002, the *Prestige* tanker suffered serious damage off the Spanish coast. The *Prestige* was a 26-year old single hull oil tanker, flying the flag of the Bahamas. The ship broke in two pieces and sank on 19 November 2002, about 130 miles off the Spanish coast, to a depth of more than 3000 meters. The *Prestige* was carrying 77,000 tonnes of heavy fuel oil, most of her cargo still on board, the rest having already spilled from the tanker during the time that attempts were made to save her. This accident caused the third major oil slick off the Galicia coast. Galicia had already been struck by a similar disaster in 1976 (Urquiola) and again in 1992 (Agean Sea). It was also – and this made a deep impression upon Europeans – the third major oil slick in less than 4 years which heavily polluted the European coastline, following on from the *Erika* (1999) and *Baltic Carrier* (2001) disasters.[42]

---

[41] The position of the Member States consists, indeed, only of disputing the legislator's Community competence to impose on them the obligation to take criminal measures in case of serious violations of environmental law. The substance of the proposal is not really disputed. The alignment between the text of the proposal for a Directive and that of the Framework Decision illustrates this. The Council Legal Service has issued an opinion that concluded that criminal competence of the Community legislator must be recognised on the basis of Article 175 EC. In these circumstances, one can wonder whether the fact that the Council refuses to adopt a common position in accordance with Article 251(2) EC does constitute a likely violation of Article 175 EC in the framework of a failure of the Council to act under the terms of Article 232 EC.

The current case-law relating to the failure to act is limited to a case relating to the common transport policy (Case 13/83 *Parliament* v. *Council* [1985] ECR 1513). In this case, the Court stated that a failure to act is admissible only if the legislator's discretionary power is strongly reduced and if the Treaty itself fixes clearly the result to be reached by the legislation. One can consider that the elements raised by the Court in the transport case would make it difficult to raise a failure to act against the Council in the present case.

[42] For further factual information see for example http://www.le-cedre.fr. Le Cedre, *Centre de Documentation, de Recherche et d'Expérimentations sur les Pollutions Accidentelles des Eaux.* The Cedre was created in 1978 as a result of the oil slick of the tanker 'Amoco Cadiz'.

6.2 The Commission's Reaction: Communication on improving safety at sea in response to the *Prestige* accident

On 3 December 2002, 2 weeks after the sinking of the *Prestige*, and by way of response, the Commission issued a Communication to the European Parliament and the Council on improving safety at sea.[43] It recalled that the Commission had already reacted swiftly after the *Erika* accident in 1999, announcing a first set of measures in a Communication on safety of the seaborne oil trade (the 'Erika I' package).[44] This had been supplemented by a second Commission Communication on further Community measures on maritime safety (the 'Erika II' package).[45]

The Communication of December 2002 mainly announced an earlier application of the measures as intended in the Erika I and Erika II packages.[46]

The Communication also announced so-called 'additional measures', including revision of certain aspects of the international regime for liability and compensation for oil pollution. The Commission considers that there should be a better balance between the responsibility of the players involved in the transport of oil by sea and their exposure to liability and a stricter application of the polluter-pay principle. The measures to be taken by Member States at the international level should be *complemented at Community level by criminal sanctions*, which should be taken against any person who, intentionally or through gross negligence, causes marine pollution, whether deliberate or accidental. The Commission announced that it would, as an immediate step, envisage Community legislation introducing criminal sanctions and, in particular, would introduce a proposal for a Directive on illegal discharges from ships.

In addition, the Justice and Home Affairs Council of 19 December 2002 agreed that complementary measures should be taken in order to *'strengthen the protection of the environment, in particular the seas, through criminal law'*. It did not give any detail on the legal basis to be employed for such complementary measures.[47]

---

43 COM (2002) 681, 03.12. 2003.

44 COM (2000) 142, 21.3.2000.

45 COM (2000) 802, 6.12.2000.

46 In particular it proposed: the early establishment of the European Maritime Safety Agency, a closer monitoring of the performance of classification societies, publication of an indicative list of substandard vessels under Directive 95/21/EC (OJ 1995 L 157/1), establishment of a trans-European data exchange network for vessel traffic monitoring and speeding up the preparation of plans to accommodate vessels in places of refuge. The Commission also requested Member States to take the following measures: recruit a sufficient number of port control inspectors, take the measures necessary to achieve a sufficient inspection rate at all ports and anchorage areas in the Union, ratify without delay the Protocol establishing a supplementary fund for compensation for oil pollution incidents (COPE fund) and ensure that the fund covers damage up to €1 billion and is fully operational before the end of 2003.

47 Statement by the Justice and Home Affairs Council of 19/12/2002.

On 5 March, 2003, 3 months after issuing the first Communication of 3 December 2002, and 3 and a half months after the *Prestige* accident, the Commission made a proposal for a Directive of the European Parliament and of the Council on ship-source pollution and on the introduction of sanctions, including criminal sanctions, for pollution offences.[48]

6.3 The proposal for a Directive on ship-source pollution and on the introduction of sanctions, including criminal sanctions, for pollution offences

The content of the proposal is twofold. Firstly, it incorporates the existing international rules on discharges for ship-source pollution into Community law. This regime is known as the MARPOL 73/78[49] standards. The proposal for a Directive provides for detailed rules related to the enforcement of these standards.

Secondly, the proposal for a Directive provides that violations of these discharge rules shall be qualified as criminal offences.

The proposal for a Directive, as regards criminal sanctions, is built on the same legal foundations as the proposal for a Directive for the protection of the environment through criminal law. It has its legal basis in Community law, being founded on Article 80(2) EC (the legal basis for Community maritime policy). The explanatory memorandum of the proposal for a Directive on ship-source pollution refers to the same reasoning as the one of the proposal for a Directive on the protection of the environment through criminal law, namely: there is no explicit Community competence in relation to criminal matters *per se*, however, to the extent that this is necessary for the achievement of Community objectives, the Community can oblige Member States to provide for criminal sanctions.[50]

---

48 COM (2003) 92, 05 3 2003; see also Commission's Press Release IP/03/316, published on the Internet at : http:// www.europa.eu.int (RAPID database).

49 The International Convention for the Prevention of Pollution from Ships, MARPOL 73/78 was adopted on 02/11/1973 as a consequence of the Torrey Canyon accident in the English Channel. The Torrey Canyon tanker spilled her entire cargo of 120, 000 tons of crude oil into the sea. This was the biggest oil pollution accident ever seen up to that time. The Convention never entered into force, the number of ratifications being too low. A 1978 protocol introduced modifications to the original 1973 treaty text. The combined instrument – The International Convention for the Prevention of Marine Pollution from Ships, 1973, as modified by the Protocol of 1978 relating thereto (MARPOL 73/78) – entered into force on 02/10/1983 for Annexes I (Oil) and II (Chemicals), the Annexes III to V covering harmful goods in packaged form, sewage and garbage, being optional. International Maritime Organisation (IMO) in London performs Secretariat functions. For further information about Marpol 73/78 and IMO, see http: /www.imo.org/.

50 See explanatory memorandum of the proposal for a Directive on ship-source pollution, in particular sub para. 2.2., COM (2003) 92, 05.3. 2003.

There is a key difference between the proposal for a Directive on ship-source pollution and the proposal for a Directive on protection of the environment through criminal law, as regards criminal sanctions and the way the two proposals are built. In the proposal for a Directive on ship-source pollution, the Community obligation – transposition of MARPOL rules and standards into Community law – is created through the new proposal. By contrast, the proposal for the protection of the environment through criminal law referred to already existing environmental Community law (the Directives and Regulations set out in the Annex).

The proposal for a Directive on ship-source pollution presents a few elements, which can be considered as innovative:

- The proposal covers both accidental and operational (deliberate) discharges. Article 2(3) of the proposal reads as follows: *'Illegal discharges' shall mean discharges in violation of Marpol 73/78 and shall include discharges resulting from damage to the ship or its equipment, which are exempted under Marpol 73/78 Annex I, regulation 11(b) and Annex II, regulation 6(b)'.* Deliberate discharges into the sea are a very common, though unacceptable practice. These discharges are covered as so-called 'operational' discharges, including tank cleaning operations and waste oil disposal.[51]
- The scope of the proposal is very wide as regards the notion of a 'ship'. Seagoing vessels, irrespective of their flag, and of any type whatsoever, operating in the marine environment, including hydrofoil boats, air-cushion vehicles, submersibles and floating craft are covered.[52]
- The geographical scope of the proposal is very wide as it covers all coastal waters of the Community and the high seas as well. The exclusive economic zone is covered to the extent that such a zone has been established, in accordance with international law, by a Member State.[53]
- The persons subject to sanctions cover the whole range of potential offenders, including both natural and legal persons. The sanctions will be applicable to any person concerned with the ship, including the master, the owner, the operator, the charterer and the classification society, who has been found to have caused or contributed to illegal pollution intentionally or by means of gross negligence. The penalties may, in the most serious cases, include custodial sentences.
- Fines are referred to in Article 6, dealing with sanctions, and may not be insured against.[54] This point is very important as owners of tankers may

[51] The explanatory memorandum to the proposal for a Directive quotes the following figures: In 2001, aerial surveillance detected 390 oil slicks in the Baltic Sea and 596 in the North Sea. A Commission study for the Mediterranean Sea reports 1638 illicit discharges in 1999.

[52] See definitions in Article 2(4).

[53] See Article 3(1) of the proposal.

[54] See Article 6(6) of the proposal.

currently limit their financial liability if the accident is their fault.

- The proposal recognises that it is important to cover the liability of legal persons. However, in certain Member States, a system of criminal sanctions against legal persons does not exist and it would create difficulties to introduce them by a fundamental change in the underlying principles of national legal systems. For this reason, as in the proposal for the protection of the environment through criminal law, Member States are entitled to provide for measures other than criminal ones, as long as they are effective, proportionate and dissuasive. The proposal for a Directive refers *inter alia* to fines (non-criminal ones), confiscation of proceeds, exclusion from entitlement to public benefits or aid, placing under judicial supervision and judicial winding up orders.[55]

The proposal for a Directive on Ship-Source Pollution refers several times to the proposal for a Directive on the protection of the environment through criminal law in order to place it within the general framework established by the latter.[56] This instrument is therefore to be considered as being specific or 'vertical', as opposed to the general or 'horizontal' proposal for a Directive on the protection of the environment through criminal law.[57] It does, however, raise several problems as regards the coherence to be maintained between the two future Community Directives, if both are to be adopted.

First of all, the proposal for a Directive on Ship-Source Pollution should, if adopted, be added to the list of instruments referred to in the Annex of the proposal for a Directive on the Protection of the Environment through Criminal Law.

Second, Article 3(a) of the proposal for a Directive on the Protection of the Environment through Criminal Law specifically covers *'the discharge of hydrocarbons, waste oils or sewage sludge into water'*. The *Prestige* was towed out into the open ocean where she sank. The *'discharge of hydrocarbons, waste oils or sewage sludge into water'* therefore clearly occurred. This proposal may therefore be considered as covering the *Prestige* case. It refers in an Annex to the main Community legal instruments covering the most important types of pollution, which can be attributed to individuals or legal persons. At the time this proposal was adopted by the Commission, the only legislation referred to in the Annex, which it is possible to envisage as covering the *'discharge of hydrocarbons'*, is the Community waste legislation and in particular the Council Directive 75/442/

---

55 See Article 6(5) of the proposal.

56 See in particular, in introduction *'In line with the Commission's proposal for a Directive on the protection of the environment through criminal law, (...)'*. Same reference in para. 4.6 *'Criminal sanctions'*.

57 The Commission underlined this point in answers to parliamentary questions. See for example: oral question of José Hernandez Mollar, H-815/02, not yet published; written question of Rosa Miguélez Ramos E-716/03, not yet published; Written question of Laura González Álvarez E-1430/03.

EEC of 15 July 1975 on waste.[58] *Prima facie*, the scope of waste legislation appears as being wider than the one of the proposal for a Directive on Ship-Source Pollution. The proposal for a Directive on Ship-Source Pollution refers to MARPOL rules and incorporates them into Community law. It is therefore limited to the substances covered by Annexes I (Oil) and II (Chemicals) of MARPOL standards, the definitions of which do not correspond to those given in Community waste legislation.[59] Moreover, the MARPOL rules, as suggested by the Commission to be incorporated in Community law, contain exceptions and specific rules, which will make their implementation in Community law difficult.

6.4 The Second Commission Communication on the *Prestige*

On 5 March, 2003, the Commission submitted to the European Council a report on action to deal with the effects of the *Prestige* disaster.[60] In particular, it insisted on mechanisms for cooperation between national authorities involving the Commission's monitoring and information center.[61]

As far as criminal sanctions are concerned, the Commission indicated that it was on the verge of adopting the above-referred 'proposal for a Directive on Ship-Source Pollution, and the introduction of sanctions, including criminal sanctions'.[62] It may be noted that, for the time being, it does not appear that the Council can adopt the proposal for a Directive on ship-source pollution, as Member States do not accept criminal sanctions to appear in the proposal for a Directive.[63] The urgency, claimed by the Head of States just after the Prestige accident, is now well far away. [64] [65]

The Commission added that the proposal was to be adopted '*without excluding the possibility of undertaking other legislative initiatives.*' Indeed, the Commission decided to complete the proposal for a Directive on Ship-Source Pollution with a Framework Decision, based on the third pillar, in order to enunciate the

---

[58] Council Directive 75/442/EEC on waste, OJ 1975 L 194/39, as amended by Directive 91/156/EEC, OJ 1991 L 78/32.

[59] On these matters see Martin Hedemann-Robinson (2003b) 89.

[60] COM (2003) 105, 05.3.2003.

[61] Council Decision 2001/792/EC/Euratom establishing a Community mechanism to facilitate reinforced cooperation in civil protection assistance interventions, OJ 2001 L 297/7.

[62] The proposal for a Directive was indeed adopted by the Commission on the same day the Communication was presented to the Council (5/3/2003).

[63] Article finalised in February 2004.

[64] See for example in *The Guardian*, November 20, 2002 'Hopes of averting catastrophe slip beneath waves as salvage team runs out of options' : '*(...) The French president, Jacques Chirac, said a draconian maritime security policy was needed (...)*'.

[65] The European Parliament supports the Commission in its first pillar approach about criminal sanctions. See A5-0388/2003.

level of sanctions and other aspects where, in the Commission's view, a third pillar instrument complementing the Directive is required. The Commission therefore adopted a 'proposal for a Council Framework Decision to strengthen the criminal-law framework for the enforcement of the law against ship-source pollution'.[66]

6.5 Proposal for a Council Framework Decision to strengthen the criminal-law framework for the enforcement of the law against ship-source pollution

The Commission had already envisaged the possibility of a first pillar instrument (the Directive) which imposes on Member States the obligation to provide for criminal sanctions in case of breach of Community environmental law, complemented by a third pillar instrument (a Framework Decision) strictly limited to third pillar aspects.[67]

This is the same approach that the Commission adopted by deciding to adopt a proposal for a Framework Decision complementing the proposal for a Directive on Ship-Source pollution. The complementary character of the Framework Decision is clearly shown in its title, which uses the same terms as the proposal for a Directive: 'Framework Decision to strengthen the criminal-law framework for the enforcement of the law against ship-source pollution'. Articles 1 '*Subject Matter*' and 2 '*Definitions*' of the Framework Decision expressly refer to the Directive on Ship-Source pollution.

The proposal for a Framework Decision deals with issues such as prison sentences and fines. In relation to prison sentences, it is established in Article 3(1) that the '*most serious cases*' listed in Article 6(4) of the proposal for a Directive will require between five and ten years' imprisonment. For other cases Member States remain free to provide for lower thresholds. The appraisal of the seriousness of cases as regards custodial sentences is left to each Member State. The proposal for a Framework Decision however provides some interpretative guidance to Member States. It gives four types of specific circumstances in which a case is to be qualified as being in the 'most serious' category.[68]

---

66 COM (2003) 227, 02.5.2003.

67 The explanatory memorandum of the proposal for a Directive on the Protection of the Environment through Criminal Law already provided that '*(...). It may be envisaged to set up a framework-decision according to Article 34(2)b of the EU Treaty. It could concern criminal jurisdiction, measures guaranteeing mutual extradition and/or coordination of prosecutions and investigations.*'

68 The first specific circumstance is where the offence is committed in the context of a criminal organisation. The three other specific circumstances refer to cases where the offence causes the death or serious injury of persons, causes substantial damage to water quality or to animal or vegetable species or to parts of them. These formulations appear, curiously enough, to come from the Framework Decision on the protection of the environment through criminal law.

Article 3(2) refers to the harmonisation of penalties and in particular the level of fines that Member States may impose in addition to or in place of a prison sentence as required by the proposal for a Directive. High level penalties are envisaged, by reference to percentages of turnover or assets – from 1% to 10% of turnover for less serious cases and from 10% to 20% of turnover for the most serious cases. It is left to national legislation how these rules will be applied.

It is to be noted that the level of sanctions is specifically addressed under the third pillar. The delimitation of competencies under first and third pillars is therefore now fixed by the Commission in the two proposals (the proposal for a Directive on Ship-Source Pollution and its complementing proposal for a Framework Decision). The Commission's interpretation about the border between first and third pillars is now known. This could be an argument to be raised before the Court by the Commission, in the action against the Council Framework Decision on the Protection of the Environment through Criminal Law, in order to show how it conceives the division of competencies between pillars. It could even be considered as an argument in favour of the Commission, that the Commission has already tried to respect the limits of these pillars.

However, it is submitted that it was not for the Commission to set in stone the distribution of the competencies between first and third pillars given that its application to the Court against the Council Framework Decision precisely calls for the Court to reach a conclusion on the limits of these respective pillars.

Moreover, in the context of the revision of the treaties by the intergovernmental conference, this exercise may be considered as premature engagement by the Commission in difficult and subtle issues of the balance of power between institutions.

6.6 Destiny of the Commission's proposals on ship-source pollution

It is too early to know what will be the destiny of the proposal for a Directive on Ship-Source Pollution and on the Introduction of Sanctions, including Criminal Sanctions, for pollution offences and its complementing Framework Decision. However, it appears that it is highly probable that the Council will manage the question as it did for the proposal for a Directive on the Protection of the Environment through Criminal Law. It will probably wish to transfer the first pillar criminal part of the proposal for a Directive to a new Framework Decision, on the model of the Framework Decision on the protection of the environment through criminal law, as adopted by the Council. The present discussions within the Council seem to show that the positions over the proposal for a Directive follow this line.[69] This would raise a problem for

[69] A document published on the public register of the Council summarises the position of the different delegations during the debates within the working groups of the Council as follows: 'It appeared from

the Commission, which should oppose this manoeuver as it did for the Council Framework Decision on the Protection of the Environment through Criminal Law.[70] However, even more than for the protection of the environment through criminal law, it will be difficult for the citizen to understand why the Commission, on pure legal matters, opposes measures which appear as being necessary in order to avoid terrible new oil slicks which devastate whole coastal regions in Europe, and for which important measures have been announced at high political level.

7 Conclusion

In environmental matters, it becomes necessary and urgent to allow a better implementation of environmental law by means of criminal law. The differences between national criminal legislation enable criminals to profit from countries where sanctions are the least heavy (creation of 'criminal havens').[71] Environmental criminality is very often transnational[72] and pollution respects no national border. It is illogical and counter-productive, therefore, to want to maintain the criminalisation of this type of infringement at national level alone. The European Union is a unified legal entity in many respects and in particular as regards the content of environmental national law, under the positive influence of Community environmental law. The rules of sanctions of environmental crime should be similar or comparable inside the Union and should not differ seriously from one country to another. This is a requirement of justice and equity – that all European citizens be treated in the same way for similar acts. At stake, also, is the effectiveness of environmental law and the effective protection of our environment.

---

the discussion in the TTE Council of 9 October 2003, in particular, that Member States were divided as regards the possibility to go beyond the existing international instruments, and that all Member States favoured a solution where the criminal sanctions would be dealt with under a parallel Framework Decision, contrary to the opinion of the Commission.' (Document 13584/03 dated 20 October 2003, See under http://register.consilium.eu.int/).

70 It is also submitted that the Commission should oppose any manoeuvre from the Member States to dilute the other innovative aspects of the proposal, which go further than the mere obligations imposed in the MARPOL Convention. If the proposal finally appeared to be a simple transposition of the MARPOL Convention, and if the obligation for the Member States to adopt criminal sanctions in case of breach of these provisions is suppressed or watered down, the added value of such a new Directive would appear be extremely limited.

71 Creation of 'paradis criminels', formula of Alessandro Benardi in Benardi (2002) 3.

72 On the same basis for example as some other forms of criminality like cybercrime or terrorism.

PART TWO – HORIZONTAL MEASURES

CHAPTER 4

Environmental Impact Assessment

A Major Instrument in Environmental Integration

Liam Cashman[1]

1 Origin and development

1.1 First European Community instrument on Environmental Impact Assessment

Whether through rational or other means, societies have always sought to predict the future and to forecast the effects of human actions.

Environmental impact assessment (EIA) is a predictive tool of the late twentieth century. Originating in the United States, it shows the influence of several different disciplines, notably land-use planning and the environmental sciences. It is one of the fruits of the rapid increase in environmental consciousness that took place in the nineteen sixties, a period that laid decisive foundations for today's policies on environmental protection and improvement.[2]

In essence, EIA is a process of gathering and using information in order to guide decisions likely to affect the environment. In its most evolved forms, it exemplifies and interweaves three of the basic principles or approaches to safeguarding the environment. It is science and knowledge-based, aiming to underpin decisions with information that is relevant, reliable and sufficient. It involves a participative process, and recognises the wisdom of making use not only of different professional disciplines but also of the fund of experience and concerns of the individual citizen and the general public. It is preventive in purpose, seeking to avoid problems from the outset, rather than addressing them once they emerge.

If the launch of the Community's first environmental action programme in 1973[3] is taken as the effective start-date of EC environmental policy, it is clear that certain of these principles and approaches were already present from the outset in the minds of the Community's first environmental policy-makers.[4]

---

1 Environment Directorate-General, European Commission. The opinions contained in the present article are strictly personal and do not engage the Commission. This Article is based on policy developments as at the end of March 2004.

2 Jendroska (note 27 below) has observed that *'In the modern affluent society we have abundance not only of material products but also of 'non-material' products: ideas, theories and visions.'* In this sense, the nineteen sixties and early nineteen seventies were especially bountiful in innovative concepts and principles for protecting the environment.

3 OJ 1973 C 112/1.

4 In its Title II, the First Environmental Action programme not only refers to the principle of preventing environmental harm at source and the polluter pays principle but also notes that *'Effects on the environment should be taken into account at the earliest possible stage in all the technical planning and decision-making processes. The environment cannot be considered as external surroundings by which man is harassed and assailed; it must be considered as an essential factor in the organisation and promotion of human progress. It is therefore necessary to evaluate the effects on the quality of life and on the natural environment of any measure that is adopted or contemplated at national or Community level and which is liable to affect these factors.'*

However, given the novelty of EIA and the lack of an express Treaty reference to the environment, it is still a measure of the boldness of those policy-makers that an initiative on EIA began in the mid-nineteen seventies. It is a measure of the legislative caution that subsequently emerged that five years elapsed between the publication of a Commission proposal in 1980[5] and the adoption of the first EIA instrument, Directive 85/337/EEC[6] on the assessment of the effects of certain public and private projects on the environment.

Delayed in adoption and limited in scope to projects, the first Community instrument on EIA nonetheless represents an important milestone and achievement. In place of the *ad hoc* practices and bits and pieces of national law on impact assessment that preceded it, Directive 85/337/EEC presents a coherent logic and framework for determining the need for, and for undertaking EIA. It is true to the features that characterise EIA in its evolved forms. In the breadth of the science and knowledge that it potentially embraces – from the modelling of air emissions and water discharges to the interpretation of historic landscapes, it has never been surpassed by any other EU environmental instrument – or, indeed, it can probably safely be said, by any other piece of secondary Community legislation. In its provisions for public participation, the Directive can be considered as the first important example of EU-derived 'environmental rights'[7] legislation. It is clear in its endorsement of the preventive principle.

Indeed, in the time since its adoption, the key conceptual strands of the 1985 Directive have, in a wider sphere, grown in importance. Specialist studies and disciplines in the field of the environment have continued to develop. Environtmental rights legislation has expanded in the direction of access to information and access to justice. The principle of prevention has been joined by the precautionary principle.

With regard to EIA specifically, the period since 1985 can be described by reference to three themes: the consolidation and refinement of rules on project-related EIA under the 1985 Directive; the appearance of new instruments and initiatives on EIA that extend the exercise to plans and programmes; and efforts to ensure that, in practice, different assessment requirements are co-ordinated with each other and with other legal requirements.

---

5 OJ 1980 C 169/14.

6 Directive 85/337/EEC, OJ 1985 L 175/40, amended by Directive 97/11/EC, OJ 1997 L 73/5.

7 Conceiving of public consultation purely in terms of environmental rights may be somewhat misplaced, since the benefits of consultation accrue to decision-makers and society at large as well as to those who participate. By providing information to public authorities and by helping to fill knowledge gaps, consultees can be considered as rendering a public service. An analogy may be made with participation in a census.

1.2 Refinement and consolidation of project-related EIA

The 1985 Directive is explained in more detailed below, but it is useful to briefly outline the main developments that followed its adoption.

The Directive allowed Member States a period of three years to take the necessary measures to respect its requirements. During the 1990s, compliance with the Directive became a touchstone issue in environmental controversies about major projects across the EC, especially in those Member States going through a phase of rapid infrastructure-building, such as Spain, Portugal, Greece and Ireland. Amongst environmental complaints submitted to the Commission and the European Parliament, the Directive established itself as the most-cited EC instrument, a position it still occupies.[8]

With the Directive gaining a high profile, legal issues arose and, following preliminary references for interpretation from national courts as well enforcement action taken by the Commission against certain Member States, the Court of Justice provided useful clarification. Its rulings confirmed the Directive's broad purpose and scope.

In 1993 and 1997, under an in-built review mechanism[9], two reports were drawn up by the Commission to provide an overview of implementation of the Directive.[10] Influenced by the findings of the first of these reports as well as the developing case-law of the Court and developments at the international level, the Commission proposed amendments to the Directive in 1994[11] and 1996,[12] and an amending Directive was adopted in 1997.[13] Without departing from the original framework, the amendments clarify and reinforce several key provisions, for example those concerning the selection of individual projects to undergo EIA. A third Commission report has since appeared.[14]

The consolidating effects of case-law, implementation reports and the 1997 revision were augmented by several other initiatives. In 1999 and 2001, the European Commission services published a series of guidelines to assist

---

8 For an account of the implementation of the Directive in this early phase, including the sorts of issues that figured in complaints to the Commission, see Krämer (1997a) 240-257. As then head of the legal unit in the Commission's environmental directorate-general, Ludwig Kramer exercised an influential role in the Directive's implementation.

9 Article 11(1) and (3). These provisions provide for an exchange between Member States and the Commission on experience gained in applying the Directive. On this basis, the Commission is required to send a report to the European Parliament and Council every five years.

10 The first report was published as COM (93)28 of 2.4.93. The second report is available at http: //europa.eu.int/comm/environment/eia-support.htm.

11 OJ 1994 C 130/8.

12 OJ 1996 C 81/14.

13 OJ 1997 L 73/5.

14 This is available at http://europa.eu.int/comm/environment/eia/report_en.pdf.

practitioners and other stakeholders on several aspects of the Directive.[15] The Commission undertook several studies and in 1997 a strategy was published for undertaking research on environmental impact assessment.[16]

The influence of developments at international level can be seen in the adoption of Directive 2003/35/EC,[17] which amongst other things, introduces specific provisions on access to justice into Directive 85/337/EEC.

1.3 New instruments and initiatives on EIA

The 1985 Directive was adopted before the EC Treaty contained any specific reference to the environment. In the following decade and a half, the Treaty underwent three substantial revisions, with eventual consequences for the role of EIA. The first of these revisions, the Single European Act (1987), was the most significant for environmental policy. It saw the insertion of an environmental chapter into the EC Treaty, which has not been radically altered by subsequent revisions. The new chapter included reference to the principle of environmental integration, *i.e.* the principle that the environment should not be dealt with as a policy apart but as an integral aspect of the design and implementation of all EC policies.[18] This principle received a further boost when stronger wording was inserted into a more prominent part of the EC Treaty by the Treaty of Amsterdam (1997).[19]

EIA is, *par excellence,* an instrument for achieving integration. The Treaty recognition that the environment should be an integral part of all EC policies considerably reinforced arguments for a wider use of EIA at higher tiers of decision-making, *i.e.* at the level of decision-making on land-use plans, sectoral plans and programmes, policies and legislation. Environmental impact assessment at this level is commonly referred to as strategic environmental assessment (SEA). The influence of the Treaty became apparent in the area of Community funding in the first half of the nineteen nineties, when a form of environmental

---

15 In 1999, the Commission services published 'Guidelines on the Assessment of Indirect and Cumulative Impacts as well as Impact interactions', ISBN 92-894-1337-9. In 2001, they published separate guidance documents on screening, ISBN 92-894-1334-4, scoping, ISBN 92-894-1335-2, and on reviewing environmental impact statements, ISBN 92-894-1336-0. These documents are obtainable at http://europa.eu.int/comm/environment/eia-support.htm.

16 See http://europa.eu.int/comm/environment/eia-support.htm.

17 Directive 2003/35/EC providing for public participation in respect of the drawing up of certain plans and programmes relating to the environment and amending with regard to public participation and access to justice Council Directives 85/337/EEC and 96/61/EC, OJ 2003 L 156/17.

18 Article 130r, second paragraph provided that *'Environmental protection requirements shall be a component of the Community's other policies.'*

19 A new Article 6 of the EC Treaty provided that *'Environmental protection requirements must be integrated into the definition and implementation of the European policies and activities referred to in Article 3, in particular with a view to promoting sustainable development.'*

assessment (*ex ante* evaluation) was introduced for proposed EC regional spending. This was intended to help avoid the sort of environmental mistakes that had emerged through poor instrument design in other areas of EC activity, notably agricultural policy.[20]

This early effort at a form of strategic EIA was disappointing in substance,[21] but it was a pointer to the general direction in which the EC was moving. In fact, the nineteen nineties were marked by a general trend towards greater analytical preparation of EC policy initiatives, evidenced not only by a recognition of the role of EIA but also of the role of other forms of assessment, such as analysis of the financial implications of new proposals. The Treaty of Amsterdam was accompanied by a declaration on SEA.[22] Against the background of a general effort to improve the formulation of EU legislation and policy, the Commission in 2002 published a communication on impact assessment.[23] This provided for the amalgamation of previous forms of impact assessment, environmental and non-environmental, and the introduction of an extended impact assessment (exIA) for Commission proposals likely to have substantial economic and/or social effects. Detailed internal technical guidelines on implementing exIA were separately introduced.

Thus, the integration principle ultimately proved a significant influence on the Communities own processes for launching policy initiatives. However, in the late nineteen eighties and first half of the nineteen nineties, the climate was not immediately propitious for a general Community initiative on the EIA of plans and programmes at Member State level. The 1985 Directive was going through a teething period, and Member States showed little inclination to accept additional EIA commitments, despite recognition amongst experts that project-related EIA often came too late in to the decision-making process to meaningfully influence outcomes.

The first significant breakthrough came with the adoption in 1992 of Directive 92/43/EEC[24], an instrument to conserve the Community's most important natural habitats and endangered plant and animal species. Although limited to the sphere of nature conservation, this introduced a specific requirement on Member States to environmentally assess plans. Chronologically, this can, therefore, be considered the second major EC instrument on EIA. It is discussed in more detail below.

---

[20] An example is widespread erosion damage in several parts of Europe linked to production subsidies that encouraged farmers to overstock land with farm animals.

[21] Evaluations tended to be meagre or superficial. An imperative to rapidly approve spending programmes militated against any rigorous quality control.

[22] Declaration 12 stated that *'The Conference notes that the Commission undertakes to prepare environmental impact studies when making proposal which may have significant environmental implications.'*

[23] COM (2002) 276 final.

[24] OJ 1992 L 206/7.

A further stimulus to the introduction of more strategic forms of EIA was provided by Community participation in initiatives launched by the United Nations Economic Commission for Europe (UNECE). Older (1947) and with a wider membership than the EU (55 Member States), UNECE has, over the past quarter century, developed into a significant source of international environmental law. During the 1990s, it sponsored two key conventions relevant to EIA.

The first was the Convention on environmental impact assessment in a transboundary context, known as the Espoo Convention after the city in Finland where it was adopted in 1991. Through the use of environmental impact assessment, the Convention aims to prevent, reduce and control significant transboundary environmental impacts from a number of activities.[25] The EC ratified the Convention in 1997. The primary focus of the Espoo Convention is on project-related assessment. However, it contained an express, albeit limited, reference to SEA.[26] The Convention subsequently served as a forum for further work on SEA, with an important protocol being concluded in 2003.[27]

The second UNECE Convention is the Convention on access to information, public participation in decision-making and access to justice in environmental matters, adopted in Aarhus in Denmark in 1998, and hence now known as the Aarhus Convention. The Convention promotes government accountability, transparency and responsiveness in the field of the environment by granting the public rights and imposing on parties and public authorities obligations regarding access to information, public participation and access to justice.[28] The European Community was one of the Convention's signatories.

Other international conventions and initiatives may also be mentioned. In 1992, at the United Nations Conference on Environment and Development ('the Rio Conference') the Convention on Biological Diversity was signed. Amongst other things, this makes reference to project EIA as well as to arrangements to ensure that the environmental consequences of programmes and policies likely to have significant adverse impacts on biodiversity are duly taken into account.[29] The Rio Conference also marked the signing of the Rio Declaration on Environment and Development which made a broad reference to the role of EIA.[30]

In their broad references to EIA, these international conventions are an example of the influence of international fora on EU environmental policy-making. They helped pave the way for an EU instrument on assessment of plans

---

25 For detailed information on the Convention, see web-site http://www.unece.org/env/eia/.

26 Article 2(7) provides that '*To the extent appropriate, the Parties shall endeavour to apply the principles of environmental impact assessment to policies, plans and programs.*'

27 For an account of the origins and development of the SEA Protocol, see Jendroska (2003) 281-293.

28 For further information on the Convention, see web-site http://www.unece.org/env/pp/. See also the article of Birgit Dette in this book.

29 Article 14. For a detailed commentary, see Glowka *et al.* (1994).

30 See principle 17.

and programmes, and the Aarhus Convention has also had an influence on subsequent EU rules on project EIA.

Against a background increasingly favourable to the EIA of plans and programmes, the Commission in 1996 published a proposal for a Directive on SEA[31], which led to the adoption of Directive 2001/42/EC on the assessment of the effects of certain plans and programmes on the environment[32], discussed in more detail below.

1.4 Wider developments requiring co-ordination of EIA and other legal requirements

The creation of a broad and wide-ranging set of EC rules on EIA has taken place while the volume of EC environmental legislation has been generally increasing. As a result, issues of co-ordination have arisen not only as between the three main EIA instruments mentioned above – *i.e.* Directives 85/337/EEC, 92/43/EEC and 2001/42/EC, but also as between substantive requirements on EIA and substantive requirements on other topics.

With the growth in assessment requirements, a challenge has emerged to make different assessment instruments interact coherently. For example, the same project may require assessment under Directives 85/337/EEC and 92/43/EEC. The Commission has tried to address this challenge in guidance documentation.[33] In addition, some specific assessment provisions are the subject of explicit cross-reference.[34] However, given that the assessment of plans and programmes has hardly yet begun to widely feature, the full extent of the co-ordination challenge across different assessment instruments is only likely to be felt in the future.

Because of the nature and scope of project-related and strategic EIA, it is inevitable that it will have cross-cutting relevance to other environmental measures. This relevance stems from the fact that certain plans and project classes covered by EIA requirements are subject to other requirements under EC environmental law. In some cases, EC environmental law obliges the making of plans or programmes or the proposal of projects that either require EIA or need to be screened for it. Examples include the making of waste management plans[35] and the proposed construction of waste-water collection systems and treatment plants.[36] In other cases, projects that require EIA will need to satisfy

[31] COM (1996) 511 final, OJ 1997 C 129/14 and COM (99) 73 final , OJ 1999 C 83.

[32] OJ 2001 L 197/30.

[33] See note 84.

[34] For example, Article 3 of Directive 2001/42/EC contains an explicit cross-reference to Article 6 of Directive 92/43/EEC.

[35] See Directive 75/442/EEC on waste, OJ 1975 L 194/39, amended by Directive 91/156/EEC, OJ 1991 L 78/32.

[36] See Directive 91/271/EEC concerning urban waste water treatment, OJ 1991 L 135/40.

other procedural or substantive obligations.[37] New landfills will need to comply with detailed authorisation requirements.[38] Industrial facilities that present a major accident risk are subject to detailed risk-assessment.[39] Integrated pollution prevention and control requirements (IPPC) apply across a broad range of activities.[40] EIA processes should therefore not be seen in isolation.

2 Present situation: Applicable rules

EIA legislation in the EU currently consists of three principal instruments: Directive 85/337/EEC, Directive 92/43/EEC and Directive 2001/42/EC. However, impact assessment techniques crop up elsewhere in Community law.

2.1 Project-related impact assessment: Directive 85/337/EEC as amended

Being the first and longest-established of the EIA instruments, Directive 85/337/EEC has, until now, commanded the greatest attention.

The essential elements of the Directive are three-fold. Its application is related to listed types of *project*. It contains rules as to *when* an EIA is required. It also contains rules as to *how* an EIA should be carried out. Questions of implementation and interpretation revolve around these elements. In addition, it is relevant to consider the *effects* of EIA, and some other issues.

2.1.1 What is a 'project'?

In considering whether an intervention is a 'project' for purposes of the Directive, regard must be had to the definition of 'project', the scope of the project lists set out in Annexes I and II of the Directive, and the case-law of the Court of Justice.

'Project' is defined in Article 1(2) to mean:

'- *the execution of construction works or of other installations or schemes,*

- *other interventions in the natural surroundings and landscape including those involving the extraction of mineral resources.*'

---

37 These additional requirements have implications for the outcome of the EIA process, *i.e.* the information generated in the process may help to determine the precise conditions that are imposed to comply with authorisation-related and similar obligations derived from other EC environmental legislation.

38 Directive 1999/31/EC on the landfill of waste, OJ 1999 L 182/1.

39 Directive 96/82/EC on the control of major-accident hazards involving dangerous substances (known as 'Seveso II'), OJ 1997 L 10/13.

40 Directive 96/61/EC (IPPC) OJ 1996 L 257/26. Article 6(2) of the Directive includes a specific cross-reference to Directive 85/337/EEC.

This indicates that an intervention must have a physical dimension. While construction will often be a central, it is not a necessary feature. It may be argued, for instance, that a significant change of use may amount to a 'project', as where it is proposed to introduce a new fuelstock to operate a power plant.

Furthermore, the intervention must fall within a class of project listed in Annex I or II of the Directive.[41] These lists are extensive. Their broad scope can be gleaned from the class categories set out in Annex II: agriculture, silviculture and aquaculture; extractive industry; energy industry; production and processing of metals; mineral industry; chemical industry; food industry; textile leather, wood and paper industries; rubber industry; infrastructure projects; other projects; tourism and leisure. Certain classes of project, such as the urban development one,[42] are potentially very wide. Although extensive, the lists are not exhaustive. For example, rural telecommunication infrastructure is not covered.

By virtue of the 1997 amending Directive, there is explicit provision for modifications of projects, Annex II.13 describing the following project class: *'any change or extension of projects listed in Annex I or Annex II, already authorized, executed or in the process of being executed, which may have significant adverse effects on the environment'.*[43] Even before this explicit provision, the Court of Justice had interpreted the original text as potentially covering project modifications.

Case-law provides additional guidance. In Case C-72/95[44], *Kraaijeveld*, the Court noted: *'The wording of the Directive indicates that it has a wide scope and a broad purpose.'*[45] This consideration argues in favour of project classes being interpreted broadly rather than narrowly, once likely significant environmental effects are identified. However, there are limits. In Case C-392/96[46], *Commission* v. *Ireland*, the Court was not convinced from the evidence submitted by the Commission that sheep grazing constituted a project for purposes of the Directive.

2.1.2 When should an EIA be undertaken?

There are several aspects to this question, which, to some extent, overlaps with the previous one. Consideration needs to be given the type of decision-making that is involved, to the date on which the project was

[41] Articles 2(1) and 4.

[42] Annex II.10(b).

[43] This is the currently applicable text. However, Article 3(8) and (9) of Directive 2003/35/EC introduce amendments which need to be transposed into national law by 25 June 2005.

[44] [1996] ECR I-5403.

[45] Paragraph 31.

[46] [1999] ECR I-5901.

initiated, to whether the project falls within Annex I or II of the Directive and to whether any exceptions apply.

In the first place, EIA is related to a decision-making process. The decisive duty is formulated as follows: *'Member States shall adopt all measures necessary to ensure that, before consent is given, projects likely to have significant effects on the environment by virture,* inter alia, *of their nature, size or location are made subject to a requirement for development consent and an assessment with regard to their effects'.*[47] This formulation, combined with the definition of *'development consent'*[48] indicates that project EIA is not required in respect of stages of consideration that, formally, convey no entitlement to execute a project. For example, a proposed intervention may figure in a plan or official programme of interventions, but still require a formal approval process before it can be carried out. For purposes of the Directive, an EIA falls to be considered at the stage when an application is made to allow the project to be carried out. In Case C-201/02[49], *Delena Wells,* the Court has provided further clarification of the notion of what constitutes development consent. It confirmed that the interpretation of what constituted a development consent lay within its jurisdiction. It further confirmed that, in a consent procedure comprising several stages, assessment must, in principle, be carried out as soon as it is possible to identify and assess all the effects which the project may have on the environment.

With regard to timing, the 3 July 1988 deadline fixed by Directive 85/337/EEC for national laws to be adapted to it became the subject of a number of Court rulings. In Case C-396/92[50], *Bund Naturschutz in Bayern and others,* the Court ruled that late adaptation of national laws was not an excuse for exempting projects from EIA, where the development consent procedure was initiated after the 3 July 1988 deadline. On the other hand, in Case C-431/92[51], *Commission* v. *Germany ('Grosskrotzenburg'),* the Court found that the Directive did not apply where the development consent procedure was initiated before this deadline. During the nineteen nineties, the latter ruling proved significant to several high-profile 'pipeline' projects, *i.e.* projects proposed before 3 July 1988 but still awaiting decision after this date. A further qualification was provided in Case C-81/96[52], *Burgemeester en wethouders van Haarlemmerliede en Spaarnwoude,* when the Court ruled that the Directive was applicable in the case of a re-initiated development consent procedure. In order to fix a clear dividing line between projects that are subject to the Directive's original requirements and those that

---

47 Article 2(1).

48 This is defined in Article 2(2) to mean *'the decision of the competent authority or authorities which entitles the developer to proceed with the project'.*

49 Not yet reported.

50 [1994] ECR I-3717.

51 [1995] ECR I-2189.

52 [1998] ECR I 3923.

are subject to the current ones, Directive 97/11/EC included an explicit transitional provision.[53]

For those projects listed in Annex I to the Directive, EIA is, as a general rule, compulsory.

For those projects listed in Annex II to the Directive, Member States must operate a screening system in order to determine whether individual projects require an EIA. The screening system may take the form of thresholds or case-by-case examination or a combination of both. Whatever the chosen form, a set of selection criteria introduced by Directive 97/11/EC must be taken into account. These are set out in the current Annex III and relate to the characteristics of projects, their location and the characteristics of the potential impact.

Even before the amendments introduced by Directive 97/11/EC, the Court confirmed that Member States' discretion with regard to Annex II had significant limits. In Case C-133/94[54], *Commission* v. *Belgium*, the Court found that Member States are not entitled to exclude generally and definitively from assessment one or more project classes mentioned in Annex II.[55] In *Kraaijveld*, the Court found that the question of whether a Member State went beyond the limits of its discretion in creating a screening system for Annex II projects cannot be determined in relation to the characteristics of a single project. It depends on an overall assessment of the characteristics of projects of that nature which could be envisaged in the Member State.[56] In Case C-392/96[57], *Commission* v. *Ireland*, which concerned the use of size thresholds for afforestation, peat extraction and land reclamation projects, the Court found that, when establishing a screening system, Member States must take account not only of the size of projects, but also of their nature and location, since certain kinds of small project in sensitive locations might warrant assessment. Furthermore, Member States must take measures to avoid a screening system being circumvented by 'project-splitting' or 'salami-slicing' (*i.e.* the fragmentation of proposed developments into component parts that fall below the thresholds set for mandatory assessment).

The Directive sets out a number of possible exceptions in relation to the need for EIA. Projects serving national defence purposes are not covered by the Directive.[58] However, in Case C-435/97[59], *World Wildlife Fund (WWF) and others*, the Court indicated that a mixed-use project – in the specific case, an airport serving both civil and military purposes, but whose main use was commercial – was not necessarily excluded.[60] The Directive does not apply to projects the

53 Article 3(2) of Directive 97/11/EC.

54 [1996] ECR I-2323.

55 Paragraphs 41-43.

56 Paragraph 52.

57 [1999] ECR I-5901.

58 Article 1(4).

59 [1999] ECR I-5613.

60 Paragraphs 64-67.

details of which are adopted by a specific act of national legislation.[61] In cases C-435/97, *World Wildlife Fund (WWF) and others* and C-287/98[62], *Linster*, the Court interpreted this exception strictly. Finally, subject to several conditions, Member States may, in exceptional cases, exempt a specific project in whole or in part from the provisions laid down in the Directive.[63] To date, very limited use has been made of this provision.

2.1.3 How should an EIA be undertaken?

For detailed information on this, the reader is referred to Commission guidance documentation.[64]

EIA under the Directive is a step-wise procedure. It may begin with an exercise in *scoping*.[65] This involves the authorities providing a developer at his request with an opinion on the information that the developer is to supply. In relation to the next step in the process, scoping may enable the developer to concentrate on the most important aspects of the project in terms of environmental impacts.

Whether or not any prior scoping is involved, the developer must submit certain environmental information to the authorities in order for the EIA to proceed further.[66] The required information can potentially extend across a wide spectrum of topics, from the effects on the environmental media and plants and animals to those on the archaeological heritage and the landscape. There is also provision for information on project alternatives. In practice, developers generally hire experts to compile the information for them, and across the EU a small service industry has grown up around the requirements of EIA.

The developer's information becomes the basis on which consultation takes place with a number of different categories of consultee, including environmental authorities and the *'public concerned.'*[67] The detailed arrangements for consulting the public are left to Member States.[68] Some projects may have effects in Member States other than the Member State where they are proposed

---

61 Article 1(5).

62 [2000] ECR I-6917.

63 Article 2(3).

64 See note 15.

65 Article 5(2).

66 Article 5 in combination with Annex IV.

67 Article 6.

68 In practice, complaints to the Commission have focused on the short length of time that some Member States give to the public to express an opinion, and on the degree of publicity given to public notices that a consultation has started. One Member State, Ireland, is unique in requiring the public to pay a participation fee to express an opinion – see Ryall (2002) 317-329. The Commission has announced a legal challenge to this participation fee.

to be located, and the Directive makes explicit provision for transboundary consultation.[69]

2.1.4 Effects of EIA and the absence of EIA

It is commonly assumed that the conduct of an EIA does not tie the hands of decision-makers and that a project may proceed despite predicted negative effects. However, certain qualifications deserve to be mentioned.

First of all, the information gathered from the developer and through consultation must be taken into consideration in the development consent procedure.[70] This duty has not yet been interpreted by the Court of Justice and it may be wondered whether, having regard to the principle of prevention underlying the Directive, decision-makers are completely free to ignore the negative findings of an EIA. In particular, the decision on the project must be a reasoned one, and include '*a description, where necessary, of the main measures to avoid, reduce and, if possible, offset the major adverse effects*'.[71] Furthermore, the findings of an EIA may raise issues of substantive compliance with other EU environmental legislation. For example, an EIA may predict that a project will lead to breaches of binding water quality objectives, or it may disclose the presence of breeding site and resting place of an animal species protected under Directive 92/43/EEC.[72] In these circumstances, it is hard to see how the findings of an EIA can be validly ignored.

EIA has implications with regard to *when* a project is executed. The Directive is a preventive instrument and allowing a project to be executed in whole or in part before the decision-making process is completed is inconsistent with its requirements.

What are the *consequences* of a failure to undertake an EIA where one ought to have been carried out?

At the Community level, the Commission can bring infringement proceedings under Article 226 of the Treaty.[73] It is, in principle, also possible for the Commission to seek interim relief, *i.e.* to ask the Court to halt a project being executed pending the completion of an EIA. In practice, the Commission has never done this. On the only occasion when the Commission sought interim

---

69 Article 7.

70 Article 8.

71 Article 9.

72 Article 12.

73 On 29 April 2004, in Case C-117/02, *Commission* v. *Portugal* (not yet reported), the Court rejected a Commission challenge to a decision of the Portuguese authorities not to submit a tourism complex in the Sintra-Cascais Natural Park to an EIA. The judgment provides valuable clarification on the standard of proof that must be met in such cases (see paragraphs 82 to 88).

relief with regard to an EC environmental obligation, it was unsuccessful.[74] As a separate matter, the Commission can suspend the payment of Community funds where no EIA is undertaken for a Community co-financed project.

With regard to the national level, the Court of Justice has provided important clarification, notably in *Delena Wells*.[75] In the latter case, it declared that:

'Under Article 10 EC the competent authorities are obliged to take, within the sphere of their competence, all general or particular measures for remedying the failure to carry out an assessment of the environmental effects of a project as provided for in Article 2(1) of Directive 85/337.'

The Court noted that a Member State is required to make good any harm caused by the failure to carry out an EIA[76] and it declared that:

'it is for the national court to determine whether it is possible under domestic law for a consent already granted to be revoked or suspended in order to subject the project to an assessment of its environmental effects, in accordance with the requirements of Directive 85/337, or alternatively, if the individual so agrees, whether it is possible for the latter to claim compensation for the harm suffered.'

The Court further clarified that, in relation to the detailed national procedural rules used to remedy a failure to undetake an EIA, a principle of equivalence and a principle of effectiveness needed to be respected, *i.e.* the rules should be no less favourable than those governing similar domestic situations and they should not make it impossible or excessively difficult to exercise rights under the Directive .

2.1.5 Access to justice

The right of an individual to invoke the Directive before the national courts is closely related to the issue of the consequences of a failure to undertake an EIA (or, *mutatis mutandis,* to otherwise comply with Directive 85/337/EEC).

In this regard, the judgement in *Delena Wells* is very significant. The Court confirmed that, under certain circumstances, an individual is entitled to invoke before a national court the provisions of Directive 85/337/EEC in relation to a failure to carry out an EIA.

---

[74] Case C-57/89 *Commission* v. *Germany ('Leybucht Dykes')* [1991] ECR I-883. The Commission sought to halt work on a sea dyke project on the basis that it would give rise to a contravention of Directive 79/409/EEC on the conservation of wild birds (OJ 1979 L 103/1).

[75] Case C-201/02, not yet reported.

[76] Paragraph 66 of the judgement.

The position established by *Delena Wells* is set to be reinforced by an amendment to the 1985 Directive. One of the aims of the Aarhus Convention is to facilitate access to justice in relation to information and participation rights.[77] In order to align Community law with this aspect of the Convention, Directive 2003/35/EC[78] inserts additional clauses into Directive 85/337/EEC.[79] Under these clauses, Member States are obliged to ensure that members of the public have access to a judicial review to challenge the substantive or procedural legality of decisions, acts or omissions subject to the public participation provisions of the Directive. Any procedure put in place to respect this obligation *'shall be fair, equitable, timely and not prohibitively expensive'*. Specific reference is made to the role of non-governmental organisations. The deadline for adapting national laws to these new clauses is 25 June 2005.

It remains to be seen how significant these clauses will prove. Complaints to the Commission sometimes refer to the current prohibitive cost of seeking judicial review of EIA in certain Member States.

2.2 Assessment of habitat impacts: Directive 92/43/EEC

Under Directive 92/43/EEC, specific assessment provisions have been created to help protect the EU's richest concentrations of biodiversity from threats posed by damaging plans and projects.

The impact assessment provisions of Directive 92/43/EEC are found in its Article 6(3) which provides that:

> *'Any plan or project not directly connected with or necessary to the management of the site but likely to have a significant effect thereon, either individually or in combination with other plans or projects, shall be subject to appropriate assessment of its implications for the site in view of the site's conservation objectives. In the light of the conclusions of the assessment of the implications for the site and subject to the provisions of paragraph 4, the competent national authorities shall agree to the plan or project only after having ascertained that it will not adversely affect the integrity of the site concerned and, if appropriate, after having obtained the opinion of the general public.'*

These provisions relate to the first step of a process governing plans or projects likely to have a significant effect on sites making up the Natura 2000 network. This EU nature conservation initiative – described as '*the EU's flagship contribution to safeguarding global bio-diversity*'[80] – aims to conserve important habi-

---

[77] Article 9 of Convention.

[78] OJ 2003 L 156/17.

[79] Article 3(7) of Directive 2003/35/EC inserts a new Article 10a into Directive 85/337/EEC.

[80] See, for example, Commission press release IP/03/1109.

tats and species' habitats and covers, in total, more than 15% of the EU's land surface. The assessment provisions form part of a wider set of site safeguards.

In practice, the importance of the assessment provisions stems from the physical extent of the network, the network's crucial role in ensuring the healthy long-term status of the EU's biodiversity, and the other substantive requirements that are linked to the assessment provisions. Their importance is further underlined by the extent of political commitments to better safeguarding biodiversity[81] and by the degree to which nature conservation figures in citizen complaints to the European Commission.

The process for considering significant plans and projects is, in part, a reaction to the decision of the Court of Justice in Case C-57/89, *Commission* v. *Germany ('Leybucht Dykes')*.[82] On the one hand, it was felt that the decision of the Court might overly constrain necessary developments in protected nature sites. On the other, it was thought necessary to define a careful and proportionate approach to considering the possibility and the acceptability of site damage.

The result was a stepwise procedure. This involves potentially significant plans and projects first undergoing assessment. If, following assessment, these are deemed to have damaging effects, they should not, in principle, be approved. However, subject to conditions, exceptions are possible under the terms of Article 6(4).[83] Where there is no alternative solution, damaging plans or projects may be approved for reasons of overriding public interest. In some circumstances, a prior opinion is required from the European Commission. Compensatory measures must be provided, *i.e.* nature must receive some recompense for the damage that results from the plan or project going ahead.

The formulation of the procedure in Article 6(3) and (4) is succinct, but it repays close attention, being substantively innovative and rich in legal content.

---

[81] At the European Council held in Göteburg in June 2001, Member States committed themselves to halting biodiversity decline within the EU by 2010.

[82] See paras 21 and 22 of the judgement. The Court ruled that the reduction of an SPA can be justified only on exceptional grounds. Those grounds must correspond to a general interest which is superior to the general interest represented by the ecological objective of Directive 79/409/EEC. In that context, economic and recreational requirements do not enter into consideration.

[83] Article 6(4) provides that '*If, in spite of a negative assessment of the implications for the site and in the absence of alternative solutions, a plan or project must nevertheless be carried out for imperative reasons of overriding public interest, including those of a social or economic nature, the Member State shall take all compensatory measures necessary to ensure that the overall coherence of Natura 2000 is protected. It shall inform the Commission of the compensatory measures adopted.*

Where the site concerned hosts a priority natural habitat type and/or a priority species, the only considerations which may be raised are those relating to human health or public safety, to beneficial consequences of primary

In 2000, the Commission published a guidance document on the legal aspects of Article 6.[84]

The *scope* of the assessment requirement is at once broader and narrower than that of Directive 85/337/EEC. It is broader in that it refers to plans and potentially encompasses all project types (instead of being limited to specified ones) and narrower in that it is solely concerned with impacts on nature. Directive 92/43/EEC was drafted within a unit of the Commission that, at the time, also had responsibility for Directive 85/337/EEC. The limitations of the earlier instrument in terms of higher tiers of decision-making, and the long-term ambition of extending assessment to plans were factors that influenced the formulation. Even thought the prospects of the Council approving a general instrument on plan assessment were judged slim at the time, it was seen as feasible to introduce plan assessment in the nature sector – correctly as it turned out.

Perhaps because of its novelty, the provision for assessment of plans has since been widely ignored, both in national implementing legislation and practice, leading to Commission infringement proceedings against several Member States. Conclusive judicial interpretation is still lacking, but in Case C-256/98[85], *Commission* v. *France*, the Advocate General remarked, with regard to the notion of 'plan':

'In the context of Article 6(3), the term plan must in my view be interpreted extensively. The sites likely to be affected by such plans are, by definition, sites of Community importance, which benefit from the protection regime established in accordance with Article 6(1) and (2); the adoption of a narrow interpretation of the term plan would be contrary to both the wording of Article 6(3) ([any] plan or project), and the conservation objectives which the designation of SACs seeks to pursue. As the possible future development of a site depends primarily on the assessment, it seems to me that the obligation ratione materiae to carry out a site assessment must therefore cover all development activities with the exception of those which are unlikely to have any significant effect, either individually or in combination with other development activities, on the site's conservation objectives. This is consistent with the principle of Community law that exceptions to the general rule (here, development activities which do not require a site assessment) are to be interpreted restrictively'.

importance for the environment or, further to an opinion from the Commission, to other imperative reasons of overriding public interest.'

84 'Managing Natura 2000 sites, The provisions of Article 6 of the 'Habitats' Directive, 92/43/EEC', ISBN 92-828-9048-1. This document is obtainable at http://europa.eu.int/comm/environment/nature/art6_en.pdf. It needs to be read with some circumspection, as subsequent case-law of the Court of Justice differs from the guidance on the applicability of Article 6(2), (3) and (4) to important bird sites that have not been designated.

85 [2000] ECR I-2487, paragraph 33.

Although, thanks to Directive 85/337/EEC, project assessment is more established, the dividing line between what constitutes a 'plan or project' and what constitutes an established activity[86] is not always clear. In 2003, a Dutch Court made a preliminary reference on the question of whether a long-established activity that is annually licensed came within the scope of Article 6(3).[87]

2.2.1 When is an assessment under Article 6(3) required?

The determination of when an assessment is required has two aspects. There is the substantive aspect of determining whether a threshold of significance has been reached. Then there is the aspect of the provisions' application date.

With regard to the substantive aspect, clear parallels can be drawn with Directive 85/337/EEC, which features the same 'trigger' formula, namely 'likely to have significant effects.'

With regard to the application date, the position cannot be described as straight-forward. The assessment requirement is linked to two distinct components of Natura 2000: sites classified under the terms of Directive 79/409/EEC on the conservation of wild birds[88] (which are referred to as special protection areas or SPAs); and sites that come forward under the multi-stage process of site nomination, listing and designation laid down in Directive 92/43/EEC itself (which will ultimately become special areas of conservation or SACs). Any determination of the application date needs to take into account differences as between these two components.

By virtue of Article 7 of Directive 92/43/EEC, the provisions of Article 6(3) and (4) of Directive 92/43/EEC apply to SPAs from the date of their classification, but many important ornithological sites deserving of protection have still not been classified. The Court has ruled that, pending classification, the latter are subject to an older protection regime – the regime applied in *Leybucht Dykes*.[89] This older regime does not specifically refer to assessment. However, in such circumstances, an assessment may be independently warranted for a project covered by Directive 85/337/EEC.

According to the strict wording of Directive 92/43/EEC,[90] the assessment requirements of Article 6(3) apply to other sites once they have been placed on a list of sites of European importance adopted by the Commission in co-operation with the Member States. Uncertainty stems from the fact that, because Member States did not respect the delays for nominating sites, the list was not adopted

86 Established activities can be considered covered by a general duty to avoid site deterioration and significant species disturbance set out in Article 6(2) of Directive 92/43/EEC.

87 Case C-127/02, *Landelijke Vereniging tot Behoud van de Waddenzee* and others, not yet decided.

88 OJ 1979 L 103/1.

89 Case C-374/98, *Commission* v. *France ('Basses Corbières')* [2000] ECR I-10799.

90 Article 4(5).

within the deadline stipulated in the Directive, *i.e.* June 1998. The list remains incomplete. Are Member States free to ignore the need for assessment – as well as other site safeguards, until the list is ready? The answer is ultimately for the Court of Justice to give.[91] There are good arguments based on existing case-law and Article 10 EC for already giving effect to the assessment requirements of Article 6(3). In practice, most Member States seem inclined to accept the current need for site safeguards.

2.2.2 How should an assessment be carried out for purposes of Article 6(3) and what are its consequences?

The Directive does not explicitly specify the methodology for assessing plans and projects. To complement the legal guidance on Article 6, the Commission published guidance documentation on how to apply Article 6(3) and (4), including the assessment provisions.[92]

A particular challenge arises from the linking of the assessment requirement to 'in combination' effects. Sometimes, nature sites will be threatened not by a single large plan or project but by a multiplicity of smaller interventions. Taken individually, these may not be consequential: taken together, they may seriously compromise a site's conservation objectives.

The Commission has taken the view that an EIA under Directive 85/337/EEC can, in principle, also satisfy the assessment requirements of Article 6(3). However, unlike the assessment requirements of Directive 85/337/EEC, the assessment requirements of Article 6(3) are an integral part of a wider set of safeguards. The decision-maker is, therefore, more constrained than in situations where Natura 2000 is not involved. Furthermore, the need to ensure that Natura 2000 retains its overall coherence suggests that the features of Member States' methodologies and the skills with which they are employed should not deviate to the extent of producing scientifically or technically inconsistent outcomes.

Added to these general considerations is the factor of specificity. Natura 2000 hosts many different types of living environments, with very different susceptibilities to human influence. Assessment methodologies should take account of this factor.

With regard to the consequences that may flow from an Article 6(3) assessment, it is important to stress the link to other obligations. In Case C-209/02[93], *Commission* v. *Austria,* the Court found that Austria was in breach of Article 6(3)

---

[91] A preliminary reference from an Italian Court is currently awaiting a decision by the Court of Justice (Case C-117/03).

[92] 'Assessment of Plans and Projects Significantly Affecting Natura 2000 sites, Methodological guidance on the provisions of Article 6(3) and (4) of the Habitats Directive 92/43/EEC', ISBN 92-828-1818-7. The document is available at http://europa.eu.int/comm/environment/nature/natura_2000_assess_en.pdf.

[93] Not yet reported.

and (4) for approving a golf course extension despite an assessment that it would have negative effects on the habitats of the Corncrake, *Crex crex*, a globally endangered wild bird species.

2.3 Environment Assessment of Plans and Programmes: Directive 2001/42/EC

From the beginning, the European Commission had seen that the rationale for environmental impact assessment did not apply solely to projects. The original proposal for a Directive on project impact assessment[94] alludes to the step by step introduction of assessment principles to decision-making land-use plans, regional development programmes and economic programmes, including those in particular sectors.[95] However, as is evident from the recitals to Directive 2001/42/EC (now commonly referred to as 'the SEA Directive')[96], the progression to an instrument covering the assessment of plans and programmes was neither direct nor rapid.

In structure, Directive 2001/42/EC has clear parallels with Directive 85/337/EEC. It sets rules for defining when individual plans and programmes should undergo assessment,[97] just as the earlier instrument did with regard to individual projects. It contains provisions governing the way in which an assessment should be carried out.[98] As with Directive 85/337/EEC, these entail public consultation and an assessment process that is to be undertaken before rather than after decisions are adopted. In addition, there is a comparable inbuilt review mechanism.[99] However, there are also differences. Of particular note is a requirement to carry out monitoring of the significant environmental effects of the implementation of plans and programmes in order, amongst other things, to identify unforeseen adverse effects and to be able to undertake appropriate remedial action. This is an advance on Directive 85/337/EEC, which contains no equivalent provision. National rules to give effect to the Directive need to be in place before 21 July 2004.[100] This is also a decisive date for determining whether individual plans and programmes should undergo strategic assessment.[101]

---

94 OJ 1980 C 169/14.

95 See fourth and fifth recitals.

96 For an extensive account of the Directive and its background, see Sheate (2003) 331-347.

97 Articles 2 and 3.

98 Articles 4 to 9.

99 Article 13.

100 Article 13(1).

101 Article 13(3).

The Directive sets out a broad definition of 'plans and programmes',[102] encompassing European Community co-financed plans and programmes,[103] as well as plans and programmes adopted through a legislative procedure. The basic requirement to carry out an environmental assessment is defined broadly in terms of sectoral and land-use plans and programmes which 'set the framework for future development consent of projects listed in Annexes I and II to Directive 85/337/EEC' or which 'have been determined to require an assessment pursuant to Article 6 or 7 of Directive 92/43/EEC'.[104] This underscores a dynamic relationship between the three Directives concerned. In addition to this basic requirement, Directive 2001/42/EC provides for the possible environmental assessment of other types of plans and programmes likely to have significant environmental effects.[105]

While greatly enlarging the scope of environmental assessment requirements under Community law, Directive 2001/42/EC is not comprehensive. In particular, financial or budget plans and programmes are excluded from its provisions.[106] This omission is of potentially considerable significance, given the influence that budgetary measures such as tax breaks may exert on activities that impinge on the environment.[107]

In 2003, the Commission services published a non-binding guidance document on the Directive.[108] This was intended to promote a clear understanding of the Directive's requirements amongst Member States, public authorities and the general public.

2.4 Other EU instruments with EIA-type provisions

Space does not permit a detailed survey of all the other EU instruments and initiatives that are relevant to assessment. In essence, two broad categories can be identified: those that provide for assessment of Commis-

---

102 Article 2(a).

103 Although excluding plans and programmes concerning the current round of Structural Funding and Rural Development – see Article 3(9). Furthermore, because addressed to Member States, the Directive relates to plan and programme-making under the responsibility of the Member States. Some programmes are initiated by the Commission itself.

104 Article 3(2).

105 Article 3(3)-(7).

106 Article 3(8).

107 For example, fiscal incentives may be created that favour new construction rather than building conservation in historic urban areas, contributing to a loss of archaeological heritage independently of land-use plans or individual projects.

108 *'Implementation of Directive 2001/42/EC on the assessment of the effects of certain plans and programmes on the environment'*, European Communities, 2003, ISBN 92-894-6098-9. This is available at http: //europa.eu.int/comm/environment/eia/home.htm.

sion or multi-lateral Community processes; and those that include assessment-relevant provisions that apply within Member States.

In the former category are the undertaking on SEA reflected in Declaration 12 accompanying the Treaty of Amsterdam and the 2002 Commission communication on impact assessment mentioned above. Implementation by the Commission of the extended impact assessments envisaged by the latter is still in an early phase. The Commission work programme for 2003 foresaw an exIA for 42 proposals, covering several domains of Community policy.

In the latter category are several environmental Directives. At the level of individual projects, mention can be made of Directive 96/61/EC ('IPPC'), which requires detailed environmental information to support a permit application.[109] Examples at a more strategic level include Directive 96/82/EC ('Seveso II'), which requires major-accident risks to be taken into account in land-use planning,[110] and Directive 2000/60/EC establishing a framework for Community action in the field of water policy[111], which requires a review of the environmental impact of human activities on river basin districts.[112]

3 Challenges for the future, including critical remarks

3.1 Project-related EIA

Although EU instruments providing for impact assessment have increased in number and scope since 1985, EU-derived assessments still overwhelmingly consist of project assessments under Directive 85/337/EEC.

Measured against the pressures that impinge on the environment, the Directive's influence has been limited. In relation to its first phase of implementation, it has been referred to in terms of unfulfilled expectations.[113] These unfulfilled expectations concern a failure to carry out EIA in the first place, as well as the limited effectiveness of the EIA process in avoiding environmental harm or promoting environmental protection and improvement.

For major infrastructure projects, such as motorways, project assessment has become routine, but for other important categories, such as the urban development one, its use tends to be exceptional. It has not, for example, acted as a meaningful check in those parts of the Community where urban sprawl occurs. Nor has it made any significant impression on continued agricultural intensification, despite Directive 85/337/EEC featuring several agricultural project categories and despite strong evidence of related environmental degrada-

109 Article 6.

110 Article 12.

111 OJ 2000 L 327/1.

112 Article 5.

113 Krämer (1997a), see note 8 above.

tion, such as nutrient enrichment of water-bodies and widespread impairment of biodiversity.

This may reflect a tendency to exclusively associate the need for assessment with large-scale infrastructural and industrial projects, despite the fact that the Court has confirmed that project assessment is potentially relevant for small-scale, non-industrial projects.[114] It may also reflect a perception that impact assessment is intended for particular types of negative environmental impact, especially air and water pollution and habitat loss.

However, there are strong arguments for using assessment as a tool for achieving enhanced environmental benefits in circumstances where a project is not instrinsically harmful, for example as a tool for architects and planners to create improved urban neighbourhoods.[115] Furthermore, impact assessment is a tool that is not only relevant for impacts on the natural environment, but also for impacts on the historic built or cultural environment.[116] This has been noted by the European Parliament.[117] Furthermore, while at EU level the importance of architectural quality has been acknowledged as a means of integrating new buildings and structures into the existing environment,[118] EIA is rarely used as a methodological tool for promoting high aesthetic and resource-use standards in residential developments.[119]

---

[114] See Case C-392/96 *Commission* v. *Ireland* [1999] ECR I-5901 In this case, amongst other things, the Commission raised the issue of damage to archaeological sites and important habitats from small-scale land reclamation projects in the Burren, an important and sensitive karst limestone landscape in the west of Ireland. Many of the projects involved only a few hectares in extent.

[115] The Commission's 2002 Communication on Impact Assessment notes that 'impact assessment identifies the likely positive and negative impacts of proposed policy actions' (emphasis added). See COM (2002) 276 final, p. 2. It is true that, in places, the text of Directive 85/337/EEC qualifies the concept of significant effects with the epithet 'adverse', as in the project modification class described at Annex II.13, first indent. However, for the most part, the concept is not qualified.

[116] See Article 3.

[117] On 16 January 2001, the Parliament adopted resolution EP N°: A5-0382/2000 on the Convention on the Protection of the world Cultural and Natural Heritage. The resolution is noteworthy for its emphasis on the role of Directive 85/337/EEC in safeguarding the cultural heritage. It calls for this to be afforded the same respect as other non-renewable resources.

[118] See Council Resolution 2001/C73/04 on architectural quality in urban and rural environments, OJ 2001 C 73/6.

[119] Stookes (2003) 145, pertinently observes that, in the UK, a total of 236 EIAs were undertaken in 1999 and a total of 367 in 2000, but that '*In contrast, in 2000/01 there were around 5,000 planning decisions relating to major dwellings development, over 10 times the number of planning proposals supported by EIAs. It would be very surprising if more than a very small proportion of those 5,000 major developments didn't, in reality, have a significant environmental impact. This is because conventional land use development in the UK is so fundamentally unsustainable, using high levels of energy and water, generating high levels of waste in both construction and use, and encouraging high levels of inefficient, environmentally damaging, travel patterns.*'

In terms of the extent to which it is used, project assessment has therefore an under-utilized potential.[120] The emergence of an information society characterised by ever-easier access to diverse sources of specialist information strengthens the case for more extensive collection and dissemination of information through impact assessment.[121] On the other hand, if its use is to become routine in the contexts mentioned, there is a need to pay close attention to the need for flexibility in the specific requirements that apply to individual assessments. In particular, there is a need, through scoping, to avoid overburdening developers with extraneous information demands. Apart from cost implications, unnecessary information can prove unhelpful, by obsuring the impacts that really count.

To the extent that impact assessments have been undertaken over the past fifteen years, it is unfortunate that empirical evidence of the benefits that have resulted is lacking. The implementation reviews carried out under Directive 85/337/EEC have undoubtedly served a useful purpose, but there is a dearth of case-studies examining the outcomes of assessment. In the author's experience, project-related EIA is often effective in mitigating environmental harm, by pinpointing likely problems and identifying and promoting better design solutions. However, its potential is undermined by factors such as an inherent developer-bias (information provided by the developer leads the process and may sometimes be uncritically accepted), a lack of participation by environmental authorities in the consultation phase and an inability or unwillingness of decision-makers to ensure quality-control. Moreover, EIA is commonly of no or limited assistance in ensuring that a project is optimally located. This can reflect a context of generally poor spatial planning (*i.e.* spatially planning that fails to steer damaging development away from sensitive or inappropriate locations) or the absence of any rigour in dealing with the aspect of project alternatives. In practice, the decision at project-level may be little more than a ratification of a prior political or plan-led choice.

Looking ahead, it seems likely that the themes of consolidation and coordination will continue to feature.

As indicated, a considerable effort has already been made to consolidate the potential of Directive 85/337/EEC, through reviews, legislative amendments and the publication by the Commission of extensive guidance documents. However, the scope for further consolidation has not been exhausted. Technological and sociological changes, such as the emergence of new forms of telecommunications and the growth of leisure pursuits, can throw up new project categories or

---

[120] Advocating a wider use of EIA, Ludwig Krämer has observed '*The European Union is a densely populated area with highly developed economic activity. It is difficult to see why any reasonable, cautious administration which is to achieve a high level of environmental protection would not make an evaluation of the environmental impact of any project listed in Annex II before it gives planning consent*'. See Krämer (2002a) 51.

[121] It may noted that Directive 2003/35/EC makes explicit reference to the use of electronic media in public consultation.

make old ones potentially more significant, so creating arguments for adapting the Directive's project annexes. As regards the *status quo*, the latest Commission five-year report[122] indicates that wide disparaties continue to exist between Member States in the national provisions made for EIA. This suggests the merits of further analysing national transposition measures and associated data in order to improve the overall consistency of implementation, through Commission infringement machinery if necessary. Preconceptions that EIA is only to address environmentally negative projects, or that it is too unwieldy and costly to address small projects, arguably still need to be challenged. In practical ways, EIA could be made more user-friendly – for instance by providing for the posting of EIA documents on the Internet to facilitate their consultation (difficulties of accessing EIA documents still regularly figure in complaints to the Commission). There is room for more guidance on dealing with particular types of impacts, for example on the archaeological heritage. Wider empirical research would be beneficial. How does practice match guidelines? What makes a good assessment? What was the level of public satisfaction with the process? In addition, while guidance is clearly useful, both as an intellectual exercise of thinking through the implications of legal provisions and of matching practical advice to legal requirements, it can never be a substitute for the legal interpretation of the Court of Justice. There remains considerable scope for further interpretative rulings, as the recent *Delena Wells* case shows.

In terms of co-ordination with other instruments, it is too early to say what effect implementation of Directive 2001/42/EC will have. It may be hoped that, by improving land-use, spatial and resource-use planning, SEA will reduce the pressures placed on project-related EIA to protect and improve the environment. However, in this benign eventuality, there will remain a crucial role for project-related EIA to fine-tune the details of projects.

3.2 Other forms of assessment

Looking beyond project EIA, environmental assessment is set to grow further in importance as a decision-making tool, if only because of the coming into effect of Directive 2001/42/EC.

Relative to the totality of plans and programmes with environmental implications, the application of Directive 2001/42/EC is likely to be a lot more extensive than the application of Directive 85/337/EEC has been relative to the totality of projects with environmental implications. It therefore presents a considerable further opportunity for decision-makers to use assessment to lessen environmental impacts and to create environmental benefits. In addition, the post-decision monitoring requirements will create a 'feed back' mechanism, allowing lessons to be learnt from mistakes and oversights.

---

[122] See web-site http://europa.eu.int/comm/environment/eia/eia-legalcontext.htm#links.

However, improved outcomes will still greatly depend on the scope, rigour and quality of assessment and the extent to which decision-making is left free to do more than simply ratify predetermined choices. There will, arguably, be a critical role for the Commission to play, at least in the early years of strategic assessment, to ensure that it does not end up as a formulaic exercise devoid of meaningful content.

Of its nature, Directive 2001/42/EC is an instrument that does not apply to the Commission's own actions. However, as has been mentioned, the Commission has committed itself to also undertaking assessments. Given its extensive policy brief, and the serious adverse effects of certain past Commission initiatives, it will be interesting to learn what results this commitment brings over the coming years.

For the foreseeable future, there will continue to be processes at societal level that will not necessarily undergo assessment. Except possibly in relation to Natura 2000, ministers for finance will not, for the present, have to submit their budgets to prior environmental assessment. Fiscal or subsidy schemes, including state aids, which act as critical determinants of certain environmental impacts, such as climate change, may continue to be formulated in the absence of proper environmental analysis. Even if these gaps are legislatively closed, volatile social and market forces are always likely to limit the role of assessment in directing change.

Nonetheless, several factors – stress on natural resources, the recognition of global environmental problems, the ever-increasing integration of the world's economies, the steps towards forms of global environmental regulation and the growth and dissemination of expertise in assessment – suggest that, at all levels of administration, the status and importance of environmental assessment is likely to grow.

CHAPTER 5

Prevention and Control of Industrial Emissions

An Overview of EC Rules and Their Specific Impact on Emissions

Alexandre Paquot[1]

1 Origin and development

1.1 Introduction and key figures on industrial pollution

Mining, energy production and manufacturing industries still generate a wide range of harmful emissions to air, water and soil. Comprehensive and comparable data on industrial pollution do not exist, but general trends of the situation can be drawn.

According to the European Environmental Agency,[2] around 75% of industrial pollution indicators (air emission, water and energy) showed improvement between 1992 and 1999. However, industrial emissions still contribute largely to the total emissions of pollutants in the various media.

Problems of water contamination by toxic and persistent substances (such as heavy metals) are generally highest near hot spots resulting from past or current industrial activities. Soil contamination from localised sources is often related to industrial plants no longer in operation.

Despite a reduction in emissions, air pollution in Europe continues to pose risks and create adverse effects on human health and the environment. Emissions and subsequent deposition of nitrogen oxides (NOx), sulphur dioxide (SO2) and ammonia (NH3) are causing acidification of terrestrial and freshwater ecosystems. Although acidifying emissions decreased by 40% between 1990 and 2000, many hot spot areas remain at risk, especially in central Europe. In 2000, energy industries contributed to 25% of total acidifying emissions in the EU and to 48% in Central and Eastern Europe.

Another problem is eutrophication, which is a result of excess input of nitrogen nutrients (NOx and NH3) which disturbs the structure and function of ecosystems, in particular by excessive blooming in surface waters and oxygen scarcity. Despite an improvement in the situation, eutrophication remains a substantial problem. In 2000, energy industries contributed to 13% of the total eutrophying compounds emitted in the EU (15 Member States) and to 22% in Central and Eastern Europe.

Air pollution also remains a problem in cities and their surrounding areas, in particular due to the increase in ground-level ozone concentration. Ground-level ozone can affect human health, and damage crops and vegetation as well as buildings. Ozone is not emitted directly, but is formed by reaction of volatile organic compounds and NOx in the presence of sunlight. Industrial emissions and use of these compounds contribute to about 60% of the total emissions of ozone precursors.

---

1 French Environment Ministry, Head of Unit in charge of contaminated sites and health impacts of industrial emissions. Worked in the Commission (DG Environment) in the years 1997-2001.

2 European Environment Agency Europe's environment: the third assessment, European Environment Agency, Copenhagen 2003, p. 36.

Overall, industrial activities remain an important source of contamination of the environment. This chapter reviews the development and current situation of Community legislation on the prevention and control of industrial emissions.

Legislation not directly or exclusively related to industrial emissions is not covered by this section.[3] This concerns, in particular, the Directive on ambient air quality standards[4] and the Directive on national emission ceilings of certain pollutants.[5] Nor are the Community policies on greenhouse gases and ozone depleting substances covered by this article.

1.2 Instruments used to prevent and control industrial emissions

Three main types of instrument have been used[6] in Community legislation to prevent and control industrial pollution. These include:

- Binding emission limit values for each individual installation, which can be established for a specific industrial sector (*e.g.* 0.1 nanograms/m^3 dioxins and furans for waste incinerators). Such values are expressed as maximum concentrations of certain targeted pollutants emitted from an installation in the air or water.
- Quality standards per media (generally air and water). Such standards do not refer directly to the effluents of the installations but to the quality of the media in the areas affected by the discharges. Such areas are not usually described precisely, leaving leeway for the control and monitoring of the effectiveness of such instruments. Quality standards also take into account the dilution of the contamination in the targeted media.
- Reduction plans (*e.g.* the reduction of volatile organic compound emissions) that can be set up at national level for a specific sector or pollutant. Such plans can also address all sources of certain emissions, setting only a general target of reduction for a pollutant. These plans do not create binding obligations for each installation. The means for achieving the objectives are left to the Member States.

1.3 Development of a Community policy on industrial emissions

As products circulate freely within the Community, the setting of harmonised rules on products has been necessary for internal market purposes. Installations, however, do not circulate and therefore, little effort has been made to regulate the environmental impacts of industry, although non-

[3] These Directives do not generally have a direct impact on the regulation of industrial installations.

[4] Directive 96/62/EC, OJ 1996 L 296/55.

[5] Directive 2001/81/EC on national emission ceilings for certain atmospheric pollutants, OJ 2001 L 309/22.

harmonisation of such standards can lead to competitive distortions and affects the circulation of goods accordingly.

Discharges into water and air with transboundary impacts were a clear signal that such issues had to be addressed at Community level. The implementation of international conventions, in particular the Convention on Long-Range Transboundary Air Pollution,[7] was also a driving force for the development of Community legislation on industrial installations.

1.4 The first Environmental Action Programmes: An attempt to regulate the main polluting industrial sectors

In the first Environmental Action Programme in 1973,[8] the Member States asked the Commission to carry out a detailed plan aimed at proposing measures based on a comparative assessment of the impacts and abatement techniques for the main industrial sectors, in particular, the paper and pulp industry, the iron and steel industry, the manufacture of titanium dioxide, the chemical industry, the leather and tanning industry, the food industry and factory-farming. The Environmental Action Programmes in 1977[9] and 1983[10] repeated the request for the preparation of Community legislation on certain industrial sectors.

Despite a number of studies on specific economic sectors were carried out by the Commission, only very few industrial sectors have actually been regulated at Community level. The titanium dioxide industry is one of these sectors.

1.5 The regulation of the titanium dioxide industry

In 1978, the Council adopted Directive 78/176/EEC[11] setting general provisions for the management of waste (mainly hazardous acid waste) generated by the titanium dioxide (TiO2) industry. The Directive did however not set binding discharge limits.

Since at that time all environmental measures had to be adopted unanimously, the proposal of the Commission[12] to establish emission limit values for the discharges generated by TiO2 industry was not adopted by the Council, mainly due to the opposition of the United Kingdom.

6 This article is based on developments up to end March 2004.

7 Council Decision 81/462 on the conclusion of the Convention on long-range transboundary air pollution (www.unece.org/env/lrtap/welcome.html), OJ 1981 L 171/11.

8 OJ 1973 C 112/1.

9 OJ 1977 C 139/1.

10 OJ 1983 C 46/1.

11 Directive 78/176/EEC, OJ 1978 L 54 /19.

12 COM(83) 189 OJ 1983 C 138/5 and COM(84) 303 OJ 1984 C 167/9.

Following a long and complex legal dispute[13] between the Council and the Commission, the Council adopted Directive 92/112/EEC, banning the discharge of TiO2 waste into waters, and establishing binding emission limit values in water and air.

Overall evaluation of the legislation on the TiO2 industry is difficult since technological changes in this industry have been mainly driven by the debates in connection with international conventions and the North Sea Conferences.

Directive 92/112/EEC is a good example of the possibility of setting, at Community level, harmonised limit values to mitigate the impacts of a specific industry. However, the long and contentious procedures needed to adopt a Community legal framework on the TiO2 industry illustrate the difficulties of regulating specific industrial sectors.

1.6 The Community failed to regulate other industrial sectors

In the context of the implementation of the 1st Environmental Action Programme, the Commission adopted in 1975 a proposal for a Directive on the reduction of water pollution caused by wood pulp mills.[14] The proposal became obsolete due to the opposition of certain Member States to establish uniform limit values for discharges into the environment from a given industrial sector.

Confronted with strong opposition from certain Member States, the Commission stated in a Communication in 1980 that it would not propose any further sector-oriented Directives.[15] The intentions of the Commission were to shift its policy from an approach based on the prevention of industrial pollution of certain industrial sectors to the regulation of the impacts on environmental media, mainly air and water.

1.7 Air emissions regulation

Pressed by the international discussions on the issue of eutrophication and dying forests due to emissions of acidifying substances, the Council adopted in 1984 a framework Directive[16] covering certain industrial installations.

Directive 84/360/EEC sets up a general authorisation procedure for these installations. An authorisation can only be issued when all appropriate preventive measures have been taken, 'including the application of the best available

---

[13] For more information see Haigh (1994) chap. 4.9 and Jans (2000) 356.

[14] OJ 1975 C 99/2.

[15] 'Progress made in connection with the environment action programme and assessment of the work to implement it', COM (80) 222 final, p. 5, quoted from Krämer (2000a) 112.

[16] Directive 84/360/EEC, OJ 1984 L 188/20.

technology'.[17] The Directive goes on to state that the use of the plant must 'not cause significant air pollution particularly from the emissions of substances'[18] listed in an annex.

The wording of the Directive is rather loose. For example, no definition is given for the term 'significant air pollution', which does not even refer to the protection of human health or the environment.

The Directive was transposed with delay in most of the Member States and has proven to have little effectiveness. The requirements imposed on the Member States were so vague that no legal case could be launched for a lack of action. In particular, the reference to 'the best available technology not entailing excessive costs' did not create an obligation on the Member States to reduce the air emissions of industrial installations. In addition, the provision inviting the Council to fix emission limit values 'if necessary' [19] has never been put into practice.

Another shortcoming of this Directive relates to the preparation by the Commission of non-binding technical documents aimed at defining the best available technology in various specific sectors. It is difficult to evaluate the concrete effect of such documents on the permits delivered by the Member States. Overall, the added-value of Council Directive 84/360/EEC remains largely to be demonstrated.

1.8 Water emissions regulation

Concerning the regulation of water emissions from industrial activities, Council Directive 76/464/EEC[20] was an ambitious framework in its intent. This Directive established two lists of substances: List I specifying substances whose discharge should be eliminated and List II those substances for which pollution should be reduced.

Member States were required to establish programmes including quality objectives for water for the purpose of reducing pollution from List II substances, but the implementation of this requirement failed, since no programmes or quality objectives were indeed established. This led to a large number of infringement procedures launched against the Member States by the Commission under Article 226 EC.

For List I substances, EU-wide emission limit values and quality standards were to be established. The combination of the two instruments is a compromise between, in particular, the United Kingdom (opposed to harmonised discharges limits at Community level) and the other Member States (which

---

17 Article 4.

18 Article 4.

19 Article 7.

20 Directive 76/464/EEC on pollution caused by certain dangerous substances discharged into the aquatic environment of the Community, OJ 1976 L 129/23.

indicated in a statement that they would only introduce emission limit values).[21] Only 17 out of the 129 substances selected by the Council[22] have been regulated at Community level in five daughter Directives including, in particular, mercury,[23] lindane[24] and cadmium.[25]

Emission limit values set by these Directives were merely based on political compromise rather than an assessment of the best available techniques. In addition, the limits were not revised on the basis of new scientific knowledge on the toxicity of the substances involved and on the 'best technical means available'.[26]

At the request of the Commission, Member States were required to provide monitoring data on the implementation of the emission limit values in the various industrial plants covered by the Directive.[27] However, the Commission has not requested such data and has not pursued any Member State due to the poor quality of the discharges of certain industrial plants.[28] The only legal action taken against Member States concerned a lack of transposition.

It is interesting to note that the European Court of Justice has a wide interpretation of the scope of Directive 76/464/EEC: in a preliminary ruling[29] concerning the indirect contamination of surface water due to the precipitation of contaminated steam emitted into the air generated by a wood treatment installation, the Court stated that the term 'discharge' must be interpreted as covering such emissions. Such interpretation is subject to legal debate[30] but demonstrates the difficulties raised by the implementation of Directive 76/464/EE.

In conclusion, as Directive 76/464/EEC and its daughter Directives have been poorly implemented by the Member States,[31] it is extremely difficult to assess their benefits to the environment.

---

[21] See Krämer (2003a) 258.

[22] OJ 1983 C 46/17.

[23] Directive 82/176/EEC on limit values and quality objectives for mercury discharges by sectors the chlor-alkali industry, OJ 1982 L 81/29; Directive 84/156/EC on limit values and quality objectives for mercury discharges by sectors other than the chlor-alkali industry, OJ 1984 L 74/49.

[24] Directive 94/491/EC on limit values and quality objectives for discharges of hexachlorohexane, OJ 1984 L 274/11.

[25] Directive 83/513/EEC on limit values and quality objectives for cadmium discharges, OJ 1983 L 291/1.

[26] Article 6 of Directive 76/464/EEC.

[27] Article 13.

[28] For instance, the metallurgical plant of Metaleurop Nord in France (the main source of lead and cadmium discharge in France) did not comply with the required cadmium limits set in Directive 83/513/EEC. See the permits of the plant dated 17 April 1989 and 13 March 1995 (see http://www.nord-pas-de-calais.drire.gouv.fr/).

[29] Case C-231/97, *Van Rooij*.

[30] See Krämer (2002a) 415 *et seq*.

[31] See Krämer (2003a) 259-261.

In 1990, the Commission proposed another 15 substances for regulation as a priority under 76/464/EEC.[32] However, because of the upcoming proposals for a Directive on integrated pollution prevention and control, the proposal was withdrawn in 1993.[33] Since 1990, the setting of emission limit values has come to a standstill.

As part of the ongoing restructuring to simplify and consolidate Community water legislation, a new policy has been developed to allow flexibility to the Member States to establish parametric values at national level in order to adapt to the different environmental conditions in different parts of the Community. In this context, Directive 2000/60/EC[34] was adopted and Directive 76/464/EEC will be repealed by 2013.

1.9 Policy shift in the Environmental Action Programmes

A shift of policy can also be seen in the Community Environmental Action Programmes (EAP). Whereas the 1st EAP strongly urged harmonised regulation of industrial sectors, the 4th EAP adopted in 1987[35] acknowledged that 'the 'source-oriented' approach as defined in the First Environment Action Programme has not made much progress, at least at Community level'. The Member States[36] remained unclear about their intentions, admitting that 'a source-oriented approach is appropriate in certain circumstances and is one of the alternative approaches available that may be worth considering again'.[37]

The 5th EAP[38] adopted in 1993 called for a 'new approach implying, in particular, a reinforcement of the dialogue with industry and the encouragement, in appropriate circumstances, of voluntary agreements and other forms of self-regulation'.[39] The Programme also announced an 'improved management and control of production processes including a system of licensing linked to integrated pollution prevention and control'.[40]

As a result of this policy, the adoption in 1996 of Council Directive 96/61/EC concerning integrated pollution prevention and control[41] (the IPPC Direc-

[32] COM (1990) 9 final, OJ 1990 C 55/7.

[33] OJ 1993 C 228/13.

[34] Directive 2000/60/EC establishing a framework for Community action in the field of water policy, OJ 2000 L 327/1. See the article of Claudia Olazabal in this book.

[35] OJ 1987 C 328/1. See chapter 3.4.

[36] The first five Environmental Action Programmes were adopted as Resolutions of the Council and of the Representatives of the Governments of the Member States.

[37] See chapter 3.4.

[38] OJ 1993 C 138/1.

[39] See paragraph 19 of the executive summary.

[40] See chapter 4.1.

[41] OJ 1996 L 257/26.

tive) shows a clear shift in Community policy on these issues. Such an approach avoids the setting of binding emission limit values at Community level. This policy has been favored by certain Member States, in particular the United Kingdom, and is in line with the entry into force in 1993 of the Maastricht Treaty, which placed the subsidiarity principle in Article 5 EC as a general principle on which to base the Community policies.

2 Current situation: Applicable rules and impact

At present, Community legislation aimed at controlling and preventing industrial environmental pollution is based – apart from the IPPC Directive – on only a few sector-oriented Directives.

2.1 Large combustion plants

Combustion plants are installations producing heat or electricity from the combustion of fuel (in particular oil, gas and coal). They account for about 50% of total SO_2 emissions and 20% of NO_x emissions in the Community.[42] Actions to reduce the emissions from such installations are therefore decisive for combatting acidification, eutrophication and ground-level ozone.

As a result, the Council regulated in 1988 air emissions from large combustion plants.[43] For new combustion plants (*i.e.* plants put into operation after 1 July 1987), Directive 88/609/EEC set air emission limit values for SO_2, NO_x and dust.

For existing installations (*i.e.* operating before 1 July 1987), this Directive required – for the first time in Community legislation – the establishment of national reduction plans for SO_2 and NO_x. No specific obligations were set for the individual installations, but each Member State was to draw up appropriate programmes for the progressive reduction of total emissions.

Due to the late transposition of the Directive, the Commission launched actions against several Member States on the basis of Article 226 EC. However, no formal action was started by the Commission for non-compliance with the requirements of the Directive of a specific plant. It is indeed very difficult to monitor the compliance of specific existing installations on the basis of an overall reduction plan.

It is also interesting to note that emission limit values only apply to new installations. In 1993, less than 2% of the total emissions of large combustion plants were generated by those installations.

---

[42] See COM (2001) 245 final – The Clean Air for Europe (CAFE) Programme: Towards a Thematic Strategy for Air Quality.

[43] Directive 88/609/EEC, OJ 1988 L 336/1.

Directive 2001/80/EC[44] replaced Council Directive 88/609/EEC. It requires that plants licensed after the entry into force of the Directive (27 November 2001) will have to comply with new emission limit values for SO_2, NO_x and dust. These limits are about twice as strict as the previous ones established in Directive 88/609/EEC.

Plants licensed after 1 July 1987 and before 27 November 2001 will gradually have to comply with the emission limit values fixed in Directive 88/609/EEC.

For installations licensed before 1 July 1987, Member States may choose, by 1 January 2008, between the following two alternatives: to comply with emission limit values or to define and implement an emission reduction plan at national level. The latter option – the least stringent – is likely to be chosen by most of the Member States.

It is regrettable that a number of pollutants (such as lead, mercury or dioxines) have not been included in the scope of Directive 2001/80/EC, despite significant emissions of these substances by combustion plants. In addition, the Directive does not cover other emissions, *e.g.* to water, which are far from negligible.

The added-valued of Directive 2001/80/EC will mainly depend on the efforts made by the Member States to enforce it, and by the Commission to monitor compliance of individual plants with emission limit values or national plans. However, such monitoring will be extremely difficult since the Directive does not require the transmission of detailed information from individual plants.

2.2 Waste incineration installations

In 1989, the Community adopted two Directives on municipal waste incineration plants[45] setting general requirements for the authorization and operation of the installations, as well as limit values for air emissions.

In 1994, the Council adopted a Directive for the incineration of hazardous waste,[46] fixing stricter emission limit values than for the incineration of municipal waste, and establishing an emission limit value for dioxins and furans (0.1 nanograms/m^3), which had not been previously regulated under the Directives on the municipal waste incineration. Obviously, from an environmental standpoint, this omission could not be justified.

In 2000, all provisions on waste incineration were grouped into a single Directive,[47] covering the incineration of both hazardous and non-hazardous

[44] Directive 2001/80/EC, OJ 2001 L 309/1.

[45] Directive 89/369/EEC on the prevention of air pollution from new municipal waste incineration plants, OJ 1989 L 163/32; Directive 89/429/EEC on the reduction of air pollution from existing municipal waste-incineration plants, OJ 1989 L 203/50.

[46] Directive 94/67/EC on the incineration of hazardous waste, OJ 1994 L 365/34.

[47] Directive 2000/76/EC on the incineration of waste, OJ 2000 L 332/91.

waste. Directive 2000/76/EC concerns incineration plants as well as co-incineration plants, such as cement kilns, steel and power plants.

Furthermore, Directive 2000/76/EC introduces stricter provisions than those found in the previous waste incineration Directives subsequently repealed. It sets air emission limit values (in particular for dust, SO_2, NOx, heavy metals as well as dioxins). Unlike the previous Directives, it also establishes controls on releases to water. Directive 2000/76/EC is therefore expected to lead to significant reductions in emissions of several key pollutants.[48]

However, the added-value of the new Directive will mainly depend on the way emission limit values are enforced for individual installations. Despite its technical feasibility in view of the limited number of installations covered (only a few hundred), no reporting on individual installations is required.

Legislation on waste incineration is a good example of the way the Community can set emission limit values for a specific sector which raises serious concern due to its harmful emissions.

2.3 Volatile organic compounds from stationary sources

Volatile organic solvents (VOCs) are emitted by mobile sources (motor vehicles) and during industrial processes. A number of VOCs are directly harmful to health. Moreover, many solvents lead to the formation of ozone. The reduction of VOC emissions is therefore a key objective of Community legislation.

Directive 94/63/EC[49] aims at preventing air emissions of VOCs during the storage of petrol at terminals and its subsequent distribution to service stations. It covers both mobile and stationary sources. The Directive does not set any emission limit values, but specifies general requirements on the use of solvents.

In 1999, the Council adopted Directive 1999/13/EC[50] on the limitation of emissions of volatile organic compounds. The scope of this Directive covers a list of industrial activities, in particular, coating, printing, surface cleaning, dry cleaning and pharmaceutical manufacture. For the different activities, the Directive sets emission limit values as well as limits for fugitive emissions.[51]

---

48 According to the Commission web site (http://www.europa.eu.int/comm/environment/index_en.htm), emissions of cadmium throughout the EU are expected to fall from 16 tonnes per year in 1995 to around 1 tonne in 2005. Over the same period, mercury emissions should fall from an annual 36 tonnes to around 7 tonnes. The Directive will reduce such emissions from Community incineration from an annual 2.400 grams in 1995 to only 10 grams after full implementation in 2005.

49 Directive 94/63/EC on the control of volatile organic compound emissions resulting from the storage of petrol and its distribution from terminals to service stations, OJ 1994 L 365/24.

50 Directive 1999/13/EC on the limitation of emissions of volatile organic compounds due to the use of organic solvents in certain activities and installations, OJ 1999 L 85/1.

51 Fugitive emissions include in particular uncaptured emissions released to the outside environment via windows, doors, vents and similar openings.

Exemptions from emission limit values have been granted for installations which achieve reductions by other means (*e.g.* by using solvent-free products). However, the use of such exemptions will be difficult to monitor since Member States do not have to report on individual installations.

In addition, instead of applying the emission limit values fixed in the Directive, Member States may design and implement national reduction plans[52] resulting in a decrease in emissions similar to that obtained by the application of the emission limits. These plans must be submitted to the Commission for approval. The Directive also provides for a negotiation procedure in case the Commission is not satisfied with the objectives of the plan. The final and binding decision is taken by the Commission.

Past experience has demonstrated that it is extremely difficult to monitor the implementation of national reduction plans. The implementation of the Directive will therefore mainly depend on the good-will of the individual Member States to reduce VOC emissions from individual installations. Once the plans are adopted, the Commission will have difficulty to monitor their effectiveness.

Under the 6th Environmental Action Programme, the Community legislator plans to adopt a Thematic Strategy on air pollution, announced by the Commission for 2005. This strategy will be based in particular on the Clean Air for Europe (CAFE) programme, launched in March 2001, for the purpose of developing long-term, strategic and integrated policy recommendations to protect against air pollution. The main elements of the CAFE programme are outlined in a Communication of the Commission,[53] which announced that the Commission would review Directive 1999/13/EC in 2004 taking into account the progress made in the CAFE programme.

2.4 The IPPC Directive

Council Directive 96/61/EC[54] applies to a number of large highly polluting industrial installations (in particular energy industries, production and processing of metals, mineral industry, chemical industry and waste management). The Commission considers that about 60,000 installations are covered by the Directive.[55]

Each installation covered by the Directive must operate according to a permit issued through an 'effective integrated approach',[56] meaning that all the operating requirements should be addressed in a single permit.

---

[52] Article 6.

[53] COM (2001) 245 final.

[54] For more information about the preparation of the IPPC Directive, see in particular Doppelhammer (2000) 246.

[55] It is interesting to note that certain Member States do not yet know how many installations are covered by the IPPC Directive.

[56] Article 7.

This permit must include emission limit values for pollutants likely to be emitted in significant quantities by the installation concerned. The emission limit values are defined as mass, concentration or level of an emission which may not be exceeded by the installation. The emission limit values are to be 'based on the best available techniques [...] taking into account the technical characteristics of the installation concerned, its geographical location and the local environmental conditions'.[57] The notion of best available techniques includes the specific economic situation of the installation.

The Directive has been applicable to 'new installations' since 1999. These refer to facilities placed in operation after 30 October 1999. 'Existing installations' (*i.e.* in operation prior to 30 October 1999) must comply with the requirements of the Directive by 30 October 2007.

2.4.1 Possibility of setting harmonised emission limit values at national or EC level

The possibility for the Member States of establishing 'binding rules' for 'certain requirements for certain categories of installations'[58] is presented as an exception and not as a general rule.

The IPPC Directive also provides for the possibility for the Council (and the European Parliament) to set emission limit values for the categories for which 'the need for Community action has been identified, on the basis, in particular, of the exchange of information'.[59] However, no criteria are set for initiating such an action.

2.4.2 Exchange of information

Member States are required to transmit to the Commission every three years the available representative data on the limit values laid down for specific categories of activity, as well as the relevant best available techniques.[60]

The first reporting under the IPPC Directive took place in 2001, and the Commission recognizes the weakness of such reporting obligation, due, in particular, to the lack of comparability between data supplied by Member States.[61] As a result, the Commission considers this reporting process be of

---

57 Article 9.

58 Article 8.

59 Article 18.

60 Article 16.

61 Member States use very different ways of expressing limit values in permits. If no common units are fixed to express the emission limit values, the comparison of few thousand permits is highly complex. Source: Report for DG Environnement – Investigation of national IPPC permitting – AEA Technology – May 2002.

limited value.[62] This problem is not very surprising and could be easily resolved by requiring harmonisation of the measuring units used to express emission limit values.

2.4.3 European Pollutant Emission Register (EPER)

The IPPC Directive requires the Member States to report emissions from individual installations[63] in order to enable the Commission to establish a European Pollutant Emission Register (EPER) to provide information to the general public. This scheme would include the collection of emissions to water and air of 50 pollutants from about 10,000 installations falling under the scope of the IPPC Directive (out of about 60,000 IPPC installations). Unfortunately, data on soil contamination is not required. The Commission and the European Environment Agency have launched in February 2004 a web site (http://www.eper.cec.eu.int) with the results of the first EPER reporting.

As a general remark, the website is an interesting tool since it provides datas and comparisons on the emissions (mostly from the year 2001) of the most polluting installations in the Community. However, it is difficult for the public to appreciate the information available since no information is given on which individual installations do not comply with the requirements of the Directive.

2.4.4 Implementation

Most Member States have experienced delays in the transposition of the IPPC Directive (deadline of 30 October 1999). In addition, in most of the Member States, the Commission has identified major shortcomings in the legislation,[64] and considers that many Member States are behind schedule for the timely implementation of the IPPC Directive. The Commission has not yet launched any legal action against a Member State for bad application, indicating that discussions with the Member States to change their legislation accordingly were at an early stage.[65]

2.4.5 How effective is the concept of best available techniques?

In order to implement the IPPC Directive, the Commission has established a work programme to draw up guidance documents (the so-called BREF or Best Available Technique Reference Document) for all sectors covered

---

62 COM (2003) 354 final – 'On the Road to Sustainable Production – Progress in implementing Council Directive 96/61/EC concerning integrated pollution prevention and control.'

63 Commission Decision 2000/479/EC on the implementation of a European pollutant emission register, OJ 2000 L 192/36; Decision taken on the basis of Article 15 of Directive 96/61.

64 See COM (2003) 354 final.

65 See COM (2003) 354 final.

by the Directive. This approach is similar to the work programme carried out under Directive 84/360/EEC, which has proven to have very little impact on the prevention of industrial pollution. BREF documents are not legally binding since the Directive does not require the application of any specific standards.

The IPPC Directive also requires that 'the competent authority follows or is informed of developments in best available techniques'.[66] In practice, such a requirement is not enforced since the BREF documents, which are very voluminous,[67] are published by the Commission in English and are not translated into other Community languages, except at the initiative of certain Member States (*e.g.* France, Germany and Austria). The distribution of BREF documents within the Member States seems to be rather limited and most of the competent authorities do not make systematic use of the information presented in these documents, when issuing a permit.

The Commission does not adopt formally the documents.[68] At the end of 2003, 15 BREF documents had been finalised and 17 were in progress or about to be launched. The Commission expects all first-edition documents to be ready by the end of 2005.

Economic implications are key factors for the application of the best available techniques (BAT) but in practice the Commission recognises that data on economic evaluation of the application of certain technologies are frequently not made available.[69]

2.4.6 General assessment

Generally, a key positive impact of Directive 99/61, if properly implemented, is the obligation for all IPPC installations to operate according to an environmental permit delivered by the competent authorities setting emission limit values.

However, on the whole, the environmental benefits of the application of the Directive can not currently be demonstrated. According to the Commission, 'it is too early to make any projections of the ecological results of the Directive'.[70]

Economic implications are a cornerstone of most of the discussions on implementation of the Directive. Authorities and industry representatives seem

---

66 Article 11.

67 For instance the BREF on pulp and paper has 660 pages.

68 The Commission adopts an executive summary of each of the BREF documents. However, the BREF documents, published in the form of a CD-ROM, are not translated into the Community languages and can not therefore be formally adopted by the Commission. A notice of each of the documents is published in the Official Journal.

69 COM (2003) 354 final.

70 COM (2003) 354 final.

to be more concerned about the possible costs of its implementation than about its environmental benefits.[71]

Although installations should operate according to the BAT, it seems to be difficult to control the implementation of such requirements, in particular since BAT can vary from one plant to another and include economic aspects. Even the Commission fears 'a possible abuse [by the Member States] of the inherent flexibility of the IPPC Directive'.[72] According to the Commission, the IPPC Directive is 'crucial to ensure a soft harmonisation of environmental standards in Europe'. The borderline between 'soft harmonisation' and 'no harmonisation' is very thin and the added-valued of the IPPC Directive still remains to be demonstrated through its enforcement.

Implementation of the IPPC Directive is likely to lead to different emission limit values fixed in the individual permits for the same types of installation. Detailed monitoring will therefore be necessary to ensure that the permit requirements are consistent across the Community. The EPER tool could in particular be used to compare the performance of similar installations. Without clear Community standards to be applied, one can fear that decisions at local level are made at the expense of environmental protection, in order to ensure that employment is not jeopardised. The Commission indicated[73] that it would consider the setting of Community-wide emission limit values if insufficient efforts are made by the authorities to implement the IPPC Directive.

In addition, a lack of consistent standards is likely to affect competition between installations. The Community therefore faces a key challenge to developing a consistent policy on the prevention of industrial pollution.

2.5 Comparison of legislation on industrial emissions

The following table summarises the obligations arising from the main Community legislation on industrial emissions.

[71] See for instance *The Impact of Best Available Techniques (BAT) on the Competitiveness of European Industry*, David Hitchens et. al, Institute for Prospective Technological Studies, November 2001 (http://eippcb.jrc.es/pages/FEvents.htm).

[72] COM (2003) 354 final.

[73] COM (2003) 354 final.

	Emission limit values (ELV)	Quality standards	National reduction plans	Others
Directive 78/176 on the TiO2 industry as amended	For certain emissions into air and water	Member States can chose to apply quality standards if the same level of environmental protection is obtained		
Directive 84/360/EEC on air pollution from industrial plants				Application of the best available technologies to avoid significant air pollution
Directive 76/464/EEC on discharge of dangerous substances into water and its daughter Directives	For the emissions of certain substances into water	Member States can chose to apply quality standards		
Directive 2001/80/EC on large combustion plants	Member States can chose to apply ELV for existing installations For certain emissions into air for new installations		Member States can chose to establish reduction plans for existing installations	
Directive 2000/76/EC on the incineration of waste	For certain emissions into air and water			
Directive 1999/13/EC on VOCs	Maximum solvent concentration in the air		Member States may draw up national reduction plans for existing installations with an equivalent result to the implementation of ELV	
Directive 96/61/EC on integrated pollution prevention and control				Individual permits to fix specific ELV based on the best available technologies and taking into account local and economic conditions

As described, very few Directives set EU-wide emission limit values into air and water for specific installations. In addition, in most of the cases, Member States can opt for less stringent approaches, in particular, the compliance with quality standards or the establishment of a national reduction plan. No real consistency can be found between the various Directives.

3 Challenges for the future and some conclusions

3.1 Data availability

Despite a general reduction in emissions of pollutants from industrial sources through the modernisation of operating conditions and the decline of certain heavily polluting sectors, industry remains a large contributor to the total emissions of toxic and dangerous substances.

Data on industrial pollution need to be improved. In its third assessment of the state of the environment,[74] the European Environment Agency points out that precise, concise and comprehensive data on industrial pollution are virtually non existent.

3.2 Emission limit values

The enlargement of the European Union will bring a number of polluting industrial installations into the scope of Community environmental legislation. It still remains to be demonstrated whether the current legal and practical framework will enable the implementation of better environmental standards in these new Member States. At present, the implementation of harmonised environmental and health protection standards mainly depends on the efforts of the Member States to enforce a high level of environmental protection.

As described, the IPPC Directive, cornerstone of Community industrial prevention and control legislation, is based on a decentralisation policy. In this context, the Commission considers[75] that a large number of Member States need to accelerate progress to implement the Directive, given the final deadline for full implementation by 30 October 2007. At present, equal competition among companies cannot therefore be guaranteed.

A number of Member States, in particular the United Kingdom, have always strongly opposed harmonised emission limit values. The implementation of such standards would probably demonstrate that existing installations in a number of Member States are far from operating according to the best available techniques.

3.3 Water pollution

As regards water pollution, Directive 2000/60/EC requires the adoption of specific measures to improve the quality of waters. These include the obligation for the Commission to submit proposals for the progressive reduction or phasing-out of the discharge of priority substances.[76] For this purpose,

[74] European Environment Agency, footnote 2 above, p. 300.

[75] COM (2003) 354 final.

[76] In 2002, a list of 33 priority substances was adopted under Decision 2455/2001 establishing the list of priority substances in the field of water policy and amending Directive 2000/60/EC, OJ 2001 L 331/1.

the Commission is supposed to propose emission limit values on a sector-by-sector basis as well as quality standards for the priority substances in waters within two years following the selection of the substances. At the end of 2003, the Commission had not yet adopted such proposals.

It remains to be seen whether the provisions of Directive 2000/60/EC related to industrial emissions will lead to the setting of harmonised emission limit values. Strong opposition from certain Member States can be expected, as experienced for the implementation of Directive 76/464/EEC. In addition, such emission limit values would not cover air emissions.

3.4 A new strategy for sector-oriented directives

The main arguments of the Commission for not proposing harmonised emission limit values are the technical difficulties involved in determining BAT for an entire sector. Such arguments could be understood for very complex sectors. However, as proven by certain national legislation, current technologies could enable the setting of minimum standards, in particular, for the following sectors: metallurgical industry, cement production, glass manufacturing and certain chemical sectors.

A consistent Community strategy in the field of industrial pollution is necessary. This should take the form of the preparation of sector-oriented Directives regulating the most heavily polluting industrial sectors. This option is envisaged by the Commission in a recent consultation,[77] which could lead to a revision of the IPPC Directive.

In this context, the development of such an ambitious policy on industrial pollution (in line with the 1st EAP of 1973) will largely depend on the political will of the Member States to reach a high level of environmental protection, and of the Commission to enforce that level. The driving force for implementing such a framework might well be the distortion of competition within an enlarged European Union.

The 6th Environmental Action Programme[78] adopted by the Council and the European Parliament in 2002 is not a very positive political signal in this direction since the preparation of a consistent industrial pollution prevention policy is not mentioned.

While the Commission has announced its intention to formulate a new European environment and health strategy – the so-called SCALE[79] strategy – it is all the more necessary that an ambitious policy on the reduction of the most toxic industrial emissions is proposed by the Commission and put into practice by

---

77 COM (2003) 354 final.

78 Decision 1600/2002 laying down the Sixth Community Environment Action Programme, OJ 2002 L 242/1.

79 COM (2003) 338 final on an European Environment and Health Stategy; SCALE stands for Science, Children, Awareness, Legislation and Evaluation.

the Member States. The European Pollutant Emission Register website, recently launched by the Commission, provides useful data to the public and the authorities to call for rapid action. For instance, how could the Community justify that the metal industry, emitting 513 tonnes of lead and 0,7 kg of dioxins in the European Union in 2001 representing respectively 83% and 57% of the total industrial lead and dioxins air emissions,[80] is not regulated by a sector-oriented legislation?[81] Action is necessary as the situation in certain EU-15 Member States and in the new Member States concerning these industrial sectors is far from being acceptable from the environmental and health point of view.

80 See http://www.eper.cec.eu.int.

81 As a comparison, the incineration installations contributed in 2001 to 17% of the total dioxins emissions and 1% of the lead emissions.

CHAPTER 6

Environmental Protection by Product Policy

Focus on Dangerous Substances

Marco Onida[1]

1 Introduction – setting the scene

Traditionally, the negative impact of human activities on the environment has been perceived mainly in terms of polluting emissions – into the air and water – and in the form of waste, in particular from industrial sources. Environmental law in modern societies seems to have been most significantly influenced by this perception. In international law, the first conflicts and legal instruments relating to environmental issues focused on transboundary emissions. At Community level, the first environmental measures having a primarily environmental character related to industrial emissions, waste and the quality of the ambient environment.[2]

Yet, important sources of environmental impairment are 'products', be it in the form of raw materials converted to traded commodities (*e.g.* fuels) or manufactured products. Traded products are not often perceived as being 'polluting emissions' although, in many cases, they are just that.[3] Products are a source of environmental contamination due to their composition (particularly, substances which come into contact with air, water and soil during the lifetime of products or when products become waste; or emissions caused by the transformation of products during their use, such as fuels), or by their characteristics (for example noise pollution by cars or machinery). Energy and raw materials, sometimes in unimaginable quantities, are used in order to manufacture products, thus these items are a source of resource depletion. Space, an increasingly scarce resource, is threatened by products, either during their use phase (*e.g.* cars) or when they become waste and go to landfill. Some products endanger biodiversity (*e.g.* those dependent on exotic hardwoods, fishing drift nets causing accidental catch of endangered species). In short, products affect the environment in many ways.

Therefore, a general objective of reducing polluting emissions into the environment cannot ignore products. Indeed Ludwig Krämer has, both in his writ-

1 Environment Directorate-General, European Commission. The opinions contained in the present article are strictly personal and do not engage the Commission. This article is based on policy developments as at the end of March 2004. Thanks to Prof. J. Jans for his valuable comments.

2 There are early examples of product-focused legislation with an environmental dimension, although these were primarily the result of market-regulating initiatives. See *infra*, section 3.2.

3 One could also see it the other way: emissions of particles into air, water and soil 'are products'. From the point of view of the environment, the distinction between concepts such as emissions, pollution, chemical substances, products and waste is often a fine one. Whether the environment is suffering from a substance which is emitted by an industrial chimney or a car, or which is leached from a waste which is disposed of in a landfill, makes little difference: the state of the environment is, in all cases, affected by something that interacts physically, chemically or biologically with the environmental media and threatens their quality. Substances such as lead or mercury are often treated differently according to the type of regulatory measure which deals with them, but in the end, whether called emission, chemical, discharge, waste or product, it is always lead or mercury which degrades the environment.

ings and in his activity as Commission official, often pointed out the interaction between products – understood as 'emissions' – and the environment.[4]

The negative effects of products on the environment can be reduced by pursuing different specific objectives, such as:[5] a) generating products which use less resources/energy or which last longer, b) increasing recycling and recyclability, c) changing consumption/production patterns, d) changing production methods, where they require the use of hazardous substances, and e) modifying the composition and design of products, influencing their demand and so on. Thus, comprehensive research on products and the environment would require examination of issues of raw material extraction, energy production, CO2 emissions, products lifetime, recycling and production methods.

In this chapter, not least for reasons of space, the choice has been made to focus analysis on one specific aspect of the general subject 'products and the environment': the development and future perspectives of product-related environmental measures in the EU, with specific reference to legal issues concerning the releases of dangerous substances from products. The chosen scope of this article is, therefore, limited to the aspect of composition of industrial commodities and consumer goods.[6]

2 The general public policy context

Western societies are based on the freedom of production and trade unless the contrary is established by law. This factor always hindered development of a pro-active environmental product policy. The starting point of any analysis concerning products and the environment must therefore inevitably be the recognition that there is a clear imbalance in the basic 'rules of the game'. Whereas, in modern western societies, the freedom to produce and to trade is to a very large extent guaranteed by the Constitutions, there is no prohibition to cause environmental impairment, including by products.

Indeed, each time the freedom to place a product on the market or to trade is at stake, we take for granted that there must be 'very good reasons' for interfering with the market, whereas no such 'test' exists for marketing and trading products which cause environmental impairment. In other words, the burden of proof is always on the environment, something that could be defined as a 'legal domination' in Max Weber's words. Accordingly, the free circulation of goods within the Single Market has been one of the main preoccupations of the EC founders and it still absorbs a great deal of resources – in terms of law making and enforcement – in the European Institutions. Several instruments have been adopted, both in primary (*e.g.* Articles 28 and 29 EC) and secondary legisla-

---

4 Krämer (1997a) 205; (1999c) 50; (1996b) 458; (2000c) 14; (2000d) 225 *et seq*; (2001) 34; (2003a) 200.

5 Krämer (1997a) 213; Godt (2000) 41; Krämer (2003b) 119.

6 For a comprehensive overview of product-related measures in EC Law, see Krämer (2003a) chapter 6.

tion (*e.g.* Directive 98/34/EC)[7] which aim to avoid national measures, including those of environmental character, hindering the free circulation of goods. In EC law, the arising of product-related measures has – at least in the beginning – largely been the reaction to national product-related measures, which affected the free circulation of goods within the internal market.

The European Court of Justice (ECJ) has contributed to partly softening this imbalance. Environmental measures which have an effect equivalent to quantitative restrictions on imports and export (practically any measure capable of hindering trade directly or indirectly, actually or potentially), prohibited by Articles 28-29 EC, may nevertheless be justified if non-discriminatory and if 'proportionate': still, whenever the assessment of the proportionality – a concept which implies some degree of subjectivity – of a national environmental measure affecting trade is at stake, extreme 'pro-market' views tend, at least in quantitative terms, to prevail.

This imbalance in the EC legal system led a group of lawyers strongly dedicated to furthering the development of environmental law in the EU and its Member States (the 'Avosetta' Group) to adopting, in October 2002, a resolution proposing the insertion of a clause in the new EU Constitutional Treaty, stating that *subject to imperative reasons of overriding public interest, significantly impairing the environment or human health shall be prohibited.*[8]

In addition, emissions from chimneys or water discharges are generally visible, while impact on the environment by products is much less visible, at least until products reach the waste phase. Also, the time occurring between the placing on the market of a product (which is not perceived at all as an environmental issue) and its disposal as a waste (which often represents one of the major environmental challenges) leads to an underestimation of the environmental effects of products.

Moreover, in an increasingly globalised economy, any issue of product-policy is inevitably influenced by considerations of free-trade at international level.

In light of such a context, it is not surprising that, in EC law, a 'product' dimension of environmental problems emerged only gradually (although up to now only in a non-systematic, rather patchwork way), when from an exclusive pollution-focused philosophy the attention started turning to a more preventive approach. Environmental law consequently evolved: aside from 'traditional' air and water pollution control instruments, regulatory means started to be developed, taking the form of regulation of the marketing and use of substances in products and in production processes (restrictions, bans, authorisation proce-

7 Directive 98/34/EC laying down a procedure for the provision of information in the field of technical standards and regulations (OJ 1998 L 204/37) requires Member States to notify to the Commission all draft technical regulations which have any impact on the free circulation of goods and suspend their adoption for at least 3 months, during which the Commission exercises a preventive control of the measures's compatibility with the Treaty (in particular Articles 28-29).

8 Jans (2003) 119.

dures, labelling rules and so on). However, such regulatory initiatives have so far been rather un-coordinated, limited in number and scope. Moreover, quantitative issues have not yet been addressed: for example, the question as to whether there should be limits to the production volumes of packaging, cars or electronic gadgets has not yet been addressed by the legislator.

It should be stressed that there are no legal obstacles to the adoption of regulatory measures which affect the marketing and composition of products. Products have been the focus of extremely voluminous internal market legislation. Moreover, they have been addressed in several EC legislation on consumers[9] or worker protection. In other words, it is certainly not a product dimension which is difficult to find in EC primary and secondary law. What is difficult to find, is a systematic approach aimed at decreasing the environmental impact of products.

This is immediately evident when we try to identify which products are problematic – even when limiting the scope of the analysis to the release of dangerous substances to the environment – since which substances are problematic for the environment, is not very clear.

A first list of 'pollutants for priority investigation' as well as 'second-category pollutants' is to be found in the Council and Member States declaration of 22 November 1973 on the programme of action of the European Communities on the environment[10] (first Action Programme), which called for the drawing up of a definitive list of pollutants by mid-1974. References to lists of pollutants/problematic products in relation to air, water and waste are to be found also in the two subsequent action programmes. Over time, the 'list approach' has been integrated in several legal acts (such as Directive 76/464/EEC on discharge of dangerous substances into the aquatic environment;[11] Directive 84/360/EEC on the combating of air pollution from industrial plants;[12] Directive 96/61/EC on IPPC[13] and Directive 96/62/EC on ambient air quality assessment and management).[14] Other lists have also been used in chemicals (Directive 67/548/EEC[15] and Regulation (EEC) 1993/793),[16] waste legislation (Directive 75/442/EEC,[17] 91/689/EEC[18] and Decision 2000/532),[19] and the Eco-label system.[20] A new list of

9 For example, under the Directive on general product safety, *producers shall be obliged to place only safe products on the market*, Art. 3(1), Directive 2001/95/EC, OJ 2002 L 11/4; see Krämer (2002g) 49-51.

10 OJ 1973 C 112/1.

11 OJ 1976 L 129/23.

12 OJ 1984 L 188/20.

13 OJ 1996 L 257/2.

14 OJ 1996 L 296/55.

15 OJ 1967 196/1.

16 OJ 1993 L 84/1.

17 OJ 1991 L 78/32.

18 OJ 1991 L 377/20.

19 OJ 2000 L 226/3.

20 Regulation (EC) 1980/2000, OJ 2000 L 237/1.

priority substances in the field of water policy, under the water framework Directive[21] has been adopted in 2001.[22] Depending on the media/problem targeted, the classification/lists used are different. The lists are often functional to the type of measure adopted and the specific media targeted, and comparisons or conclusions are difficult to draw.[23] Apart form a few recurring substances (*e.g.* lead, cadmium, mercury),[24] one can easily draw the conclusion that a single fit for all lists of 'products or substances in products' which are problematic for the environment has not yet been achieved. The recent Commission Communication on an 'integrated product policy'[25] does not touch on this issue.

3 Environmental requirements for products at EC level

Various product-related environmental requirements have been enacted in relation to different media and sectors. This mirrors the administrative structure of the Commission and of the competent ministries in most of the Member States (typically, different departments are in charge of air, water, chemicals, waste, agriculture, energy and so on) and sector-specific legislation developed accordingly. Hereafter, some of the product-related restrictions are presented and briefly discussed. As mentioned above, reference is made primarily to measures on the composition and use of products, and the intention is not to provide an exhaustive overview of all relevant measures but rather to try to discuss some interesting legal features of environmental product-policy in the Community.

3.1 Effects on product composition through controls on chemicals

Directive 76/769/EEC[26] lists, in Annex I, a number of substances whose marketing or use is subject to restrictions in the Community. When considering restrictions on marketing and use of substances, one might be tempted to take this Directive as the only relevant piece of legislation, or at least as the overarching one. True, this Directive was conceived in the mid-seventies as a 'horizontal' Directive for the harmonisation of restrictions of marketing and use of some hazardous substances with the aim of protecting the

---

21 Directive 2000/60/EC, OJ 2000 L 327/1.

22 Decision 2455/2001, OJ 2001 L 331/1.

23 These lists had no direct influence of product-related provisions but where rather aimed at framing Community policy for the limitation of the emission of pollutants into the environment, see Krämer (2003a) 205.

24 CO2 should also be mentioned, given it implications for climate change.

25 COM (2003) 302 of 18 June 2003.

26 Directive 76/769/EEC on the restriction on marketing and use of chemicals, OJ 1976 L 262/201.

internal market, human health and the environment[27] and indeed it provides for a number of environmental-based restrictions. However, this Directive neither represents the only relevant tool for product-related restrictions (as it will be shown hereafter), nor is it clear that this Directive has fulfilled the expectations which led to its adoption. Twenty-five years after its entry into force, the Commission highlighted substantial shortcomings in the functioning of this system and suggested a new strategy[28] for chemicals policy which led, in 2003, to the proposition of a complete set of new regulatory measures.[29]

Article 1 of Directive 76/769/EEC establishes that this Directive is without prejudice to the application of other relevant Community provisions, thus showing clearly that the legislator has deliberately intended to provide for restrictions other than those laid down in this Directive. Moreover, the issue has arisen whether substances not targeted by Directive 76/769/EEC are to be considered as 'positive' substances compared to the restricted substances, meaning that their use cannot be restricted by individual Member States. On 11 July 2000, the Court clearly answered in the negative, establishing that, with reference to Directive 76/769/EEC, *it clearly presents no obstacle to the regulation by Member States of the marketing of substances that do not fall within its scope*.[30] Therefore, Member States may subject the placing on the market of substances not addressed by Directive 76/769/EEC to restrictions, provided they comply with Articles 28-30 EC.

3.2 Product policy in the air sector: vehicles and fuels in the spotlight

Product-related measures which affect air quality have essentially targeted road vehicles and their fuels. No measures have yet been brought forward in relation to airplanes, whereas a Commission proposal on fuel quality for ships is presently being discussed by the Council and the European Parliament (EP).[31] Although not adopted with a view to restricting the use of specific products, ambient air quality legislation has, in some cases, also affected products.[32] Product-related requirements have also been adopted, in response to international action, on substances which deplete the ozone-layer.[33]

---

27 Recitals 1 to 4.

28 White Paper of 27.2.2001, COM (2002) 88 final.

29 COM (2003) 644 of 29.10.2003. For a thorough focused analysis of Directive 76/679/EEC and the need for reforming it, see Winter (2000).

30 C-473/98 *Kemikalieninspektionen* [2000] ECR I-5681, par. 30.

31 COM (2002) 595 of 20/11/2002.

32 Examples: in the early 1990 Ireland, in order to comply with the ambient standards for particulates set by Directive 80/779 (OJ 1980 L 229/30) prohibited the use of bituminous coal in domestic heating. By Ordinance of 27/5/03 the Tyrol Region of Austria intended to prohibit the circulation of certain heavy goods vehicles on part of the Brenner highway. This Ordinance did not come into effect as, by

The first measures in relation to car emissions appeared in the early seventies. These are the first product-related Community rules to have an impact on the environment. However, their declared aim was to ensure the smooth functioning of the internal market, rather than the control of polluting emissions. Directive 70/220/EEC[34] (tackling carbon monoxide and hydrocarbons emissions from motor vehicles) was adopted in 1970 as a reaction by the EEC to potentially 'protectionist' national measures adopted in Germany and France in the late Sixties.[35]

The limit values of Directive 70/220 were progressively tightened and its scope was extended to nitrogen oxides (1977) and particulate from diesel engines (1988). In 1994, the EP and the Council adopted Directive 94/12/EC,[36] on the basis of a Commission proposal presented shortly after the signature of the UN Framework Convention on Climate Change, which called, *inter alia,* for the improvement in fuel quality in view of reducing emissions of CO2 and dangerous substances (in particular benzene). In addition, in 1992, the Commission had set up a technical work programme together with the automobile and oil industries (the 'Auto-Oil' programme), based on the 'need for an objective assessment the most cost-effective ways to reduce emissions from the road transport sector in order to achieve the new air quality standards that were under development'.[37] As a result, two new Directives on emissions from cars and fuel quality were adopted in 1998.[38]

Ordinance of 30/7/03 of the Court of Justice issued following an action brought by the Commission for alleged breach of EC internal market rules, the Court ordered Austria to suspend its application (C-320/03, not yet decided on the substance).

33 Regulation 2037/2000/EC, OJ 2000 L 244/1.

34 OJ 1970 L 76/1.

35 See Recitals 1 and 2 of Directive 70/220/EEC. This Directive forms part of the so-called 'type-approval' system (Directive 70/156/EEC, OJ 1970 L 42/1), establishing that a vehicle type-approved in any Member State in compliance with this Directive would not need to be type-approved in the other Member States, in adherence to a 1958 UNECE Agreement, in which no trace of environmental objectives may be found. Directive 70/156/EEC has undergone several amendments in order to be adapted to the technical specifications (more than 100) agreed upon within the UNECE agreement. However, out of the 57 'daughter Directives' that constitute the type approval system, only three have some environmental implications: Directive 70/220; Directive 72/306/EEC on pollutants from diesel engines (OJ 1972 L 190/1) and Directive 80/1268/EEC on fuel consumption (OJ 1980 L 375/36) (which sole objective is to harmonize the conditions under which fuel consumption is to be measured, in order to ensure comparability of different vehicles; no requirements for limiting fuel consumption are set). Some environmental implications are also to be found in Directive 71/320/EC (OJ 1971 L 202/37) which, in an amendment of 1998 (Directive 98/12/EC, OJ 1998 L 81/1) banned asbestos in brake-linings.

36 OJ 1994 L 100/42.

37 Communication from the Commission, *A Review of the Auto-Oil II Programme,* COM (2002) 626, p. 4.

38 Directive 98/69/EC (OJ 1998 L 350/1) and Directive 98/70/EC (OJ 1998 L 350/58).

Directive 98/69/EC deals with emission limit values from cars, whereas Directive 98/70/EC relates to the quality of petrol and diesel fuels, amending provisions which had been developed by the EEC from 1975[39] with the free circulation of fuels as the main objective. The maximum level of sulphur in gas-oil has been gradually reduced from 0.5% (1976) to 0.05% (1996). In 2001 the Commission proposed the introduction of sulphur-free petrol and diesel by 2005.[40] This led to the adoption of Directive 2003/17/EC, which requires the marketing of petrol and diesel fuel containing a maximum of 10 mg/kg of sulphur by 1 January 2005 on an appropriately balanced geographical area of the Member States territory and to make the use of such fuels mandatory after January 2009. Member States may require that, in specific areas, petrol and diesel fuels may be marketed subject to more stringent environmental specifications than those laid down in the Directive. As regards petrol, a Directive of 1978[41] set the maximum content of lead at 0.40 g/l from 1 January 1981. Gradually, these limits have been lowered. Under Directive 98/70/EC lead in petrol was to be phased out completely by 1 January 2000.[42]

Despite the fact that Directive 94/12/EC called for the reduction of CO_2 emissions from cars, no binding limit values have been adopted. A strategy was presented by the Commission in 1995,[43] laying down the objective of reducing CO_2 emissions from newly registered cars to 120 g/km by 2010 at the latest. In order to meet this target, action was foreseen at three parallel levels: (1) a self-commitment by the automobile industry on fuel economy improvements; (2) fuel-economy labelling of cars[44] and (3) promotion of car fuel efficiency by fiscal measures (not yet applied).

Pursuant to point (1) the European Automobile Manufacturers Association (ACEA) committed to collectively achieve a target of 140 g/km by 2008, while its individual Members would place on the market, by the year 2000, vehicles emitting 120 g/km. Its Japanese and Korean homologues (JAMA and KAMA) committed to the 140 g/km target for 2009 and the placing on the market of cars emitting 120 g/km at the earliest possible date after the year 2000. Intermediate targets have also been set. The Commission endorsed these commitments by three Recommendations (non binding instruments) based on Article 155 EC.[45] In order to monitor the progress towards achieving the targets, 'joint statements', are published yearly. According to the last report, dated 11 Febru-

---

39 Directive 75/716/EEC (OJ 1975 L 307/22).

40 OJ 2003 C 213E/255.

41 Directive 78/611/EEC, OJ 1978 L 197/19.

42 Italy, Spain and Greece failed to adapt their petrol distribution system in time and were given two extra years time. See *infra*, section 6.

43 COM (1995) 968.

44 Directive 1999/94/EC OJ 2000 L 12/16.

45 Recommendations 1999/125 of 5.2.1999 (ACEA), OJ 1999 L 40/49; 2000/303 and 304 of 13.4.2000 (KAMA and JAMA), OJ 2000 L 100/55-57.

ary 2004,[46] the value achieved in 2002 was 166 g CO2/km, compared to 186 g in 1995. In 2002 about 5% of ACEA cars (3% for JAMA) have been registered in the EU which emit 120 g/km. Thus, it appears clearly that the key to reaching the 120 g/km overall target depends heavily on the large number of cars not complying with this limit, which are still being put on the market. Here, the question arises whether vehicles which are far from complying with the set targets should nevertheless be allowed on the market or whether quotas should be set, for example for the most fuel-consuming or polluting cars.

3.3 Product policy and water protection

Community legislation in the field of water protection progressively laid down a number of quality standards (*e.g.* bathing water, drinking water), obligations to designate vulnerable areas in relation to specific pollutants coupled with corresponding pollution reduction programmes or requirements to take measures to reduce this pollution (*e.g.* nitrates, waste water) and emission limit values for polluting discharges (Directive 76/464/EEC).[47] Unlike in the air sector, no environmental product-related restrictions have been adopted in specific legislation aimed at protecting water.[48] Rather, the restriction of substances harmful for the aquatic environment has been left to Directive 76/769/EEC. However, we do find some implications for products in water-related legislation.

Directive 76/464/EEC requires Member States to take measures to eliminate discharges of 'list I' substances and reduce discharges of 'list II' substances. In relation to list II substances, Member States were to draw up pollution reduction programmes. Article 7(4) states that these programmes may lay down requirements for the composition and use of substances and products. This shows that the importance of products for water pollution had already been recognized in 1976. It is also worth stressing that this Directive defines 'discharge' as the introduction into waters of any substances in list I or list II of the Annex.[49] In the *Nederhoff* case,[50] the ECJ found that this term covers any act attributable to a person by which one of the dangerous substances listed in Annex I or II to the Directive is directly or indirectly introduced into the waters to which the Directive applies. As a consequence, a decision by a Dutch authority to refuse permission to use wooden posts impregnated with a pesticide (creosote, containing polycyclic aromatic hydrocarbons – PAHs, which are substances of list I of the Annex) was found by the ECJ to be consistent with the Directive. The Dutch

---

46 http://europa.eu.int/comm/enterprise/automotive/pagesbackground/pollutant_emission/index.htm

47 OJ 1976 L 129/23. See the articles of A. Paquot and C. Olazabal in this book.

48 To the extent that drinking water can be considered as a product, Directive 80/778/EEC (OJ 1980 L 229/11) and 98/83/EC (OJ 1998 L 330/32) should be seen as product-related measures with implications for human health.

49 Article 1(2)(d).

50 C-232/97 [1999] ECR I-6385.

refusal had been based on the substitution principle (economic operators asking for permission to use dangerous substances must in the first place look for more ecological alternatives), which was deemed by the ECJ to be in line with the Directive and in particular its Article, 10 allowing Member States to take more stringent measures than those provided for under the Directive. The ECJ did not endorse the argument that creosote is also regulated by Directive 76/769/EEC, which allows for the use of creosote under certain conditions, thus Member States would not be allowed to take further restrictions, given that Directive 76/769/EEC applies without prejudice to the application of other relevant Community provisions. In short, given that Directive 76/464/EEC requires Member States to eliminate pollution of waters by substances of List I and reduce pollution by substances of List II, the Court's interpretation of the term 'discharge' implies that – for products destined to be used in contact with waters – Member States are under an obligation to take measures on the use of such products.

In this context, it is also worth mentioning Directive 91/676/EEC[51] which, in so far as it encourages the substitution of chemical with organic fertilizers in Member States with manure surplus and nitrate problems, can be mentioned as a Directive with implications on certain products.

A list of priority substances in the field of water policy, pursuant to Directive 2000/60/EC[52] (the water framework Directive) has been adopted in 2001,[53] calling for specific measures with a view to the cessation or phasing out of discharges, emissions and losses within 20 years of their adoption. It is not clear whether among these measures, product-related provisions will be found. This possibility is explicitly mentioned by the Commission in relation to SCCP[54] and in relation to MTBE.[55] Several (unsuccessful) actions against Decision 2455/01, in relation to specific listed substances, have been lodged before the Tribunal of First Instance by the chemical industry.[56]

---

51 OJ 1991 L 375/1.

52 Note 21 above.

53 Note 22 above.

54 Commission decision 2004/1/EC on national provisions on the use of short-chain chlorinated paraffins notified by the Netherlands under Article 95(4) EC, OJ 2004 L 1/20.

55 Methyl tertiary butyl ether, a toxic chemical which is blended into petrol in order to boost its octane rating. In its proposal of 11.5.2001 on the quality of petrol and diesel fuels amending Directive 98/70/EC, the Commission recognized that MTBE has been found in groundwater, but it decided not to propose any restriction of this substance in fuels, and to consider it 'within the water framework Directive' (COM (2001) 241 final, *explanatory memorandum*, not published in the OJ, page 9).

56 T-45/02 [2003] ECR II-1973; T-46/02, T-57/02, T-70/02 (OJ 2003 C 184/35).

3.4 Product requirements in the waste sector

Waste policy inevitably deals with products, since waste is 'products'. Behind the legal definition of waste, we find exactly the same consumer or industrial goods which – before being discarded and becoming waste – have lived their life as products. It is therefore not surprising that it is in the waste sector that environmental requirements are closest to products. The first stage of Community waste legislation focused mainly on the environmental impact of the disposal and the transport of waste.[57] The waste-specific legislation, such as the 1975 waste oils Directive,[58] the 1976 Directive on the disposal of PCB-PCT[59] or the 1985 Directive on containers of liquids for human consumption[60] limited themselves to regulating issues of collection and disposal/recovery of specific waste streams while not containing provisions on the composition of products. In 1989, the Commission adopted its first structured orientations on a waste management policy, according to which priority should have been given to waste prevention and calling, though in rather vague terms, for product-related measures.[61] In 1990 the Council invited the Commission to accelerate work in relation to packaging, batteries, and PCB's.[62] Time was therefore ripe for product-related legislation in the field of waste. The first Directive where this bridge was built was Directive 91/157/EEC on batteries,[63] which besides establishing collection and labelling obligations, prohibited the placing on the market of batteries containing mercury in excess of given thresholds.[64] This prohibition was intended to be inserted in Annex I to Directive 76/769/EEC.

In 1992 the Commission presented a new proposal for a Directive on packaging,[65] which included a provision aimed at limiting the maximum concentration of lead, mercury, cadmium and hexavalent chromium in new packaging.

---

57 Directive 75/442/EEC on waste, OJ 1975 L 194/39; Directive 78/319 on toxic and dangerous waste, OJ 1978 L 84/43; Directive 84/631 on the supervision and control within the European Community of the transfrontier shipment of hazardous waste, OJ 1984 L 326/31.

58 Directive 75/439/EEC OJ 1975 L 194/23.

59 Directive 76/403, OJ 1976 L 108/41, now repealed by Directive 96/59/EC, OJ 1996 L243/31.

60 Directive 85/339/EEC, OJ 1985 L 176/18.

61 SEC (1989) 934 final of 14 September 1989.

62 Resolution of 7 May 1990, OJ 1990 C 122/2.

63 Directive 91/157/EEC on batteries and accumulators containing certain dangerous substances, OJ 1991 L 78/38.

64 Directive 98/101/EC (OJ 1999 L 1/1), amending Directive 91/157/EEC, has completely phased-out mercury in batteries covered by this Directive. On 24 November 2003 the Commission adopted a proposal for a new Directive on batteries [COM (2003) 723)]. In terms of product-rules, this proposal confirms the ban on mercury already contained in Directive 91/157/EEC and does not propose restrictions on other substances. In spring 2004 the European Parliament voted in favour of banning cadmium in batteries (PE 340.787 www.europarl.eu.int).

65 OJ 1992 C 263/1.

This eventually became Article 11 of Directive 94/62/EC.[66] The product-related provisions of this Directive were based on the so-called 'new-approach' (until then not used in the field of environmental legislation): aside from the provision on the four mentioned heavy metals, it set a number of other requirements for eco-design, whose compliance was to be shown by adhering to CEN standards. However, out of the 5 standards approved by CEN in 2000 on a mandate from the Commission, the Commission only endorsed and published in the Official Journal some minor parts.[67] No published standards yet exist in relation to compliance with the requirements on prevention, reusability, general heavy metal contents and recyclability (as materials or energy). It is widely recognized that Directive 94/62/EC did not have an impact on the composition of packaging put on the market.

In 1996, the Commission reviewed the Community Strategy for Waste Management.[68] Ludwig Krämer was at that time head of the waste Unit of DG Environment. In the 1996 Review, the need for more product-oriented measures was clearly spelled-out: the Commission called for EC-wide rules to limit the presence of heavy metals in products or ban specific substances. The EP responded by asking for measures limiting the use of substances such as heavy metals, in particular cadmium and mercury, as well as chlorine[69] and PVC. Also the Council asked the Commission to bring forward recommendations to deal with environmentally dangerous substances.[70]

The most important innovations in this Review were the priority given to material recycling over waste incineration and the principle of producer responsibility, which had made its appearance in some Member States but not yet in Community law. The Commission acted to apply these principles in a proposal for a Directive of 1997[71] on end of life vehicles (ELV). The ELV Directive was adopted in September 2000 (Directive 2000/53/EC)[72] and it was then followed by a 'twin' Directive on waste from electrical and electronic equipment[73] (WEEE).

Article 4(2) of the ELV Directive bans lead, mercury, cadmium and hexavalent chromium from vehicles placed on the market from 1 July 2003. A number of derogations have been provided for in Annex II based on the principle of substitution: derogations may only be included in that Annex (which may be modified by the Commission via Committee procedure)[74] if there is no techni-

66 OJ 1994 L 365/10. This Directive repealed Directive 85/339/EEC.

67 Commission Decision 2001/524/EEC of 28 June 2001, OJ 2001 L 190/21.

68 COM (1996) 399 final.

69 Letter 'l', Resolution A4-0364/96, OJ 1996 C 362/241.

70 Resolution of 24 February 1997 on a Community Strategy for Waste Management, OJ 1997 C 76/1.

71 OJ 1997 C 337/3. On the origin of this proposal, see Onida (2000) 276.

72 OJ 2000 L 269/34.

73 Directive 2002/96/EC, OJ 2002 L 37/24 and Directive 2002/95/EC, OJ 2002 L 37/19.

74 On details of this Committee procedure, see Onida (2003) 203.

cal substitute for a given application containing a banned substance. Economic considerations have been deemed by the co-legislator not to play a role in this substitution process. One of the immediate results of this provision has been that vehicle manufacturers have become aware of the composition of 'their' vehicles in terms of hazardous substances.

The ELV Directive is based on Article 175(1) EC meaning that individual Member States may well decide to impose stricter requirements in accordance with Article 176. For electrical and electronic equipment (EEE) another approach was followed: the product-related provisions were placed in a separate Directive on Restrictions on Hazardous Substances in electrical and electronic equipment (Directive 2002/95/EC; RoHS). The RoHS Directive is based on Article 95(1), meaning that Member States may only take stricter measures on the basis of Article 95(4-5). It is precisely because the legislator wanted to prevent Member States from taking stricter measures than those laid down in the Directive that the RoHS Directive was based on Article 95(1). As a consequence, identical products (*e.g.* lead solder) are subject to different legal rules depending on whether they are used in cars or in electronic appliances. The RoHS Directive goes further than the ELV Directive in so far as it also bans certain brominated flame retardants (PBB and PBDE) and provides for a mechanism for applying the substitution approach to other substances.[75] However, the ELV Directive sets out rules on the design of vehicles (recyclability),[76] whereas no similar provision is to be found in the WEEE/RoHS Directives. Eco-design requirements for electric and electronic equipment are proposed in a Commission proposal of 2003 for a framework Directive on eco-design for energy using products (EuP).[77]

3.4.1 Recent developments on 'integrated product policy'

Decision 1600/2002/EC[78] laying down the Sixth Environment Action Programme calls for further measures on waste prevention by, *inter alia*, the phasing out of certain materials and substances through product-related measures. At present, discussion on further product-policy measures in relation

---

75 Hedemann-Robinson (2003a) 56.

76 COM (2004) 162 final of 11 March 2004. The proposed recyclability requirements, in practice, correspond to existing ISO standards.

77 COM (2003) 453. This proposal draws from the 'new approach' where monitoring of compliance with design requirements is essentially left to standardisation bodies. The aim is more to prevent Member States from adopting national product-related requirements than to propose design requirements at EC level. 'Implementing measures' laying down 'generic eco-design requirements' in accordance with Annex I and II of the Directive shall be adopted by the Commission under a Committee procedure. To what extent these generic requirements, if adopted, will be sufficiently precise in order to constitute full harmonisation measures remains to be seen.

78 Art. 8(2)(ii)(d), OJ 2002 L 242/1.

to waste is being conducted mainly in the framework of the Integrated Product Policy (IPP). A 2003 Commission Communication,[79] building on a Green Paper of 2001,[80] openly recognises the need for product-related environmental measures.[81] However, the approach followed has been rather general, spelling out the five concepts on which the IPP approach is based (life-cycle thinking; working with the market; stakeholder involvement; continuous improvement rather than setting thresholds or targets; and a variety of policy instruments) and calling for action mainly in two directions: 1) targeting products with the greatest potential for improvement (still to be identified) and 2) establishing framework conditions for the continuous environmental improvement of all products. Here, though legislation is mentioned as a residual tool, focus is mainly on market-related instruments, such as taxes, voluntary agreements, standardisation and public procurement, information, awareness-raising and labelling. Thus the philosophy is to tackle the environmental impacts which, under a cost-effectiveness perspective, present the greatest potential for enhancement, rather than systematically provide for substitution of hazardous substances in all products. This economic approach is also the basis of the Commission Communication of 2003 'Towards a Thematic Strategy on the Sustainable Use of Natural Resources',[82] where it is stated that the focus of the legislator should be on the issues with the greatest potential for environmental improvement. Thus, a clear shift can be identified from a waste-related product policy focused on products and substances which are intrinsically hazardous – applying the principles of producer responsibility and substitution – to a more economic-based philosophy whereby measures are to be taken only if 'cost-effective'.

3.5 Product-related requirements in relation to soil

There are no specific Community environmental measures aimed at protecting soil as such, although a number of product-related provisions have a direct consequence on soil. Directive 86/278/EEC[83] restricts the use of sludge[84] in agriculture if certain concentration limits of heavy metals in sludge are exceeded. Marketing and use restrictions which have a direct

---

79 COM (2001) 68 of 7.2.2001.

80 COM (2003) 302 of 18.6.2003.

81 Page 3: *'Up to now, product-related environmental policies have tended to focus on large point sources of pollution, such as industrial emissions or waste management issues'..Now, however...they need to be complemented by a policy that looks at the whole of a product's life cycles....It should also mean that environmental impacts are addressed at the point in the life cycle where they will best and most cost-effectively reduce the overall environmental impacts and resource use.'*

82 COM (2003) 572 of 1.10.2003.

83 OJ 1986 L 181/6. See the article of L. Marmo in this book.

84 Sludge is, however, a *sui generis* product, which is produced as the outcome of waste water treatment.

85 Directive 91/414/EEC OJ 1991 L 230/1.

bearing on soil have been adopted in relation to pesticides,[85] and animal feed stuffs,[86] although the aim is more to protect water than soil. Also legislation on the deliberate emission of GMOs (Directive 2001/18/EC)[87] constitutes product-related legislation aimed, *inter alia*, at protecting soil, biodiversity and eventually human health. Discussions on whether there should be maximum concentrations for cadmium in fertilizers have been ongoing since Austria, Sweden and Finland jointed the EU in 1995.

3.6 Other examples of product requirements having environmental implications

There is no single definition of 'environment', as a result the identification of environmental rules is somewhat arbitrary. Many examples of product-related environmental requirements may be found in areas not typically defined as 'the environment'. In the energy sector (which does not have a specific legal basis in the Treaty, therefore use is made of Article 175) Directive 2002/91/EC[88] on the energy performance of buildings can be considered to be product-related legislation, to the extent that it affects the choice of construction materials. Lead capsules were phased out for wine bottles in 1992 by a Regulation based on Article 43 (now 37, the agriculture legal basis) and 100A (now 95).[89] For internal market reasons, the composition of detergents has been regulated since 1973.[90]

Finally, a number of EC provisions have been adopted which, although not directly affect the marketing and use of products, are aimed at influencing the demand by consumers. The Directives on labelling of energy products[91] and on car fuel consumption[92] are cases in point. On the basis of the eco-label Regulation[93] several ecological criteria, often referring to substances which must not be used if the eco-label is used, (such as PVC in shoes)[94] have been adopted. Work is ongoing in relation to standardisation[95] and green technologies.[96]

86 *E.g.* Directive 2002/32/EC on undesirable substances in animal feed, OJ 2002 L 140/10.

87 OJ 2001 L 106/1.

88 OJ 2003 L 1/65.

89 Regulation (EEC) 3280/92, OJ 1992 L 327/3.

90 Regulation (EC) 648/2004, OJ 2004 L 104/1.

91 Directive 92/75/EEC, OJ 1992 L 297/16.

92 Directive 1999/94/EC, OJ 2000 L 12/16.

93 Regulation (EC) 1980/2000, OJ 2000 L 237/1.

94 Decision 2002/231/EC OJ 2002 L 77/50. Point 5 of the Annex states: '*The footwear shall not contain PVC.*'

95 On 25 February 2004, the Commission adopted a Communication on the integration of environmental aspects into European Standardisation (COM (2004) 130 final), which aims at raising awareness *for the need to integrate environmental aspects into European standardization, a voluntary, stakeholder-driven process.* No concrete action is proposed at this stage, the Communication rather invites stakeholders to develop concrete actions.

96 COM (2004) 38 of 28.1.2004 available at http://europa.eu.int/comm/environment/etap/etap.htm.

4 The role of Member States

Some words should be spent also on the role of product policy measures at national level, from two main points of view, firstly the room for such measures under the constraint of EC free-trade rules and secondly the propulsive role of these measures.

4.1 The room for Member States action

The rather incoherent set of product-related environmental requirements existing at EC level has an impact on the possibility for Member States to take individual measures. Measures relating to the internal market are generally under the exclusive competence of the EC. However, there are several cases where product restrictions at EC level have been based on Article 175(1) EC, thus allowing Member States to take more stringent measures on the basis of Article 176. Reference is made, for example, to product restrictions on substances which deplete the ozone layer (Regulation 2037/2000)[97] or to the ban on heavy metals in cars (Directive 2000/53/EC), both based on Article 175(1).

Furthermore, not all areas have been 'harmonised', and in these cases Member States are free to take measures which restrict the free circulation of goods on the basis of Article 28-30 EC. With some risk of oversimplifying a very complex subject, we may recall that trade restrictive measures can be justified in three ways; 1) under Article 30 EC,[98] to the extent that the targeted environmental concerns fall under the concept of 'protection of life and health of animals and plants'; in this case, it is up to Member States to determine the level of protection which should be given to human health and life, whilst taking into account that the measure must not constitute a means of arbitrary discrimination or a disguised restriction on trade between Member States;[99] 2) under the *Rewe*[100] doctrine, when they are necessary in view of mandatory requirements (including the environment), provided they apply indistinctly to domestic and imported products and no less trade-restrictive alternatives leading to the same result are available (proportionality test). In recent case-law, where the environmental aim of the national measure in question was clear, the ECJ has not been strict on the proportionality condition,[101] suggesting that there is indeed more

---

[97] OJ 2000 L 244/1.

[98] Provided they do not *constitute a means of arbitrary discrimination or a disguised restriction on trade between Member States* (Article 30 EC).

[99] Case 272/80 *Frans-Nederlandse Maatschappij voor Biologische Producten BV* [1981] ECR 3277, paragraph 12; C-293/94 *Brandsma* [1996] ECR I-3159 paragraph 11; C-400/96 *Harpegnies* [1998] ECR I-5121, paragraph 33; C-125/88 *Nijman* [1989] ECR 3533, paragraph 14.

[100] Case 120/78 *Rewe* [1979] ECR 649; 302/86 *Commission* v. *Denmark* [1988] ECR 4607.

[101] C-473/98 *Kemikalieninspektionen* [2000] ECR I-5681; C-67/97 *Bluhme* [1998] ECR I-8033; C-379/98 *PreussenElektra* [2001] ECR I-2099. On this point, see Jans (2000) 251; Krämer (2000a) 79-80; Wiers (2002) 72-83.

room for national environmental trade-restrictive measures than traditionally thought. In other words, it seems that, when the environmental objective of the measure is clear, the Court does not require a comparison between the trade-restrictive national measure and the environmental objective pursued, unless it is very clear that less trade-restrictive alternatives exist. The Court has also acknowledged that the integration principle, laid down in Article 6 EC, plays an important role in assessing the compatibility with the Treaty of trade-restrictive measures.[102] Finally (3), certain trade-restrictive measures not representing 'measures affecting trade' (*e.g.* advertising or selling rules)[103] may fall out of the prohibition in Article 28 EC.[104]

Procedurally, national measures which affect the free movement of goods in non harmonised areas have to be notified to the Commission at the draft stage, at least three months prior to their entry into force ('standstill period' pursuant to Directive 98/34/EC). The Commission and other Member States may comment on the draft measure or issue a detailed opinion, in which case the 'standstill' is prolonged to 6 months.[105] In the past, the Commission has considered detailed opinions to be equivalent to letters of formal notice under Article 226 EC (the first step of the infringement procedure),[106] thus it has sometimes followed detailed opinions issued under Directive 98/34/EC with reasoned opinions issued pursuant to Article 226 EC. The Court has ruled out this practice.[107]

In sectors which have been harmonised by means of provisions based on Article 95(1) EC, stricter national environmental rules may only be maintained or introduced under the conditions, respectively, of Article 95(4) and 95(5). They must be approved by the Commission. This derogatory clause, as amended by the Treaty of Amsterdam (TOA) leaves very little room for Member States wishing to introduce stricter measures after a Community harmonisation measure is adopted, since Member States have to prove that new scientific evidence has arisen, after the adoption of the harmonisation measure, on grounds of a problem specific to that Member State. More room would seem to exist for maintaining stricter national rules, where the condition of the new scientific evidence on grounds of a problem specific to the Member State is not a formal pre-condition for the Commission's approval.[108]

---

[102] C-379/98 *PreussenElektra* [2001] ECR I-2099.

[103] Jans (2000) 236.

[104] C-267-8/91 *Keck and Mithouard* [1993] ECR I-6097.

[105] Art. 9, Directive 98/34/EC.

[106] See the article from S. Grohs in this book.

[107] C-230/99 *Commission* v. *France* 2001 [ECR] I-1169. The Court declared the practice inadmissible given that a detailed opinion issued pursuant to Directive 98/34/EC is based on draft legislation, and at this stage it cannot yet be inferred that a Member State has breached Community legislation.

[108] C-3/00 *Denmark* v. *Commission* [2003] ECR I-2643.

Since the 1st of May 1999 (date of entry into force of the TOA), Article 95(4) has been invoked, in relation to environmental concerns, five times, leading in all cases to the approval of the national measures by the Commission.[109] Article 95(5) was invoked six times (one approval, four rejects, one case withdrawn).[110] In two cases[111] – both not concerning the environment but health protection – Commission decisions rejecting national derogatory measures have been challenged before the ECJ by the addressee Member State (respectively Germany and Denmark) and in one case this action has lead to the Decision being annulled.[112] Legal conflicts on this important topic regularly arise, showing the that the division of competences between the Community and Member States, in environmental matters, is of a dynamic nature.[113]

An interesting legal question relates to the power of Member States, in applying environmental legislation on air or water quality (based on Article 175(1)), to make product-related requirements which may conflict with harmonisation Directives.[114] For example, can a Member State which needs to take measures to comply with air quality standards, restrict the use of cars in certain areas/days? Could a Member State restrict the placing on the market of a car which is deemed to emit too much CO2? These questions can only be answered by assessing each specific situation according to its own merits and a legal analysis of this topic goes beyond the scope of this article. However, it is submitted that, in order to protect the environment, considerable space exists for Member States in this area. It is likely that, in light of the increasing recognition of the role of products on environmental critical matters, legal conflicts will increase in the future.[115]

---

[109] Decision 2002/366 (OJ 2002 L 132/65); Decision 2002/398 (OJ 2002 L 138/15); Decision 2002/399 (OJ 2002 L 138/24); Decision 2002/884 (OJ 2002 308/30); Decision 2004/1 (OJ 2004 L 1/20).

[110] Decision 2002/59 (OJ 2002 L 23/37); Decision 2000/509 (OJ 2000 L 205/7); Decision 2001/570 (OJ 2001 L 202/37); Decision 2003/1 (OJ 2003 L 1/72); Decision 2003/653 (OJ 2003 L 230/74).

[111] Decision 1999/836 (OJ 1999 L 329/100); Decision 1999/830 (OJ 1999 L 329/1).

[112] Note 108 above.

[113] Wanneras (2003) 169; De Sadeleer (2003) 889 *et seq.*; Jans (2000) 121-132; Sevenster (2000) 291-310; Verhayen (2000a) 71-75; Verhayen (2000b) 178-187; Bär-Albin (2000) 119-134; Bär-Kraemer (2000) 315-330; Krämer (2003a) 122-131; Onida (2004).

[114] See note 32 above. See also the interesting legal discussion in the House of Lords on the 'London Lorries case' (dealing with the compatibility of local authorities restriction on heavy lorries in certain streets versus harmonization Directives), in Fitzpatrick (1992) 121.

[115] For example, in Annex I to Decision 2004/279/EEC (OJ 2004 L 87/50) concerning guidance for implementation of Directive 2002/3/EC on ozone in ambient air (OJ 2002 L 67/14), the Commission published a number of experiences at national level, some constituting product-related restrictions.

4.2 The interaction between Member States initiatives and EC legislation

National environmental rules always played a crucial role in the development of EC measures. Historically, the first harmonisation measures were taken by the Community as a reaction to national measures which created problems for the internal market. The use of the term 'harmonisation' implies in itself that the Community should only act in areas where at least one Member State has already acted (although in legal terms this is certainly not a precondition for Community action and in fact the term 'harmonisation' is also used where the Community takes the initiative in advance of any Member State).

This crucial role is still relevant, despite the fact that nowadays Community harmonisation covers many areas and may give the impression that Member State action is only 'residual'. There appears a tendency from Member States not to take action in relation to products but to wait for Community action, even where a need to take measures for environmental concerns has been widely recognised (*e.g.* PVC).[116] Directive 76/769/EEC is often seen as a 'monopoly' of product-related restrictions. However the relationship between EC and Member States initiatives is more complex than it would appear *prima facie*. Directive 76/769/EEC achieves less than is sometimes presumed. Substances and uses not targeted by this Directive may be tackled by Member States.[117] Thus, prior to concluding whether Member States have room for restricting a certain substance or a use thereof, careful attention should be paid to understanding to what extent the subject has already been harmonised by the Community. Moreover, restrictions enacted by Member States usually have an impact on the development of EC measures. White asbestos was banned in the EC in 1999, by an amendment[118] to Directive 76/679/EEC, after some 9 Member States had taken restrictions at national level. Several other cases exist where products have been restricted by a number of Member States and although no Community restrictions have been put in place yet, the pressure for the Community to act is growing (*e.g.* lead hunting shot, totally banned in NL and DK, partially banned in the UK and several other Member States, and also banned in the US; cadmium in fertilizers, which is subject to restrictions in 9 Member States).[119] In this context, it is important that Member States which aim at a high level of environmental protection take the necessary initiatives, which will eventually trigger action from the EC regulatory mechanisms.

The role of pro-active Member States is also important in relation to already harmonised areas. Whenever the Commission approves a national derogatory

---

116 COM (2000) 469.

117 See note 30 (C-473/98 *Kemikalieninspectionen*).

118 Directive 99/77/EC, OJ 1999 L 207/18.

119 http://europa.eu.int/comm/enterprise/chemicals/legislation/fertilizers/cadmium.htm. On lead shot, see Thomas & Owen (1996) 358-364.

measure under Article 95(4-5), by virtue of Article 97(7) it must immediately examine whether to propose an adaptation to the EC measure. It is true that the conditions set in Article 95(4-5), particularly the latter, are strict.[120] However, it should be observed that even in cases where the Commission rejects national requests for derogations (and therefore there is no obligation to revise the EC provision in question), this sometimes triggers new discussions which, in certain cases, leads to reconsideration (for the better) of the harmonisation measure.[121]

5 The international dimension

In some cases, Community restrictions on the marketing and use of products are the direct consequence of discussion in international fora. Examples can be found by referring to the PARCOM/OSPAR Convention (in relation to SCCP),[122] the IMO anti-fouling Convention (in relation to TBT used as an anti-fouling agent for ships),[123] the Vienna Convention and Montreal Protocol on ozone-depleting substances and the Stockholm convention on POPs.

Yet, the contribution of international environmental legislation to product-related measures in the EU is not very significant. More often, draft national or Community restrictions are criticised for alleged breach of free-trade rules under the WTO system. Trade and environment within the WTO is a complex subject, which cannot be summarized in a few pages. However, what is important to underline in this context, is that even under the WTO rules (GATT and TBT), room for environmental product-related measures exist: contracting parties may pursue the level of environmental protection they wish, and constraints come into play only when national technical regulations are misused for purposes which are not of environmental but of protectionist character.[124]

---

[120] Krämer (2000) 103; Wannerås (2003) 169.

[121] For example, after rejecting the German notification on Azo-dyes (Decision 2003/829, OJ 2003 L 311/46), the Commission adopted Directive 2003/3/EC (OJ 2003 L 4/12) which, with some differences in terminology, provides practically the same restrictions as the German notified law. The refusal in 2003 of measures envisaged by Austria on GMOs (ban of GMO cultivations in Upper-Austria, Decision 2003/653, OJ 2003 L 230/34) has led to further discussion on co-existence between conventional and GMO crops and in this context the Carinthia Region has obtained Commission approval for its envisaged co-existence provisions notified under Directive 98/34/EEC (notification 2003/327/A).

[122] Note 54 above.

[123] Directive 2002/62/EC, OJ 2002 L 183/58; Regulation (EC) 782/2003, OJ 2003 L 115/1.

[124] Wiers (2002), in particular parts three and four; Sands (2003) 940 *et seq;* Krämer (1996d) 444 *et seq.;* Trebilcock-Howse (1995) 395 *et seq.*; Birnie-Boyle (2002) 697 *et seq.*; Montini (2001) 253 *et seq.*

6 Substitution

The Community has produced several lists of substances which threaten the environment. In one case it went further: in 1988, the Council adopted a resolution on an action programme to combat environmental pollution by cadmium,[125] stating the use of cadmium should be limited to cases where suitable and safer alternatives do not exist. However, substitution has been applied by the Community legislator in a rather unsystematic way: obligations to replace substances with less hazardous ones can be found in very few binding acts (Directive 90/394/EEC[126] on workers protection and 1999/13/EC[127] on emissions of volatile organic compounds from organic solvents -but in these two cases the grounds for substitution is human health – and two waste-related Directives, ELV and RoHS). The reasons for this are mainly economic. Substitution is a complex and controversial subject. In many cases substitutes are available to the market, but the concerned economic sector opposes substitution until all or most of the individual economic operators have switched to the alternative material, or until stocks have been exhausted and past investments have been sufficiently exploited. In some cases, slowness on the side of industry to comply with phase-out provisions leads to the measures being reconsidered. In 1997 the Commission proposed, and in 1998 the Council and the European Parliament agreed, to ban lead in petrol from 1 January 2000. Notwithstanding this obligation, the concerned economic operators were late in making lead-free petrol available in Italy, Spain and Greece. At the eve of the date of entry into effect of the ban, the Commission had to agree on a two-year delay for these Member States, since it would not have been possible to phase-out lead in petrol in the absence of sufficiently available lead free petrol. An equivalent situation is arising for the ban on heavy metals in vehicles and electrical goods where delays in implementation have come to be expected by the relevant economic operators. Thus, it is important that clear signals are given, that the progress towards phase-out are monitored and failure to take the necessary measures to substitute are duly sanctioned.

Opposite opinions often exist within the same trade associations: individual, more pro-active, companies are often ahead in substituting, but the associations tend to defend the 'lowest common denominator', which in certain cases are even codified in standards. This slows down the substitution process considerably and penalises the front-runners.[128]

---

[125] OJ 1988 C 30/1.

[126] OJ 1990 L 196/1.

[127] OJ 1999 L 85/1.

[128] When launching the Environmental Technologies Action Plan (footnote 96 above), Commissioner Wallström (*ENDS Daily*, 3 February 2004) quoted the example of a Swedish Cement manufacturer which can cut by half CO_2 emissions but, lacking the adaptation of the relevant industrial standards, which are dominated by firms using conventional processes, may not use this technology. She also mentioned-

Although it is clear that changes in production patterns have a cost, pursuing a systematic replacement of substances and products identified as problematic would not be in contradiction with an approach based on cost-effectiveness. On the contrary, if pro-active companies were rewarded – by increasing their market quotas – this would greatly benefit both industrial innovation and the environment. To do this, there is a need to break into the resistance of certain corporate interests comfortably doing business as usual.

In addition, monitoring of the presence of hazardous substances in air, water, waste and soil has a cost. If these substances are removed at source from products, in the long run monitoring costs will decrease. This is one of the grounds on which, in 1998, Denmark notified to the Commission, under Directive 98/34/EC, a draft law providing for a general ban on lead intentionally used in products. This followed a similar initiative taken in 1994 on mercury. Denmark considered that, in light of the presence of lead in a great number of products, it is impossible and uneconomic to solve the problem of the propagation of lead through products by means of waste collection schemes. The Danish law eventually won the approval of the Commission.[129]

7 Concluding remarks

The objective of this article was to show that EC law sets out, directly or indirectly, a number of product-related environmental requirements. However, a coherent environmental product policy – even limited to hazardous substances in products – is still to be developed. Questions regularly arise, such as why is cadmium prohibited in batteries for electric vehicles and not in portable batteries or in fertilizers; why has lead been phased out from petrol, cars, electronic appliances and wine capsules but it is still widely spread in the environment by its use in hunting shot[130]; why are several substances (*e.g.* PVC in shoes) not allowed in products which flag the European Ecolabel but their use is nevertheless allowed in all other cases; why heavy metals restrictions in cars are based on Article 175(1) and in electronic goods on Article 95(1). One reason for this lack of coherency is the fact that attempts to protect the environment by taking product related measures – including substitution measures – tend to be increasingly assessed on grounds related to risk-assessment, cost and benefit, competitiveness tests and so on,[131] even when no such requirement exists in legislation. This leads sometimes to increased legal uncertainty, weakening of the legislation and measures being adopted without a coherent framework.

---

cars on the market which use 3 litres of fuel per 100 Km, and pointed at the possibility that performance targets should be set for specific types of products.

129 Notification 98/595/DK.

130 Thomas & Guitart (2003) 144.

131 See Krämer (2003a) 203.

As well illustrated by Gerd Winter,[132] a possible way forward would be to refer to a list of substances – even limited to a few 'usual suspects' (heavy metals, substances which are ecotoxic, persistent and bioaccumulative), whose marketing and use is to be substituted, regardless of results of risk-assessments or economic analysis. In legal terms, the substitution principle would imply reversing the burden of proof, which today is generally placed on those who want to restrict the marketing or use of a product. The precautionary principle has not substantially changed this situation.[133] This would also give clearer signals to economic operators, who would expend less energy on lobbying for prolonged use of substances and would put more resources in the development and testing of substitutes. There is already a sufficiently large list of 'usual suspects' to start with.

---

[132] Winter (2000) 183.

[133] In some cases, when the substitutes to well known toxic substances have not been sufficiently tested, the precautionary principle is even invoked as grounds to oppose the substitution of toxic substances. See Stolzenberg-Ahlers (2003) 394.

PART THREE – MEDIA-SPECIFIC ENVIRONMENTAL POLICIES

CHAPTER 7

The European Union and Protection of the Marine Environment

Some Reflections on Developments in Law, Policy and Practice

Martin Hedemann-Robinson[1]

1 Introduction

The marine environment has been an area in relation to which the European Union has devoted until most recently relatively little serious focused political attention. True, the advent of environmental policies in the early 1970s and constitutional commitments to attaining a high level of environmental protection through changes effected to the Treaty of Rome 1957 (EC Treaty)[2] in 1986 have culminated over time into a range of environmental measures at EU level that have served either directly or indirectly in contributing to the enhancement of systems intended to protect European marine environments. However, the development of policy underpinning the range of legal obligations now in place has followed a unduly complex, protracted and difficult route.

Policy initiatives have been largely adopted in an uncoordinated and segmented fashion, often with the result that measures affecting the marine environment have been developed and implemented with marine protection issues being a subordinate or ancillary factor. Responsibility for these measures has been dispersed amongst the various Directorate-Generals (DGs) of the European Commission, depending upon the dominant purpose underlying the measure at hand, *e.g.* fisheries, agriculture, transport, environment. Little coordination between the Commission services has existed in terms of pooling together the impact of these measures and ensuring a consistency of approach in terms of ascribing policy priorities. Issues connected with national sovereignty have resulted in notable resistance emanating from certain Member States' in relation to suggestions or initiatives for greater EU involvement in the sphere of marine protection. Littoral Member States (such as the UK and France) have often traditionally perceived themselves as having unlimited and/or exclusive access to neighbouring marine resources located within their respective territorial and sovereign areas. Issues of ownership of and access to marine resources, as opposed to responsibility for safeguarding the marine environment for its own sake, have dominated international discourse between states for years and this approach has proven to be stubbornly resistant to change. Legal factors have also served to undermine possibilities for extensive development and application of policy instruments on marine protection. In particular, continuing legal uncertainties over the proper geographical scope of internal EU environmental legislation have tended to bolster the predominance of intergovernmentalist decision-making practices in the marine sector, with relatively few common internal EU policies being reflected or fostered at broader international level in the context of discussions and negotiation with third

---

1 Lecturer in Law, Brunel University, London. The author recently returned to Brunel after working two years as a legal desk officer in the European Commission's technical unit for waste issues in DG Environment.

2 Notably through the Single European Act 1986.

countries. In its 2002 Communication *'Towards a strategy to protect and conserve the marine environment'*[3] the European Commission has really for the first time acknowledged some of the above-mentioned long-standing failings and short-comings, including the limited impact of measures adopted so far at EU level; it has recognised in particular that at Union level the non-existence of any 'overall, integrated policy for marine protection' and identified the need to adopt what it terms to be 'a more integrated approach to policy making and management' (ecosystem-based approach). The Communication, published under the auspices of the EU's Sixth Environmental Action Programme (EAP), is to be followed up in 2005 with a thematic strategy on the marine environment.

This chapter seeks to focus on some of the key legal and political issues that have had a significant influence on the development and implementation of EU political and legal strategies connected with marine environmental protection. In particular, it will consider the main legislative and policy developments that have so far come to make up the core body of EU marine protection instruments. Given the relatively short length of this paper, it is not intended here to provide a detailed or extensive overview of EU environmental legislation on the marine environment. Readers are referred to more detailed and thorough analyses and overviews provided elsewhere, such as the excellent review by Professor Krämer[4] himself, to whom this book is dedicated. Instead, attention here will be to focus on key overarching influences on the shaping and pace of previous and current policy development, with a view to drawing hopefully some lessons for the future.

2 EU policy developments on marine environmental protection

Although the EU has taken a range of environmental measures in order to enhance protection for the marine environment over the span of the last 30 or so years since the launch of the First EAP of the former European Economic Community in the early 1970s, it has been the case that the overall policy approach of the Union has been fractured and uncoordinated. Marine environmental matters have tended to be parcelled up as ancillary or subordinate policy issues in the context of development of environmental protection policy at EU level. In many respects, this is not surprising given that the seas have traditionally been perceived at international and national levels, not least amongst several industrialised nations, to be a predominantly anthropocentric domain, with policy concerns focusing largely on issues to do with economic glean (typically resource exploitation and highway controls for vessels) as opposed to ecological sustainability. The constitutional framework of the European Union itself has only relatively recently in its history made a paradigm shift from its

[3] COM (2002) 539 final, 02.10.2002.

original vision of a regional economic community of states in 1957 to one of a Union of countries that now incorporates a mandate to achieve a high level of environmental protection as an integral component of its policy objectives.[5] The dearth of EU policy measures directed specifically towards protecting the marine environment reflects a deeply rooted cultural and political reluctance to acknowledge that the (marine) environment should be worthy of protection as an ecological entity in itself, irrespective of anthropocentric interests (such as economic worth or health impacts of pollution on humans).[6] Gradually, though, and notwithstanding this challenging context, the Union has over time begun to develop a range of policy measures that cumulatively address a broader range of marine pollution sources. However, it remains to be seen within the context of the current Sixth EAP of the EU (2001-2010) to what extent these initiatives may be coordinated into an effective integrated strategy. The 2002 interim Communication from the European Commission on the marine environment has been a breakthrough in terms of seeking to take stock of existing *acquis* and advocating a list of objectives and actions that are to be co-ordinated at Union level across the various policy sectors that deal directly or indirectly with marine protection issues.[7]

In terms of the legislative instruments that have been adopted by the Union thus far which have addressed marine environment issues either directly or indirectly, it is perhaps possible to detect at least three phases of differing policy approaches or emphasis which have served collectively to make up the current core bundle of marine environment protection instruments at Union level.

2.1 Key phases in constructing a strategy on the marine environment at EU level.

The first phase of EU legislation, principally passed in the 1970s, appeared to focus predominantly on issues concerned with very visible sources of water pollution, including marine pollution, as well as addressing health concerns of humankind as a result of such pollution. Other measures were also introduced, whose direct or indirect benefits for the marine environment were less obvious and not clearly identified as being necessary for an effective strategy to address sea pollution. The following is a selected list of key first wave measures relevant in this regard:

- Directive 75/439/EEC on used oils;[8]
- Directive 75/440/EEC on the quality of surface water intended for abstrac-

[4] Krämer (1997a) 259 *et seq.*

[5] Article 2, 6 and 174-6 EC, Article 2 first indent EU.

[6] See *e.g.* Gillespie (2002).

[7] COM (2002) 539 fin, see paragraphs 8 and sections 7-8 especially.

[8] OJ 1975 L 194/1.

tion of drinking water;[9]
- Directive 75/442/EEC on waste;[10]
- Directive 76/160/EEC on the quality of bathing waters;[11]
- Directive 76/464/EEC on pollution caused by certain dangerous substances discharged into the aquatic environment of the Community;[12]
- Directive 78/176/EEC on waste from the titanium dioxide industry;[13]
- Directive 79/923/EEC on quality objectives for shellfish waters.[14]

This initial body of legislation, much of which remains in force today, has been dogged by a number of limitations. The absence of a clear and coordinated launch of a marine environment strategy has led to a fragmented and inevitably limited approach to tacking marine pollution issues. This has been compounded by the fact that, from early on, the Union has placed an undue reliance and responsibility upon the role of international conventions as playing a key if not principal role in delivering enhancement of minimum quality standards.[15] This served to displace responsibility for marine pollution controls away from the Union to the international community as a whole at an early and crucial stage in EU environmental policy development. Historically, regulation of anthropocentric interaction with the seas and oceans has been considered appropriate to be set in a context of international discussion and regulation of a global commons. The right to roam and exploit the marine environment permeates very deep in the predominant political and legal cultures of industrialised nations and is a lasting influence that casts a long shadow over EU involvement in marine affairs. This deeply rooted attitude is crystallized (albeit in a tempered form) in the UN Convention on the Law of Sea 1982 (UNCLOS), the major global framework treaty on international maritime law. Specifically, whilst the convention provides for possibilities and duties of states to undertake measures to preserve and protect the marine environment[16], any (unilateral or collective) measures by such states are made subject to the overriding principle of so-called 'innocent passage' of international maritime traffic, including in respect of passage through coastal waters.[17]

Brevity of space does not allow for a detailed or indepth discussion here of the interaction between the EU and the international community in relation to marine environmental protection. Suffice it so say that the relationship has to

---

[9] OJ 1975 L 194/34.

[10] OJ 1975 L 194/47.

[11] OJ 1976 L 31/1.

[12] OJ 1976 L 129/23.

[13] OJ 1978 L 54/19.

[14] OJ 1979 L 281/47.

[15] See First EAP, OJ 1973 C 112/1.

[16] See especially Articles 21, 42, 56, 73 and Part XII of UNCLOS.

[17] Article 19 UNCLOS.

this date never been adequately clarified to the detriment of policy development. In particular, the Union has never been engaged in a transparent discussion as to the geographical extent of its jurisdiction[18], and the European Commission has appeared to have been hesitant to assert application of a number of pieces of maritime-related EU environmental legislation[19] within the exclusive economic zones and continental shelf spaces assumed by individual Member States. In addition, the European Commission has not appeared to track or follow up enforcement of internationally agreed norms, to which the European Community has been a party, notwithstanding that such provisions constitute an integral part of the EU legal order in respect of which the Commission has a basic duty[20] to ensure Member State adherence.[21]

In many respects the EU has crafted its environmental protection legislation on the premise that it is fundamentally for the international community and individual nation states and not for the EU to supervise marine environmental protection. Accordingly, in deference to UNCLOS, express or implied jurisdictional limitations were imposed upon the geographical reach of Union legislation from the earliest phase in relation to marine protection. This placed severe limitations on the ambition of subsequent EU policy development. For instance, the scope of Directive 76/464/EEC on pollution caused by certain dangerous substances discharged into the aquatic environment of the Community is confined to inland surface, territorial and internal coastal waters and does not cover economic exclusion zones (Article 1).

The most important instrument to emerge from this initial phase was the Dangerous Substances Directive 76/464/EEC. This Directive was ambitious in its intent. It divided up substances into two groups, Lists I and II with the former identifying the most toxic families and groups of substances. For List I groups, EU-wide maximum emission limit values were to be established (Article 6) and for List II substances, Member States were to set up programmes for the purposes of reducing water pollution (Article 7). Until emission limits were to be set for List I substances, they were to be subject to List II-type controls Out of some 129 substances identified by the Commission by the early 1980s to be candidates for List I-type controls, only 17 substances have been subject to legislative regulation at EU level in five daughter Directives.[22] Many infrac-

[18] See Article 299 EC.

[19] Notably Directives 79/409/EEC on wild birds (OJ 1979 L 103/79) and 92/43/EEC on habitats (OJ 1992 L 206/7).

[20] Article 211 EC.

[21] For instance, none of the annual reports on environmental law enforcement published by the European Commission has ever provided a scoreboard of compliance on international environmental agreements to which the EC and Member States are parties.

[22] Directives 82/176/EEC (OJ 1982 L 81/29) and 84/156/EEC (OJ 1984 L 74/49) (mercury); Directive 83/513/EEC, OJ 1983 L 291/1 (cadmium); Directive 84/491/EEC (OJ 1984 L 274/11) (HCH) and Directive 86/280/EEC (OJ 1986 L 181/16) (carbon tetrachloride, DDT, PCP, aldrin, dieldrin, endrin, isodrin, hexochlorobenzene, hexochlorobutadiene, chloroform, EDC, TRI, PER, and TCB).

tion proceedings under Article 226 EC have been taken against Member States in respect of failures in relation to national programmes.[23] The recent Water Framework Directive 2000/60/EC,[24] succeeding Directive 76/464/EEC, is to reinvigorate targeting of priority hazardous substances for the purpose of establishing discharge controls in respect of individual pollutants with a view to achieving concentrations near background levels for naturally occurring substances and close to zero for man-made synthetic substances by 2020 (Article 16). Thirty three priority substances or groups of substances have been identified so far for prospective priority list treatment.[25] A recent report from the European Environment Agency on selected hazardous substances in the marine environment has highlighted shortcomings on data availability.[26] Whilst noting decreasing trends in concentration levels of six hazardous substances in mussels in the north-east Atlantic and Mediterranean, the EEA has reported increases in lead concentrations in the Baltic Sea fish and persistently high concentrations of PCB in north-east Atlantic blue mussel.

A subsequent second phase of Union measures addressing pollution issues affecting the marine environment may be identified as having emerged by the 1990s. Whilst the earliest generation of environmental protection instruments tended to focus on specific sources and effects of marine pollution, with a view to introducing mandatory emission limit controls, the subsequent phase of measures sought to address diffuse sources of water pollution, in particular focusing on the problems of eutrophication of waters emanating from various inland industrial activities, as well as seeking to adopt measures to foster regionalised as opposed to centralised integrated pollution control of industrial installations. In addition, the second phase marked a significant shift towards decentralisation towards Member States in terms of definition of specific implementation standards in respect of policy objectives. Three measures stand out in this regard:

- Directive 91/271/EEC concerning urban wastewater treatment (UWWD);[27]
- Directive 91/676/EEC concerning the protection of waters against nitrate pollution;[28]
- Directive 96/61/EC on integrated pollution prevention and control (IPPC).[29]

---

[23] Krämer (1997a) 273.

[24] OJ 2000 L 327/1.

[25] Decision 2455/01/EC, OJ 2001 L 331/1.

[26] *Hazardous substances in the European marine environment: trends in metals and persistent organic pollutants* (EEA, Copenhagen 2003)

[27] OJ 1991 L 135/40, as amended by Directive 98/15/EC, OJ 1998 L 67/29.

[28] OJ 1991 L 375/1.

[29] OJ 1996 L 257/40.

Eutrophication has been reported by the European Environment Agency to affect many marine areas of the Union.[30] Chief causes are identified to be nitrogen run-off from agricultural land brought to the sea via rivers, emanating from extensive fertiliser and livestock presence in soils, as well as untreated emissions from waste water treatment plants. Directive 91/271/EEC phases in requirements for the management of urban waste water, stipulating that by the end of 2005 secondary treatment should be in place for most sewage collection plants servicing a population equivalent of 10,000 or over (Article 4). Stricter treatment was to be in place by the end of 1998 in respect of discharges from plants servicing agglomerations of 10,000 or over in areas identified by Member States to be 'sensitive', namely in areas with water bodies actually or likely to become eutrophic for various reasons (Article 5). Sludge disposal to surface waters was banned at the end of 1998 (Article 14). Directive 91/676/EEC stipulates that Member States were, inter alia, to designate zones vulnerable to nitrate pollution by the end of 1993, establish action programmes to reduce pollution by the end of 1995 and implement them within four years thereafter (Articles 3 and 5). European Commission reports have revealed that the implementation track record for both Directives has been dismally behind schedule, with many Member States failing to ensure compliance with basic obligations.[31] Since 1994, the Commission is reported to have opened some 56 infraction proceedings in relation to implementation failures pertaining to the nitrates Directive alone. At least seven Member States have been already condemned by the ECJ, with some 23 cases still pending at the end of 2002. As far as the UWWD is concerned, by 2001 the Commission had identified some 14 ongoing infringements, many of which related to failures to designate sensitive areas. The IPPC Directive 96/61/EC aims to prevent and control pollution arising from large-scale industrial activities, incorporating provisions designed to prevent or reduce emissions in the air, water and land, as well as measures concerning waste generation and efficient use of raw materials, energy and water. Substantial transitional periods have been programmed in the IPPC Directive in respect of existing installations until 2007 with respect to key permit requirements (Article 5), making it too early to comment on the implementation of this instrument. The permit requirements themselves will be predicated upon the principle of Best Available Technology (BAT), determined locally in accordance with 'economically and technically viable conditions', as opposed to precise EU-wide emission limit values. The prospects for proper compliance already look bleak, with the Commission recently publishing a communication about lack of progress on the part of Member States towards preparing for full implementation of the Directive.[32]

---

[30] *Eutrophication in Europe's coastal waters* (EEA Copenhagen, 2001)

[31] See Implementation Report of Council Directive 91/271/EEC (European Commission, OOPEC, 2002) and Implementation Report of Council Directive 91/676/EEC (European Commission, OOPEC, 2002).

[32] IP/03/865, Brussels, 19.6.2003.

Accompanying the first and second phases of water legislation at Union level have been a number of other significant pieces of EU environmental legislation that have served to provide important direct and indirect benefits for the purposes of enhancing legal protection for the marine environment. Recently, these initiatives have come to play an increasingly important flanking role in practice, as it is increasingly recognised that they are not confined to environmental issues on land but have a wider geographical scope of application, namely also the marine environment.[33] They include notably:

- Directive 79/409/EEC on wild birds;[34]
- Directive 85/337/EEC on environmental impact assessment (EIA);[35]
- Directive 90/313/EEC on the freedom of access to environmental information[36] (repealed with effect from 14.2.2005 and replaced by Directive 2003/4/EC on public access to environmental information[37]);
- Directive 92/43/EC on the conservation of natural habitats and of flora and fauna (Habitats Directive).[38]

All of these instruments are relevant in relation to all spaces of the EU marine environment, including within the 200 nautical mile exclusion zones asserted by the Union and its constituent Member States. None of them are specifically confined to apply to territorial waters, unlike a number of EU instruments pertaining to water pollution.[39] This potentially opens up a number of significant opportunities for the European Commission to widen the geographical scope for Union policy on protection for the marine environment. The requirements to designate special areas of conservation for listed marine species such as cetaceans and special protection areas for sea birds under the wild birds and habitats Directives constitute particular important legislative initiatives in this regard. The same applies in respect of EIA requirements for developments projects affecting marine spaces. To date, however, the Commission has not endeavoured to clarify this important issue of EU legislative 'reach' unambiguously and this needs to be rectified. The Commission's interim 2002 Communication on development of a marine strategy has indicated that it will implement

---

33 See *e.g.* *Report on Implementing the Habitats Directive in marine and coastal areas* (European Commission, DG XI, OOPEC, 1997) and Commission Working Document on Natura 2000 (Brussels, 27.12.2002) available on DG ENV website.

34 OJ 1979 L 103/1.

35 OJ 1985 L 175/40 as amended by Directive 97/11/EC, OJ 1997 L 73/5.

36 OJ 1990 L 158/56.

37 OJ 2003 L 41/26.

38 OJ 1992 L 206/7.

39 See, *e.g.* Articles 1 of the Directive 76/464/EEC on dangerous substance discharges (OJ 1976 L 129/23) and of the Water Framework Directive 2000/60/EC (OJ 2000 L 327/1).

the wild birds and habitats Directives in the exclusive economic zones (EEZs), such as through adaptations to annexes to the latter Directive.[40]

A third phase of policy approach to tackling water pollution issues may be detected to have started in earnest with the recent adoption of the Water Framework Directive 2000/60/EC (WFD), due to be implemented by 22 December 2003. This measure represents the first really genuine attempt by the Union to address water pollution issues in a more coordinated, coherent and holistic perspective. The ultimate aim of the WFD is to achieve in the long term elimination of priority hazardous substances and contribute to achieving concentrations in the marine environment near background values for naturally occurring substances.[41] In seeking to establish an integrated framework for the improved protection of inland surface, transitional coastal as well as groundwater, Member States are to develop a system of river basin management planning and supervision. The WFD sets an overall bottom-line deadline for the achievement of implementation regarding BAT emission controls and limit values as well as diffuse impact controls prescribed by existing Union water-related legislation by the end of 2012 (Article 10), aiming to achieve the environmental objective of 'good surface water status' by the end of 2015 (Article 4(1)(a)). Member States must establish for each river basin district programmes of measures in order to implement the minimum requirements set by the WFD by the end of 2009 and to make them operational by the end of 2012 (Article 11), complemented by river basin programmes (Article 13). In so doing the aim is to ensure there will be comprehensive and more co-ordinated delivery on implementation of current water pollution legislation (namely, first and second phase EU Directives).[42]

2.2 Impact of the Sixth Environment Action Programme

The Sixth EAP of the Union[43], spanning 2001-2010, appears to mark a significant change in appreciation of the variety of challenges that need to be squarely addressed in terms of crafting a credible policy for enhancing protection systems for the marine environment. In the past, EAPs have tended to focus heavily on the need to tackle the most visible or well-known sources of marine pollution, such as direct discharges and dumping of waste from ships and land-based point sources into the aquatic environment. Yet it has become evident that the main sources of marine environmental pollution derive from a wider range of sources, more diffuse and less directly connected with the sea

---

[40] See 'Action 2' relating to conserving biodiversity and ensuring habitat protection in COM (2002) 539, at page 21.

[41] Recital 27 to WFD.

[42] Listed in Part A of Annex VI to the WFD.

[43] COM (2001) 31 final *Commission Communication on the Sixth Environment Action Programme 2001-2010 'Environment 2010: Our future, our choice'* (24.1.2001)

environs. It has been estimated, for instance, that vessel discharges only account for 12% of marine pollution, with atmospheric depositions (33%) and run-off from land (44%) constituting significantly larger quantities of pollutant inputs.[44] The European Commission Communication for the current programme recognises that protection of the marine environment needs an 'integrated strategy' to cope with the variety of causes of pollution and degradation of marine habitats and coastlines, ranging from eutrophication pressures from urban development to point source pollution from direct discharges and dumping into water environments.[45] Action in relation to protection of the marine environment under the auspices of the Sixth EAP is to include specifically promotion of greater integration of environmental considerations in the Common Fisheries Policy, a thematic strategy for the protection and conservation of the marine environment by the autumn of 2005, promotion of integrated management of coastal zones as well as further promotion of marine areas, such as through the Natura 2000 network being developed under the auspices of the habitats Directive.[46]

The objectives set out in the Sixth EAP have been to some extent fleshed out in further detail by the recent 2002 interim European Commission Communication on development of a marine strategy.[47] Various 'policy actions' have been identified which are set to lay the foundations for prospective EU involvement in the area. These include prioritisation of European Commission focus on the following aspects of marine environment protection, summarised below, to be coordinated principally through DG Environment:

- *Conservation of biodiversity and ensuring habitat protection*
  (development of ecosystem benchmarks/targets, full implementation of nature protection legislation, sustainability commitments for fisheries, work on preventing introduction of non-indigenous species from vessel ballast tank washing)
- *Hazardous substances*
  (implementation of WFD, development of integrated chemicals and pesticides policy and monitoring)
- *Eutrophication*
  (more 'vigorous' implementation of nitrates and urban waste water legislation, date development, reduction of vessel NOx emissions)
- *Radionuclides*
  (review of measures pertaining to discharges from nuclear-fuel reprocessing plants)
- *Chronic oil pollution*
  (Exploration of ways to improve surveillance of illegal discharges, elabora-

44 Sands (2003) 428 and 438.

45 COM (2001) 31 at 35.

46 Article 6(2)(g) of Decision 1600/2002/EC laying down the Sixth EAP, OJ 2002 L 242/1.

47 COM (2002) 539 final.

tion of a strategy to eliminate oil discharges from all sources, with special focus on port reception facilities)

- *Litter*
(report by 2004 on extent and sources of litter affecting marine environment)
- *Maritime transport*
(in conjunction with European Maritime Agency to undertake an ongoing review of EU laws on maritime safety, support initiatives to minimise environmental harm)
- *Health and environment*
(In 2006 to propose maximum contaminant levels in food safety legislation, revision to bathing water legislation, support entry into force of MARPOL commitments on sewage discharges from vessels)
- *Enhancing co-ordination and co-operation*
(within the EU to establish co-ordination type initiatives to ensure consistency of policy approach across services and sectors, especially regarding fisheries and access to EU funds; globally, to secure better co-ordination and understanding of marine protection issues in relevant international organisations).

3 Critique of developments

Notwithstanding the shift by the EU to develop a more integrated approach in relation to protection of the marine environment and the establishment over time since the early 1970s of a range of policy measures that have important direct and indirect benefits for delivering improvements to the state of Europe's marine environment, question marks still remain concerning the adequacy of changes that have been put in place. In addition, notwithstanding the impressive political statements and general policy commitments outlined in the recent 2002 interim Commission Communication on a marine strategy, it is not yet evident whether in practice the Commission services will have the requisite range of resources, initiatives and political backing at EU and national levels in order to deliver necessary substantive changes to enhance marine environmental protection standards and their enforcement.

Firstly, it is highly questionable that the European Commission is in a position to deliver the commitments set out in the Sixth EAP. In particular, DG Environment does not possess sufficient staff to even form a dedicated marine protection unit. Instead, DG ENV's organigram is structured so that marine policy issues are to be principally tackled within the unit dealing with water, marine and soil issues which comprises very few marine specialists.

Secondly, it is evident that a number a marine-related issues are spread around and within the various Directorates-General of the Commission (agriculture, fisheries, transport and energy, industry, trade and so on). In the author's experience, cross- and intra-departmental co-ordination between and within DGs on environmental issues is still relatively undeveloped. Few DGs have dedicated resources to ensuring that their particular policy spheres meet the environmental integration commitment set out in Article 6 EC and the author is unaware of any accounting systems having been introduced in order to seek to assist in monitoring of compliance with this treaty requirement. There appears to be a widespread cultural perception within the Commission that environmental issues are to be dealt with principally if not solely by DG Environment. Responsibility for environmental protection has not yet been adequately internalised by other Commission services as a joint and several responsibility, notwithstanding the constitutional requirement set out in Article 6 EC that environmental protection requirements must be integrated in to the definition and implementation of Community policies and activities.

Thirdly, it is clear that non-environmental interests play a significant role in determining the pace and shape of EU policies on the environment, and the marine area has been and is no exception.[48] It cannot be overstated that the constitutional structuring of the EU does not place environmental protection to be a pre-eminent policy goal for the Union; instead environmental protection is set to compete and negotiate in a predominantly market-oriented and market integrationist context. This is reflected most markedly in the context of communications and negotiation between the various Commission services over policy development, where it is standard practice to find that DG Environment is deemed to be solely or predominantly responsible for representing environmental protection issues. Mainstreaming of environmental protection issues within the Commission's services as a whole remains an underdeveloped institutional commitment, to put it diplomatically.

Fourthly, in many respects the EU's actions in relation to the marine environment continue to fail to address a number of sources of pollution. The absence of EU norms on radioactive discharges into marine environments are obvious examples. Whilst the Sixth EAP expressly identifies releases of radioactive substances as a key pressure on the marine environment, no mention is made of following this up with specific measures. Traditionally, nuclear related questions have been considered as falling principally within the scope of the EURATOM Treaty, as a specialist international agreement. However, it is highly questionable whether its legal structures, historically biased in favour of the promoting the development of the nuclear industry, are at all suitable to meeting the environmental protection requirements now inscribed within the general EC Treaty.[49] Article 38 EURATOM constrains the powers of the Commission to making recommendations to the Member States with regard to the level of radio-

---

48 *E.g.* Fitzmaurice (1992) 216 *et seq.*; Saetevik (1988) 99.

49 In this regard, one might note the EU's recent rejection of accrediting nuclear projects in the context of implementing the Kyoto Protocol's provisions on clean development mechanisms and joint implementation projects.

activity in the air, water and soil, save in 'cases of urgency' when the Commission is to issue a Directive requiring a Member State to take necessary measures to prevent infringement of the 'basic standards and to ensure compliance with regulations'. As the Commission has recently acknowledged, it has to date made no such recommendations in relation to discharges into the marine environment;[50] it is set to review this area.[51] There is no legal reason why environmental measures on radioactive discharges should not be developed on the legal basis of Article 175(1) EC, given that some EC Treaty environmental measures already exist on nuclear installation development.[52] However, EU involvement remains unlikely in the face of strong UK and French political opposition to challenges in an area considered by governments of these countries to be of a quasi-sovereign nature. Since 2001, DG Environment does not retain any unit dealing specifically with nuclear issues. By way of another example, only very recently has the EU begun to address the need for addressing environmental concerns in relation to the development and approval of chemicals released into the environment with the REACH initiative,[53] a package of recently proposed measures intended to install risk assessment controls in respect of chemicals placed on the open market.

Fifthly, the development of a coherent EU marine protection strategy has been limited by a widespread attitude on the part of Union institutions and Member States that ultimately the appropriate fora for many discussions on marine issues should be located and driven in the context of the broader international relations arena on the basis of intergovernmentalism. There has been a marked reluctance to accept that marine policy should be conducted on the basis of internal decision-making (qualified majority voting); the result has been that the EU has been slow to develop common positions on several many marine issues discussed in a variety of different international organisations that focus on regional seas and/or global marine pollution issues.[54] The perception that marine issues are ultimately matters 'external' to the EU has been a factor favouring the subordination and suppression of Union involvement in policy development; in addition, uncertainties over legal and political boundaries between 'internal' and 'external' competence of the EU on marine affairs

50 COM (2002) 539, para.41.

51 COM (2002) 539, see 'Action 10' on 23.

52 See *e.g.* the EIA Directive 85/337/EEC, (OJ 1985 L 175/40), as amended by Directive 97/11/EC (OJ 1997 L 73/5) and Article 2(1)(b)(i) of the Waste Framework Directive 75/442/EEC (OJ 1975 L 194/47) as principally amended by Directive 91/156/EEC (OJ 1991 L 135/32) which takes the trouble to expressly exclude radioactive waste from the scope of the waste definition.

53 See COM (2003) 644 final Commission proposal for regulation on registration, evaluation, authorisation and restriction of chemicals (REACH), establishing a European Chemicals Agency and amending Directive 1999/45/EC and Commission proposal for a Directive amending Directive 67/548/EC. Commission press release IP/03/1477, Brussels 29.10.2003.

54 Krämer (2000a) 201.

has not assisted in providing a suitable basis to develop common approaches to particular issues.

4 Some conclusions

From the above very brief discussion, it may be seen that possibilities for development of an EU marine environment protection strategy has been and still is beset by a number of fundamental limitations and problems. Ultimately, the credibility of such a strategy will depend upon a number of key factors. Specifically, it is evident that the Union needs to assert both its existing legal competencies as well as develop political confidence to enhance protection measures so as to have the capability to begin to address the full range of marine pollution issues and challenges in a far more comprehensive and co-ordinated fashion. It appears, however, that it is more accurate to speak of a number of strategies still existing at EU level. These need to be moulded into a coherent whole and which need to be firmly rooted in the environmental principles set out in the EC Treaty. It is fair to say though that improvements on this front have been signalled with the Sixth EAP and the recent 2002 interim Commission Communication on development of an EU marine strategy seeking to foster an integrated ecosystem based policy approach. The development of an EU voice on marine protection issues is important for a number of reasons, not least because it meets the constitutional requirement and mandate set out in the EC Treaty for development of an environmental policy of the Union characterised by a high level of protection, a policy principally to be based on qualified majority voting and not on unanimity. Finally, the level of awareness of the general public about their responsibilities in relation to marine pollution and protection issues should be raised by the EU, particular by the European Commission, which so far has completely failed to promote information initiatives either through consumer protection[55] or European educational strategies.[56] It remains to be seen though whether the prospective thematic strategy on the marine environment in 2005 will take the opportunity to foster these and other under explored possibilities. The silence of the Commission's 2002 interim Communication on a marine strategy indicates that this is most unlikely.

---

[55] The eco label scheme developed under Regulation 880/92/EEC (OJ 1992 L 9/1) could be extended to provide greater consumer information on impacts of products to the marine environment. A plethora of unregulated claims on the market already exist, such as 'dolphin safe' labels on tuna tins, which provides but confusing signals.

[56] See Article 149 EC, which requires Community action on education, vocational training and youth, inter alia, to develop the 'European dimension in education'. The inherently transboundary nature of environmental aspects ties in well with this mandate.

CHAPTER 8

Community Legislation on Water Protection

An Assessment of its Evolution and Possible Future

Claudia Olazábal[1]

1 Introduction – how Community water policy has evolved[2]

The European Community adopted its first five-year environmental action programme in 1973[3] setting out the principles and priorities that would guide its policies in the future. This action programme already provided for a number of measures to protect fresh waters and sea water from certain pollutants. Almost concurrently to the first Action Programme on Environment and the first International Environmental Agreements, the first pieces of Community environmental legislation addressed, *inter alia*, the protection of water. As the main driving force for the European integration in the 70s was the achievement of an economic community, it is not surprising that the first two Directives addressing water protection were actually Directives regulating products. That is, where a harmonised framework needed to be put in place in order to avoid distortions of the internal market. These were the Directive on detergents (1973)[4] (concerning their biodegradability) and the Directive on drinking water[5] (Proposal from the Commission adopted in 1975 and Directive adopted by the Council in 1980). Drinking water is obviously a vital and sensitive product for citizens and its quality had to be harmonised not only to prevent distortion of competition (*e.g.* marketing of food produced with water of different quality) but also to ensure that the population was not subject to different margins of risk because of different national measures, which would create ethical concerns.

Air quality protection had also been tackled in the early 70s, but there again with the main concern of harmonising the standards for a smooth functioning of the internal market by limiting at Community level the emissions to air of certain motor vehicles.[6] However water, as an environmental medium, was regulated before air and long before soil, which is only starting to be addressed now at Community level.[7] Nevertheless, the legislation was mainly conceived with the aim of ensuring that the quality of water was suitable for its intended purpose. Indeed, during the 70s and early 80s, the fit-for-use approach produced several Directives addressing the quality of water for different uses such as surface water intended for the extraction of drinking water,[8] the drinking water,[9] bathing water,[10] shellfish waters.[11] In this context, water was just perceived as a

---

1 Environment Directorate-General, European Commission. The views expressed in this article are exclusively the ones of the author.

2 Marine international conventions and marine Community legislation will not be addressed in this article; see the chapter from Martin Hedemann-Robinson in this book.

3 OJ 1973 C 112/1.

4 Directive 73/404/EEC, OJ 1973 L 347/51.

5 Directive 80/778/EEC, OJ 1980 L 229/11.

6 Directive 70/220/EEC, OJ 1970 L 81/15.

7 See the chapter from Luca Marmo in this book.

8 Directive 75/440/EEC, OJ 1975 L 194/26.

9 Directive 80/778/EEC, OJ 1980 L 229/1.

10 Directive 76/160/EEC, OJ 1976 L 31/1.

medium supporting different human activities or satisfying human needs and it was preserved mainly as far as its suitability for the different uses could be threatened. It can be argued that Directive 78/659/EEC on the quality of waters to support fish life[12] was not based on this anthropocentric approach and aimed indeed at the protection of certain freshwater fish species and fish biodiversity. This would be a fair argument, though the results of the implementation of this Directive remain modest, as rightly pointed out by Krämer,[13] and many of the species targeted were commercial species such as salmon and trout.

Consequently, in order to achieve such quality levels for the different water uses, it was necessary to put in place a range of measures to prevent or reduce polluting discharges. Water legislation became a bicephalous creature, with one head looking at quality for different water uses and the other focused on preventing discharges of particular substances whose presence could hamper those uses. This led to the adoption of a number of Directives regulating emissions to water of a wide number of substances from different sources. The main instrument was Directive 76/464/EEC on pollution caused by certain dangerous substances discharged into the aquatic environment of the Community,[14] with a 'black list' and a 'grey list' as Jans[15] very illustratively described to list the various pollutants contained therein, but also the Directive on groundwater.[16] On this issue, it is relevant to refer to the sharp analysis by Ludwig Krämer[17] on the combination in the Directive of provisions on emission limit values and quality standards as a result of a compromise between the United Kingdom and the rest of the Member States at the time of adoption. This Directive was followed by legislation on emissions of mercury,[18] cadmium,[19] HCH,[20] some halogenated hydrocarbons and pesticides (carbon tetrachloride, DDT, pentachlorophenol, aldrin, dieldrin, endrin, isodrin, hexachlorobenzene, hexachlorobutadiene, chloroform, 1,2-dichloroethane, trichloroethylene, perchloroethylene and trichlorobenzene)[21] and nitrates[22] among others.

Having established some quality standards and emission limit values, in order to be able to compare monitoring data, identify trends, check compliance with legislation and draw up comparisons between Member States, it was necessary to develop a whole set of standardising tools. New pieces of legislation were

11 Directive 79/923/EEC, OJ 1979 L 281/47.

12 Directive 78/659/EEC, OJ 1978 L 222/1.

13 Krämer (2003a) 257.

14 Directive 76/464/EEC, OJ 1976 L 129/23.

15 Jans (2000) 342.

16 Directive 80/68/EEC, OJ 1980 L 229/11, as last amended by Directive 98/83/EC, OJ 1998 L 330/32.

17 Krämer (2003a) 258.

18 Directive 82/176/EEC, OJ 1982 L 81/29 and Directive 84/156/EEC, OJ 1984 L 74/49.

19 Directive 83/513/EEC, OJ 1983 L 291/1.

20 Directive 84/491/EEC, OJ 1984 L 274/11.

21 Directive 86/280/EEC, OJ 1986 L 181/16.

thus adopted to complement the obligations of Member States and to give the Community the apparatus to harmonise the reporting and analytical techniques required to enforce the quality standards adopted. These pieces of legislation could be called 'technical tools' and they address issues such as the exchange of information on the quality of surface water, the methods and frequencies of sampling and testing drinking water.[23]

Therefore during the 70s we witnessed the adoption of legislation on quality standards for certain uses of water. During the 80s and early 90s, the legislative exercise focused on limiting the emissions of certain dangerous substances. However from the late 80s and through out the 90s a new conceptual approach was slowly developing.

In fact, a wider knowledge and awareness of ecology, ecosystems and resource management brought to life a new conception: water was no longer considered to be only a platform for human activity, but also a component of very wide ecosystems on which human life was only one element. This is a much more 'purist' approach aiming at protecting water for its own sake and not exclusively for human activities and needs. Furthermore water was no longer seen as a juxtaposition of disconnected water bodies but rather an integrated flowing hydrological system.

This new approach was progressively reflected in Community legislation and it found its full-blossomed expression in Directive 2000/60/EC establishing a framework for Community action in the field of water policy[24] – the Water Framework Directive (WFD) which gradually repeals many of the existing fragmented legislation[25] under its Article 22. This legislation integrates the different types of water bodies to protect seamlessly the entire dynamic hydrological systems, incorporating the concept of River Basin Management. Furthermore, as explained in greater detail later on, the WFD aims to ensure a good chemical quality of water bodies but also a good ecological status to perform as an ecosystem support.

In this new integrated context, the transboundary dimension of water legislation means that co-operation between Member States and streamlining of their respective national implementation are no longer just a desirable achievement

[22] Directive 91/676/EEC, OJ 1991 L 375/ 1. Directive 91/271/EEC, OJ 1991 L 135/40.

[23] Decision 77/795/EEC, OJ 1977 L 334/29. Directive 79/869/EEC, OJ 1979 L 271/44.

[24] Directive 2000/60/EC, OJ 2000 L 327/1.

[25] Some Directives will be repealed seven year after the entry into force of the WFD, such as Directive 75/440/EEC on the quality required of surface water intended for the abstraction of drinking water, Decision 77/795/EEC establishing a common procedure for the exchange of information on the quality of surface freshwater, Directive 79/869/EEC concerning the methods of measurement and frequencies of sampling and analysis of surface water intended for the abstraction of drinking waters. Some other will be repealed 13 years after the date of entry into force of the WFD, such as Directive 78/659/EEC on fresh fish waters, Directive 79/923/EEC on shellfish waters, Directive 80/68/EEC on groundwater, Directive 76/464/EEC, with the exception of Article 6, which shall be repealed with effect from the entry into force of the WFD.

but now an obligation for water bodies spread over different countries. Indeed, although bilateral or multilateral agreements existed for the joint management and protection of some watercourses (*e.g.* Danube, Elbe, Rhine, Oder), transnational co-operation only fully bloomed in 1996 with the entry into force of the Helsinki UN-ECE Convention on the Protection and Use of Transboundary Watercourses and International Lakes. This new framework of co-operation was mirrored in the WFD on the basis of Article 13 establishing the obligation of adopting a *single* river basin management plan for water bodies extending over different Member States. Therefore, water policy evolved from a water-body-specific and fit-for-use approach to a wider transboundary chemical and ecological protection and management of all water bodies.

2 Some of the main Directives on Community water policy

Following the general introduction on the development of EU water legislation, it is worth spending more time focusing on key Directives which have not been covered by other sections of this book with the aim of illustrating for each of them the main achievements, gaps and challenges for the future. Some other important legislative instruments such as Directive 76/464/EEC on pollution by certain dangerous substances and Directive 91/271/EEC concerning urban waste water treatment, to prevent among others, bacteriological discharges are addressed in other chapters.

2.1 Bathing Water Directive

In a summarised way, Directive 76/160/EC introduces a definition of bathing waters, establishes mandatory sampling, testing and monitoring and sets binding quality standards for 19 parameters. It requires Member States to take all necessary measures to achieve the required quality standards though it does include a derogation clause for the achievement of such standards under certain conditions.

Implementation was greatly enhanced in the 90s with significant improvements of bathing water quality, particularly for fresh waters. Further progress can certainly be expected as the implementation of Directive 91/271/EEC on urban waste water treatment also advances. Almost all infringement cases, opened by the Commission on the basis of Article 226 EC in relation to Directive 76/160/EEC, concerned the alleged failure of Member States to correctly implement its Articles 3, 4 and 6 that is to achieve the quality standards, to take all necessary measures to achieve them, and to comply with the monitoring requirements. Indeed, departures from the required levels can only be identified where they have been indeed monitored, hence the importance of having a proper monitoring scheme in place.

Thus, not surprisingly, many disputes between the Commission and the Member States have arisen concerning the definition of bathing waters and the grounds to grant derogations to the achievement of the quality standards. Some Member States contend that the targeted water bodies not fulfilling the quality standards did not fall within the scope of the Directive's definition and consequently were not subject to these obligations. Similarly, Member States often argued that their 'faulty' water bodies could be derogated from the quality standards obligations in accordance with the provisions of the Directive, whereas the Commission interpreted more stringently the conditions upon which derogations could be granted.

The European Court of Justice tended to interpret the definition of bathing water in a wide manner[26] and the possibilities for derogations to the limit values in a restrictive manner.[27] One of the most interesting cases for this Directive was Case C-307/98 *Commission* v. *Belgium* of 25 May 2000. Therein, the ruling of the Court clarified a very important point by concluding that it could not be inferred from the objective of the Directive, nor construed from a combination of different Articles, that although not explicitly, the Directive contained a ban on bathing in waters not fulfilling the quality standards. Thus the Court rejected the argument from the Commission who advocated that the Directive called for an implicit ban on bathing in inapt waters as one of the necessary measures to be taken by Member States when the limits were not achieved. This issue is very important as intuitively a big share of the public may have thought that the Directive would impose an obligation across the EU to ban bathing in unsuitable waters. However this was not the case and it was left to the Member States to decide upon it.

The Commission has since adopted a proposal for a revised Directive concerning the quality of bathing water.[28] The revision aims at taking on board progress on epidemiological knowledge and managerial methods. Its main features are: a wider definition of bathing waters (in line with previous case-law) but not so wide as to include 'recreational waters';[29] the establishment of two types of quality standards – the obligatory ('good') standard and a tougher ('excellent') standard to be encouraged ; the reduction of the number of quality standards (from 19 parameters to 2) making those more stringent; the assumption that bathing water quality will increase through the implementation of the WFD – therefore establishing a synergy with the WFD; and finally a much bigger involvement of the public coupled with stronger information obligations.

---

26 *E.g.* C-307/98 *Commission* v. *Belgium* [2000] ECR I-3933.

27 *E.g.* C-92/96 *Commission* v. *Spain* [1998] ECR I-505.

28 COM (2002) 581, OJ 2003 C 45/127.

29 Recreational waters are those where recreational activities other than bathing take place, such as kayaking, surfing, sail-boarding etc.

There has been heated debate on the issue of including recreational waters under the scope of the Directive. On one hand, recreational water sports practitioners or learners can fall into the water while exercising and hence be exposed to the same risk as bathers. On the other hand, it was argued that some of these sports often take place a long-way offshore far beyond where swimming normally takes place, are often practised in locations where bathing does not take place or are not compatible with bathing, hence including those would put a too high monitoring burden upon Member States.

It is worth noting, that although it had been made clear that the current Directive did not include (explicitly or implicitly) a ban on bathing in unsuitable waters, much to the regret of the Commission, the latter has not included such a provision in its proposal for a revision, which did not include an explicit call for a ban on bathing.

Recently, a very important ruling on the basis of the bathing water Directive was issued by the Court in the Case C-278/01,[30] according to which Spain will have to pay a an annual penalty of €624,150 for each percent of bathing areas in Spanish inshore waters which will have been found not to conform to the limit values laid down under the Directive for the year in question, starting from the year 2004. Only two cases, both pertaining to environmental legislation, have so far been the subject of fines for Member States under Article 228 EC, these are Case C-387/97[31] (also known as the *Kouroupitos* case) and the Spanish case mentioned above.

2.2 Drinking Water Directive

Legislation on the quality of drinking water has also evolved in the last 25 years. The Community already expressed an intention to legislate on quality standards for drinking water in the first and the second programmes of action on the environment in 1973 and 1977[32] respectively. A step by step approach led to ruling the quality of the surface water that would be used to abstract drinking water[33] and subsequently to regulate the quality of the drinking water itself. The initial proposal from the Commission was adopted in 1975, but the Council Directive 80/778/EC[34] was only adopted five years later. Worth noting is the fact that Directive 80/778/EEC excludes natural mineral waters from its scope as these are regulated through another piece of legislation[35] which, not coincidentally, was adopted on the same day.

---

30 *Commission* v. *Spain* (not yet reported).

31 *Commission* v. *Greece* [2000] ECR I-5047.

32 OJ 1977 C 139/3.

33 Directive 75/440/EEC, OJ 1975 L 194/26.

34 Directive 80/778/EEC, OJ 1980 L 229/11.

35 Directive 80/777/EEC, OJ 1980 L 229/1.

In short, Directive 80/778/EEC laid down the requirements to be met for drinking water quality by defining legally binding organoleptic, physical and chemical as wells as toxic and microbiological parameters. To ensure that such criteria are fulfilled, it set a basic monitoring and reporting regime.

Almost twenty years later, on the basis of better toxicological knowledge and more advanced water management schemes, the Council and the European Parliament adopted a new Directive on drinking water[36] which repealed the old Directive as of December 2003. The new version was reinforced with key elements. It strengthened and streamlined the parametric values largely on the basis of WHO Guidelines and the opinion of the Scientific Committee on Toxicity, Ecotoxicity and Environment (reduction from 66 parameters to 48, out of which 15 are new parameters), increased transparency and public information, and introduced a very important feature: it became a 'Tapwater Directive', which means that the point of use is the point of compliance with the quality standards (the quality of the surface water of origin being in principle ensured by the Water Framework Directive). A clearer distinction between micro-biological and chemical parameters has been made and indicator parameters have been introduced for monitoring purposes. On the other hand, it also broadened considerably the possibilities for Member States to exempt some types of water from the Directive such as for instance hot tap water and toilet-water on trains or planes. The new version sought to be integrated in a wider framework of pollution prevention and built upon other pieces of legislation such as Directive on plant protection products,[37] the Biocides Directive[38] (relevant for the reduction of the impacts of pesticides and biocides in the environment) and the Directive on construction products[39] (relevant for materials used in the production and distribution of drinking water).

Though implementation of drinking water legislation has significantly improved, the main obstacles to good quality come from diffuse pollution, namely the presence of pesticides and the migration of materials from piping systems. The limit value for pesticides, strongly influenced by analytical detection limits, was the subject of heated debates because their total phase out might require strong upstream measures in agricultural practices. Similarly, the progressive phase out of lead will entail in some Member States the execution of lead pipe replacement programmes.

The evolving nature of drinking water legislation was crystallised in Article 11 of Directive 98/83/EC which establishes the obligation to review its parameters at least every five years in the light of scientific and technical progress. In that context, discussions have started to assess the need to revise the Directive and although it would be very premature to conclude what the outcome of such

---

36 Directive 98/83/EC, OJ 1998 L 330/32.

37 Directive 91/414/EEC, OJ 1991 L 230/1.

38 Directive 98/8/EC, OJ 1998 L 123/1.

39 Directive 89/106/EEC, OJ 1989 L 40/12.

discussions will be, what seems to transpire so far[40] is the lack of a strong call for an immediate amendment. However, the next revision will have to address major challenges for the future such as tackling the presence of new substances, *e.g.* endocrine disruptors, which may have effects at very small doses of intake, of protozoa (*e.g.* Legionella) and the adaptation of current limit values, based on average adult exposure, to more vulnerable human groups (*e.g.* children, babies, elderly people, pregnant women, ill patients). It remains to be decided whether all limit values will be tightened to protect systematically the most vulnerable groups.

2.3 Groundwater Directive

Just as for other environmental compartments but more so in this case, the protection of groundwater at Community level has to be seen as the result of a mosaic of provisions emanating from different pieces of legislation. The entire pattern can only be perceived when all the components are read together. Besides Directive 80/68/EEC on the protection of groundwater against pollution caused by certain dangerous substances and the WFD, groundwater protection also features in other environmental legislation and policies, *e.g.* Directive 1999/31/EC on landfilling of waste,[41] Directive 98/83/EC on drinking water, the Nitrates Directive, Directive 91/414/EEC on plant protection products and Directive 98/8/EC on biocides. These elements are linked to the activities carried out on and above the ground which would have an impact on the water beneath.

Directive 80/68/EEC provides for two types of framework: a protection framework and a harmonisation framework to prevent distortion of competition between Member States having different national regimes for the discharges of pollutants. It aims at this by: for high priority pollutants (substances listed in List I to that Directive), banning their direct discharge and subjecting their indirect discharges to an authorisation; for other pollutants (substances listed in List II to that Directive) subjecting their direct discharge to an authorisation procedure preceded by a thorough investigation on a case-by-case basis. Monitoring is compulsory only for those specific cases when authorisation is required and not generally for all groundwater bodies.

The Water Framework Directive establishes that, among other pieces of legislation, Directive 80/68/EEC shall be repealed in 2013. After that date, the protection regime for groundwater will be continued through the Water Framework Directive and the new Groundwater Directive, which had to be proposed under the mandate of Article 17 of the Water Framework Directive. Hence there is a period between the entry into force of the Water Framework Directive and

[40] This article is based on developments up to end March 2004.

[41] Directive 1999/31/EC, O J1999 L 182/1.

the repeal of Directive 80/68/EEC when both pieces of legislation will apply concurrently to ensure groundwater protection.

The Water Framework Directive includes in its articles many elements pertaining to groundwater protection and it sets the objective of achieving good chemical status of groundwater bodies. Hence, it would appear that the most straightforward way would have been to take on board and complement the provisions of Directive 80/68/EEC in the context of the Water Framework Directive. In this manner upon repeal of the old Directive, only the latter would have taken over to regulate the protection of groundwater. However in the context of the very difficult discussions in Council and Parliament for the adoption of the WFD it was not possible to find a consensus for some aspects of groundwater protection. Hence this discussion was postponed and Article 17 was introduced in the Water Framework Directive stipulating that at a later stage the European Parliament and the Council on the basis of a proposal from the Commission will adopt specific measures to prevent and control groundwater pollution. The proposal would have to include the following elements: criteria for assessing the good chemical status of groundwater, for identifying significant and sustained upward trends and for defining a starting point for trend reversal. The Commission has recently adopted a Proposal for a new Directive on the protection of groundwater against pollution,[42] thus fulfilling two aims: the achievement of the mandate established under Article 17 of the WFD and the closure of different legal loopholes which arose.

It is worthwhile analysing the issue of quantitative management of groundwater, as this is a very important matter both from a sustainable development point of view and from a legal point of view. Indeed, Article 175(2) EC lists the 'measures affecting quantitative management of water resources or affecting, directly or indirectly, the availability of those resources' as one of the few environmental domains where the Council would need unanimity to adopt a legislative act. The quantitative management of water is perceived as falling fully within the scope of subsidiarity. This issue was the subject of Case C-36/98[43] brought to the European Court of Justice by Spain against the Council of the European Union. Actually in the Nice Treaty, the wording of Article 175 was modified to reflect the ruling of the Court in that case and to specify that *only* the quantitative management of water was to fall under the unanimity regime[44]. The Water Framework Directive does not address the quantitative management of *surface* water, which is left to Member State discretion. However, excessive extraction of groundwater lowering the level of groundwater tables can cause not only supply problems but also may lead to sea water intrusion and salinisation of the groundwater as well as mobilisation of dangerous substances. Thus,

42 COM (2003) 550 (http://europa.eu.int/eur-lex/en/com/pdf/2003/com2003_0550en01.pdf).

43 *Spain* v. *Council* [2001] ECR I-779.

44 Before the Nice Treaty entered into force, Article 175(2), second indent, referred to the 'management of water resources'.

excessive abstraction may hinder the achievement of the good quality status of that groundwater body. Furthermore in many rivers, between 50% and 90% of the flow may come from groundwater, hence the deterioration of groundwater quantity and quality and may directly affect also the quality of other *related surface* aquatic and terrestrial ecosystems. For that reason, it was justified for groundwater to introduce elements of sustainable use and quantitative management in Article 4(1) of the Water Framework Directive (under a co-decision procedure not requiring unanimity in Council) in order to be able to achieve the quality objectives therein.

2.4 Water Framework Directive

The development of Community legislation for water has followed the reverse trend that was followed by waste community legislation for instance. In the case of waste, a framework Directive was adopted in the 70s[45] as the foundation upon which more specific legislation on shipments of waste, on the management of specific waste stream and on treatment operations were built. For water, as conveyed above, early Community policy was based on the adoption of very specific legislation targeting particular uses or discharges of certain substances. Only in 2000, the Community decided to apply a more integrated approach encompassing all water categories (rivers, lakes, transitional waters, coastal waters, groundwater) and all water uses and aiming at guaranteeing a high level of protection to all water resources in the European Union. The Water Framework Directive is the result of a certain environmental maturity, which has allowed the Community to depart from a fairly anthropocentric approach to embrace a more ecological one.

International conventions on the protection of specific watercourses such as the Danube, Rhine and Oder have paved the way to develop what will constitute the backbone of the WFD: the protection and management of water at river basin scale under the River Basin Management regime. This new approach allows to tackle in an integrated manner all the pressures exerting an impact on the quality of the entire aquatic system. This is linked to one of the most fundamental feature of the WFD, namely that water quality is now given a different meaning as it covers not only chemical quality but also ecological quality. It introduces on stage the most important novelty: the ecological status of surface waters, which defines the quality of the structure and functioning of aquatic ecosystems. This element is crucial and ambitious as it encompasses different types of ecosystems dependent on water, not only covering human activities, *e.g.* flora, fauna, including to some extent the preservation of valuable terrestrial habitats.

---

[45] Directive 75/442/EEC on waste, OJ 1975 L 194/39, as amended by Directive 91/156/EEC, OJ 1991 L 78/32.

In a nutshell the main objectives of the WFD are to reduce and prevent water pollution, to promote sustainable use of water, to protect the aquatic environment, to improve the status of aquatic ecosystems and to mitigate the effects of floods and droughts. In order to achieve these goals, Member States had to identify river basins, establish river basin districts and designate a competent authority for each one by December 2003. At a later stage, within four years of the date of adoption, by December 2004, Member States have to assess the situation of these river basins, based on the characteristics of the river, a review of the impact of human activity and an economic analysis of water use. Moreover, Member States have to register areas of special protection and identify the sites which are used for extraction of drinking water.

On the basis of such characterisation they have to adopt and publish by December 2009 a customised River Basin Management Plan for each river basin based on a programme of measures to ultimately achieve, by 2015, good chemical and ecological status for all surface waters and to prevent deterioration and depleting of groundwater. Good chemical status is defined as the status required to meet the environmental objectives where concentrations of pollutants do not exceed the quality standards established. Good ecological status is an expression of the good quality of the structure and functioning of aquatic ecosystems associated with surface waters. This status is defined on the basis of requirements established in accordance with Annex V.

Furthermore, the Directive also requires the development of fair water pricing policies by 2010 (see also the communication from the Commission on 'Pricing policies for enhancing the sustainability of water resources'[46]) and broadens widely the participation of civil society in particular in the production, review and updating of the river basin management plans.

The WFD includes a combined approach for pollution from local sources, based on emission limit values, and pollution from diffuse sources, based on quality criteria in the receiving water body, thus putting an end to the old dispute on these two antagonist approaches. In this context a list of priority substances has been established,[47] for which the Commission will propose community-wide water quality standards and emission controls. Furthermore, among this list of priority substances the Commission has identified priority hazardous substances which are of particular concern and which will be subject to cessation or phasing out of discharges, emissions and losses within an appropriate timetable that shall not exceed 20 years. Hence the WFD has an enormous potential to reduce diffuse pollution by means of quality criteria.

Certain authors[48] have made a distinction between the different obligations pursuant to the WFD establishing a two level classification: general objectives constituting the ideal aims that have to be achieved and much more specific

---

46 COM (2000) 47 final, OJ 2000 C 177 E/74.

47 Decision 2455/2001/EC, OJ 2001 L 331/1.

48 Grimeaud (2001) 45 & 135; Thieffry (2001) 4.

concrete objectives compulsory in a given time (also called in the literature soft and hard objectives). In this context it has also been argued[49] that some Member States, for instance the Netherlands, regard the objectives of the Directive not as obligations of results but rather as obligations to perform to the best of one's abilities.

The negotiations to adopt this piece of legislation are known to have been particularly complex and intricate. Following the discussions within the European institutions and among Member States, for certain cases, an escape route from the ambitious objectives of the Directive found its way on the final text. Indeed, the original proposal[50] of the Commission did include a possibility to establish less stringent environmental objectives than those required for the good surface water status and for the groundwater quality for some instances 'severely affected by human activity and where improvements in status are proven to be impossible or prohibitively expensive'. However the adopted text introduces the concept of 'heavily modified water body'. It thereby sets a regime to exempt some waters from the achievement of the good ecological status and aim instead at achieving 'good ecological *potential*,' though they would still have to reach a good chemical status. As the definition of 'heavily modified water body' in Article 2 of the WFD is very broad, namely 'a body of surface water which as a result of physical alterations by human activity is substantially changed in character', it can be foreseen that it might become the basis of a variety of interpretations which may lead to be challenged in Court in order to determine the water bodies which can be subject to such an exemption regime.

However, this is not the only aspect of the WFD in need of a common approach and interpretation. Various experts have suggested that[51] the underdetermined terminology which can be found scattered through the legal text is likely to weaken enforceability and hence regrettably reduce the protection bestowed to water bodies. The vague wording of some important provisions, the fruit of long and complex negotiations, makes it essential to develop a shared understanding among all parties concerned in order to guarantee the achievements of the objectives of the Directive in a coherent and equal manner among Member States.

It is estimated that there will be between 100 and 120 river basins districts identified in the enlarged European Union (EU 25). The international basin districts will require a single management plan to be drawn up jointly by two or more Member States. Hence it has been deemed necessary to establish a Common Implementation Strategy,[52] in the framework of which, a dozen technical guideline documents and reports have already been elaborated. An

---

49 Van Rijswick (2003) 287.

50 COM (97) 49 final, OJ 1997 C 184/20.

51 Grimeaud (2001) 135; Fairley (2002) 233.

52 Strategic Document issued on May 2001 - http://forum.europa.eu.int/Public/irc/env/wfd/library?l=/framework_directive/implementation_documents&vm=detailed&sb=Title.

empirical scheme has been put in place to test and validate these guidelines on a network of pilot river basins. In this exercise for the common implementation, the crucial concept of good ecological status deserves particular attention and thought. Indeed, even assuming that the best ecological status of all water bodies would be pristine conditions, that is the state of these bodies before any human impact, it might be difficult to establish precisely in all cases what these immaculate conditions might have been. Therefore already in the concept of 'good ecological status' is inherently embedded to a certain degree the existence and influence of human activity. Moreover, while every water body performs common ecological functions, each one supports different ecosystems and species, some being more vulnerable than other to human pressures. It becomes an extremely complex exercise to ensure that the definition of high, good and moderate ecological status[53] is applied homogenously between for instance a Scandinavian fjord and a southern European estuary. An intercalibration system has been set up in accordance with Annex V, the purpose of which is to ensure comparable ecological quality assessment and harmonized ecological quality criteria for surface waters in the Member States. This is a fundamental need as the agreed ecological quality criteria will constitute the common target for restoration.

Although the WFD includes an obligation of recovery of costs for water services with the aim that water-pricing policies will provide incentives for users to utilize water resources efficiently as well as the requirement in Article 11(3) of adopting measures for the efficient use of water under the programme of measures, the WFD provides mainly a qualitative protection of water. Deliberately the WFD does not cover the quantitative management of surface water at Community level. As explained above, the adoption of measures on this domain would require a unanimous position from Member States in Council according to the EC Treaty. Quantitative restrictions or any limitations on the use of their aquatic resources are perceived by Member States as an extremely delicate issue touching upon one of the most intimate national competence. The long-lasting and extremely heated debate about the Spanish National Hydrological Plan and in particular the Ebro river transfer of water from one northern region to a number of southerner regions is the most illustrative example of how hundreds of thousands of people on either side spark a popular mobilisation to defend what they consider to be their water needs. Indeed, the right to free access to water is strongly anchored in European public opinion. One of the major challenges of the future would be to continue to evolve in the political and legislative process and ultimately reach the maturity to regulate the rational and sustainable quantitative use of water at Community and national level. Such an approach would entail an enormous adaptation effort from all society to change consumption and production patterns in order to stop taking water for granted.

---

[53] In Annex V, for each parameter there is a three-level classification possible depending on the quality: high, good and moderate. Waters achieving a status below moderate shall be classified as poor or bad.

In order to illustrate who would have to make the biggest efforts, it might be useful to provide the average water consumption per sector: OECD households consume 8% of total freshwater withdrawals, compared to 65% for industry (44% for power generation and 21% for other industry) and at least 30% for agriculture.[54]

For the energy sector, certainly due to climate change concerns among others, we have witnessed recently the development of Community legislation on rational utilization and conservation of energy, introducing energy efficiency requirements (*e.g.* on the energy performance of buildings,[55] on summer-time arrangements,[56] on energy efficiency requirements for household electric refrigerators, freezers,[57] on the performance of heat generators[58] and on limiting carbon dioxide emissions by improving energy efficiency).[59]

A similar development could be foreseen for the progress of water efficiency measures and rational water use at Community level. As it stands now, the WFD already contains the seeds to grow into a legal instrument that could in the future also rule the quantitative management of water. Indeed it already lays down some quantitative restrictions for groundwater and requires that water pricing includes external costs of water services which ought to induce users to reduce their water consumption. We may witness that the leap towards quantitative management of water resources might be triggered indirectly by the obligation to secure a flow rate and a flow regime necessary for the different water bodies to achieve a good ecological status of the water to support the species therein.

3 Conclusions

In has become clear[60] that although in principle its main objective is water protection, water legislation has, and even more so as the implementation of the WFD progresses, an enormous impact on other Community policies such as agriculture, regional development, nature protection and product policy and on national policies such as land use planning. The achievement of the objectives of water legislation entails inescapably the necessity to integrate water protection aspects in a wide range of other environmental and non-environmental sector-based policies.

---

54 OECD, *The price of Water: Trends in OECD Countries* (Paris 1999).

55 Directive 2002/91/EC, OJ 2003 L 1/65.

56 Directive 2000/84/EC, OJ 2001 L 31/21.

57 Directive 96/57/EC, OJ 1996 L 236/36.

58 Directive 78/170/EEC, OJ 1978 L 52/32

59 Directive 93/76/EEC (SAVE), OJ 1993 L 237/28.

60 Van Rijswick (2003) 288.

Water legislation is an evolving organism which has not yet reached its final state. One of the compelling ingredient for further progress could be the wider political discussion triggered by the enlargement of the European Union to 25 and subsequently 27 members. Indeed, it is perceived that there is a need to reduce the number of domains where unanimity in Council is required, in order to avoid a total legislative paralysis and ensure a dynamic functioning of the Community. If that political path is followed, it may well lead to a change in the procedure needed to adopt community legislation on quantitative management of water resources. This, though it would simplify the procedure to establish Community legislation in that domain, would certainly not render it less delicate or sensitive.

Another cause for the evolution of water protection will be the legal interpretation of various definitions which are currently wide. Indeed the definition of water is very straightforward and coming from the chemical formula of a molecule, though in practice of course it also includes minerals and other substances dissolved therein. However, the definitions of , for instance, 'bathing water', 'drinking water', 'heavily modified water body' as they are laid down in Community legislation belong to the realm of politics. Existing case-law illustrates how often these definitions are the subject of different interpretations and court proceedings. Furthermore, given that the scope of these definitions determine the application of the obligations and/or the derogations allowed, it will ultimately be the European Court of Justice which will actually shape the real protection regime for water in the Community in the years to come.

Finally, the issue of wider public participation and public information is growing in importance as reflected by recurring provisions in new legislation. This development deserves particular attention. Indeed, public participation and public information requirements can either be found embedded in water legislation as we have seen for the WFD, the Drinking Water Directive, the proposal for the revision of the Bathing Water Directive or they can follow from Community legislation such as the EIA[61] or the IPPC[62] Directives as well as provisions derived from the Aarhus Convention . The impact of a much stronger involvement of the public and organised civil society, even if slow to build, coupled with the use of new technologies such as the Internet would be well worth a comprehensive analysis. From the comfort of their home any EU citizen or stakeholder will soon be able to retrieve information on the status of the water bodies to which she or he feels related, on the drinking water she or he has access to, consult the progress of measures and plans adopted by the competent authorities, request to be provided with the information on the basis of which plans, programmes and measures have been elaborated and last but certainly not least, they will be able to provide input and try to influence the decision making. This

---

61 Directive 85/337/EEC, OJ 1985 L 175/40 as amended by Directive 97/11/EC, OJ 1991 L 73/5.

62 Directive 96/61/EC, OJ 1996 L 257/2.

participation could raise awareness on the importance of resource conservation and lead consumers to adopt more rational and efficient water use patterns.[63]

Nevertheless, it is fairly easy to fall into the trap of overrating the possible impact of these access possibilities. Indeed all this potential will not be fully exploited and properly used if it is not combined with a thorough training of civil society and the public on consultation. Such training and education on decision making ought to provide all parties involved with the proper tools to navigate these enormous tides of information without drowning, in order to finally reach the shores of an informed yet self-digested opinion.

[63] Leprince (2001) 869.

CHAPTER 9

Developments on Soil Protection in the EU

Luca Marmo[1]

1 Introduction

This paper is about the development of a soil policy at EU level with the main emphasis on the contribution of waste management to soil protection. In particular, it aims to show how Community waste legislation has contributed either directly or indirectly to the protection of soil quality. Certain aspects of the Common Agricultural Policy relative to soil protection are also illustrated. Future perspectives are indicated and special attention is paid to the regulatory framework now in place and to its evolution perspectives.

2 Origin and development of waste and soil policies in the EU

The number of pieces of EU environmental legislation and indeed other legislation and policies that affect directly or indirectly the soil ecosystem is very large. Their analysis is beyond the scope of this paper. Legislation on air pollution and industrial installations, as in the case of the European Pollutant Emission Register (EPER),[2] mineral fertilisers, with the lengthy discussions on a possible limit on cadmium in phosphate fertilisers,[3] and organic farming, just to name a few, would deserve the same degree of attention.

2.1 Setting the scene

Soil is a precious resource, vital for food production and generally taken for granted. All the Earth's vegetation is dependent on soil for the supply of nutrients and water and for root fixation. Soil is a great storehouse of minerals, organic matter, water and energy. It is a water filter, a transformer of gases and a gene pool for a huge variety of organisms formed by mineral particles (sand, silt and clay), organic matter, water, air and living organisms. It is an archive for human and geological history, which may have an important archaeological interest. The complex interaction between climate, geology, vegetation, time and land use establishes its structure and its character. Soils are

[1] European Commission, DG Environment. Opinions expressed are personal to the author.

[2] Decision 2000/479/EC on the implementation of a European pollutant emission register (EPER) according to Article 15 of Council Directive 96/61/EC (IPPC), OJ 2000 L 192/36. It should be noted, however, that the EPER does not include emissions to soils.

[3] Upon accession of Austria, Finland and Sweden to the EU in 1995, the Community undertook a commitment to consider introducing a limit on cadmium impurities in mineral fertilisers. Despite many years of discussions, the elaboration of a targeted risk assessment, and the twice renewed derogation to those three Member States to keep their national limits notwithstanding the Internal Market rules, the Commission has so far (February 2004) not yet presented a proposal to the Council and the European Parliament on the matter.

extremely variable, over 320 major soil types have been defined in Europe alone, with remarkable differences in their chemical and physical properties even at a local level. It is of particular importance to be aware of the fact that soil formation processes are active over geological periods of time and that the formation of a fertile soil layer needs thousands of years. This in practice means that soil is a non-renewable resource.[4]

In Community legislation environmental compartments such as water, air or natural ecosystems now benefit of a global protective approach that can be exemplified by mentioning Directive 2000/60/EC on water policy,[5] Directive 96/62/EC on air quality[6] and Directive 92/43/EEC on natural habitats.[7] This is not (yet?) the case for soil, which often seems to be still considered as a simple support for various activities, an interface between air and groundwater, without its own value and unworthy of global protection. No policy aiming at preservation of its quantity (by limiting erosion and its destruction for urban or transport purposes, for example) has been set, and no standards exist on its chemical and biological quality. This is not to suggest that there is not in real terms a soil policy, as the summation or result of many other policies dealing not just with air and water, but with agriculture, transport, regional and urban planning, industry and energy do have an impact (positive or negative) on soil quality.

It is interesting to note that the issues of soil and soil protection, although present in many pieces of Community legislation, are very seldom focused upon and dealt with in their own right. If we take the Fifth Community Environment Action Programme,[8] we will not find a specific chapter on soil. Of course, many of the targets of the programme have a bearing on soil and soil eco-systems one way or the other. But they do so in an indirect manner.

This is partly due to the fact that the soil compartment is a much more difficult medium than air or water to characterise and soil distress takes a long time to show its negative effects. Moreover, from a psychological point of view, soil is a much less problematic medium, as we do not breathe it like air and we do not drink it like water. As historically the main driver for environmental concerns has been human health protection, water and air have attracted much more interest than soil. Although soil quality does have an impact on human health, it does so in an indirect and much mediated way via, for example, leaching of

---

4 'Soil genesis is a long process – the formation of a layer of 30 cm of soil takes from 1,000 to 10,000 years. It is formed so slowly that soil can be considered as a non-renewable resource', Stanners & Bourdeau (1995) chapter 7.

5 Directive 2000/60/EC, OJ 2000 L 327/1, hereinafter 'the Water Framework Directive'.

6 Directive 96/62/EC on ambient air quality assessment and management, OJ 1996 L 296/55.

7 Directive 92/43/EEC, OJ 1992 L 206/7, hereinafter 'the Habitat Directive'.

8 Resolution of the Council and the Representatives of the Governments of the Member States, meeting within the Council of 1 February 1993 on a Community programme of policy and action in relation to the environment and sustainable development – A European Community programme of policy and action in relation to the environment and sustainable development, OJ 1993 C 138/1.

pollutants to groundwater, uptake of contaminants by plants or intake of toxic substances by grazing animals.

Partly this may also be due to the fact that Article 175(2) EC requires unanimity for measures affecting[9] land use. This in practice has meant that soil-related issues have been regarded as a matter of national competence, even if the European Court of Justice has clarified that 'the territory and land of the Member States and their water resources are limited resources and the second indent of the first subparagraph of Article 130s(2) of the Treaty therefore refers to the measures which affect them as such, that is measures which regulate the quantitative aspects of the use of those resources or, in other words, measures relating to the management of limited resources in its *quantitative* aspects and not those concerning the improvement and the protection of the *quality* of those resources'.[10] Which in practice means that measures adopted for soil protection in a general sense are (will be) subject to the provisions of Article 130s(1) (now 175(1)) EC and therefore require qualified majority and not unanimity in Council.

However, the situation has now started to change. The Sixth Community Environment Action Programme[11] calls for the development of a Thematic Strategy on soil protection with particular attention to preventing erosion, deterioration, contamination and desertification. In 2002 the Commission has adopted a Communication 'Towards a Thematic Strategy on soil protection'[12] whose purpose is to build on this political commitment and to outline how the Commission intends to proceed in order to develop the Strategy. This Communication is the first occasion on which the Commission has addressed soil protection for its own sake and therefore it is both broad and descriptive in approach.

Both the Council[13] and the European Parliament[14] have responded to the call made by the Commission highlighting their political concerns.

---

9 In the earlier versions of the Treaty up to and including Amsterdam, the word used was 'concerning' instead of 'affecting'. This semantic change may be an indication that the application of the unanimity rule should be interpreted in a narrow sense. It would not be sufficient that a Community act relates to land use (or, for that matter, any other of the environmental policy areas referred to in Article 175(2)), but it would need to specifically regulate quantitative aspects of land use.

10 Case C-36/98 *Spain* v. *Council* [2001] ECR I-779, para. 52 (emphasis added).

11 Decision No 1600/2002/EC laying down the Sixth Community Environment Action Programme, OJ 2002 L 242/1.

12 COM (2002) 179 final, 16.4.2002.

13 Council Document 10800/02 of 18 July 2002 on conclusions adopted by the Council on 25 June 2002 (not yet published in the OJ).

14 European Parliament Resolution on the Commission communication 'Towards a Thematic Strategy for Soil Protection' adopted on 19 November 2003 (A5-0354/2003) (not yet published in the OJ).

2.2 The development of EU waste legislation

Waste management always has a bearing on soil protection either directly when waste is landfilled or landspread, or indirectly, as in the case of waste incineration, because the incineration residues (fly and bottom ash) have to be disposed of and the pollutants emitted in the atmosphere will eventually deposit on the soil.

Waste represents an enormous loss of resources both in the form of material and energy. According to the Commission,[15] total waste generation in the EU is about 1.3 billion tonnes per year (excluding agricultural and forestry waste). This means that total waste generation in the EU amounts to approximately 3.5 tonnes per capita per year. Five major waste streams make up the bulk of these 1.3 billion tonnes: mining and quarrying waste (29%), manufacturing waste (26%), construction and demolition waste (22%) and municipal solid waste (14%). To these, the amount of agricultural and forestry waste needs to be added, an estimation of which is particularly difficult.

A concentrated effort to create a coherent and complete legislative framework on waste has been made since the first Community Strategy for Waste Management[16] was adopted in September 1989. The main strategic guidelines were maintained in the 1996 review of the Community Strategy,[17] adding that preference should in general be given to the recovery of material over energy recovery.

The Community has adopted stringent regulations for reducing environmental pollution due to the landfilling[18] and incineration[19] of waste. Soil protection is explicitly mentioned as a goal in the Landfill Directive. Although soil protection is not explicitly mentioned in Directive 2000/76/EC, its rules should ensure that the negative effects on soils due to waste incineration operations are minimised. There is at least a piece of EU waste legislation that has an important bearing on soil protection, namely Directive 86/278/EEC on sewage sludge.[20]

As regards the spreading of waste on soils, with the exception of the rules pertaining to the use of sewage sludge (in any case limited to agricultural soils) and restrictions on nitrogen input to agricultural soils[21] (although the latter are principally meant to protect groundwater quality and limit the euthrophication

---

15 'Towards a thematic strategy on the prevention and recycling of waste', COM (2003) 301 final, 27.5.2003, p. 9.

16 'Community waste strategy', SEC (89) 934 final, 18.09.1989.

17 'Review of the Community strategy for waste management', COM (96) 399 final, 30.07.1996.

18 Directive 1999/31/EC on the landfill of waste, OJ 1999 L 182/1, hereinafter 'the Landfill Directive'.

19 Directive 2000/76/EC on the incineration of waste, OJ 2000 L 332/91.

20 Directive 86/278/EEC on the protection of the environment, and in particular of the soil, when sewage sludge is used in agriculture, OJ 1986 L 181/6, hereinafter 'the Sewage Sludge Directive'.

21 Directive 91/676/EEC concerning the protection of waters against pollution caused by nitrates from agricultural sources, OJ 1991 L 375/1, hereinafter 'the Nitrate Directive'.

of surface water), the Community has not yet specifically regulated this activity. This means that the recovery and/or disposal of waste involving landspreading operations need to be assessed and regulated in light of the provisions of Directive 75/442/EEC on waste,[22] in particular its Article 4, which states that waste is to be recovered or disposed of without endangering human health and without using processes or methods, which could harm the environment.

2.3 The beginning of EU soil policy

Soils are coming under increasing threat from human activities. Some threats are well known historically such as erosion, which means the removal of soil particles by water or wind and their transportation elsewhere. Erosion, which is often linked to other degradation processes especially in the Mediterranean area, can eventually lead to desertification when soil is no longer able to carry out its functions and the land becomes increasingly valueless. The slow build up of contaminants through air emissions from industry, transport and some farm practices can result not only in soil pollution but also in the contamination of water and food. Other soil problems are linked to industrial sites, to declining organic matter in some agricultural soils, to the sealing of soil for infra-structural and housing purposes, the compaction of land and the effects of floods and landslides. The issue of the decline in soil organic matter is central and a clear picture of its extent is necessary. Soil organic matter is an important reservoir of carbon and soils are now considered as sinks in relation to climate change. Reversing trends in organic matter decline brings many benefits for soil functions and can contribute to carbon sequestration.

The issues of contaminated sites and diffuse contamination now feature prominently in the aforementioned Communication 'Towards a thematic strategy for soil protection' aimed at putting soil protection at the heart of sustainable development.[23] The Communication includes a number of new legislative initiatives of specific benefit for soil protection that should be adopted by the Commission in coming years, including a proposal for a Directive on mining waste,[24] a proposal for the revision of the rules concerning sewage sludge, a proposal for a Directive on biowaste and a proposal for a Directive on soil monitoring. The latter three are now understood to form, together with a Communication to further soil protection aspects in EU policy making, a 'package' of measures composing the Soil Thematic Strategy expected for April 2005.

---

22 Directive 75/442/EEC on waste, OJ 1975 L 194/39. Directive as amended by Directive 91/156/EEC, OJ 1991 L 78/31, hereinafter 'the Waste Framework Directive'.

23 A description of the legal aspects relative to contaminated sites in the EU is in Krämer (2002c).

24 Scheduled for 2002, in reality adopted on 2 June 2003 (COM (2003) 319). For an analysis of the legal aspects surrounding the Aznalcóllar accident, one of the events at the origin of this proposal, see Krämer (1999a).

The Communication 'Towards a thematic strategy for soil protection' is a step taken by the Commission for putting high on the political agenda the protection of soils within the EU. After so many years of environmental policy dealing with water and air, but neglecting this precious non-renewable medium, it is now time to focus on a better way to ensure sustainability of soil management, while at the same time allowing economic growth and social development. One could argue that it is not such a bold step after all, as it stops short of advocating the need for a comprehensive Directive on soil protection at EU level. However, the ball is now rolling and it will be up to the discussions between the European Institutions in coming years to muster the political will to do more.

3 Some instruments at EU level relevant for soil protection

3.1 The Waste Framework Directive

Article 4 of the Waste Framework Directive is central to existing EU legislation on the landspreading of wastes and requires that 'Member States shall take the necessary measures to ensure that waste is recovered or disposed of without endangering human health and without using processes or methods which could harm the environment, and in particular: without risk to water, air, soil and plants and animals; without causing a nuisance through noise and odours; and without adversely affecting the countryside or places of special interest. Member States shall also take the necessary measures to prohibit the abandonment, dumping or uncontrolled disposal of waste'.

Annexes IIA and IIB of the Waste Framework Directive list the operations which may lead to disposal or recovery of waste, including disposal operation D2 – 'Land treatment (*e.g.* biodegradation of liquid or sludgy discards in soils etc)', as well as recovery operations R3 – 'Recycling/reclamation of organic substances which are not used as solvents (including composting and other biological transformation processes)', and R10 – 'Land treatment resulting in benefit to agriculture or ecological improvement'. What is 'benefit to agriculture' or 'ecological improvement' is not further specified.

It is worth noting that the Directive itself does not define recovery and disposal, as there is only a tautological reference to Annexes IIA and IIB in Article 1. Moreover, both recovery and disposal operations have to fulfil the requirements of Article 4, *i.e.* they must not endanger the environment. Seen in relation to soil protection, this could mean that the Community legislature has made a distinction between lansdpreading of waste leading to actual benefit to the soil, which would be classified as recovery, and landspreading that is 'neutral' in terms of soil quality, which would be classified as disposal (in theory, there should be no harm to the environment in either case, so disposal leading to the worsening of soil quality must be excluded).[25]

Thus the question of whether in practice there can be landspreading of waste that is neutral in terms of soil quality and still respects the conditions of Article 4 arises. It is difficult to imagine that such an event does indeed happen in practice, as one would tend to believe that landspreading of waste has always positive and negative effects mixed together. It is their overall balance that leads to benefiting the soil or worsening soil conditions. In the latter case, the operation should not take place.

All this may seem rather academic. In reality the classification of a waste operation as recovery or disposal may have important consequences in terms of waste shipment, for the fulfilment of specific recovery targets, and for the actual operation happening or not. It is well known that the Waste Shipment Regulation[26] offers more opportunity to Member States to restrict the shipment of waste to another Member State in case of disposal operations. Certain Directives (*e.g.* the Packaging and Packaging Waste Directive[27]) set recycling targets for waste and therefore the issue of the classification of an operation is of consequence.

However, it should be observed that Article 4 of the waste framework Directive does not lay down specific technical requirements to be followed when waste is landspread. Nor does it specify what kind of waste is suitable for a landspreading operation. It is more an Article that should 'inspire' the competent authorities, when granting an authorisation in accordance with Articles 9 or 10 of Directive 75/442/EEC, to require the appropriate treatment and processes in order to ensure that waste is spread on land for purposes of agricultural benefit or ecological improvement. Unless they do so, this Article is dead letter.

A landmark ruling on the extent and applicability in concrete situations of Article 4 can be considered the case concerning an illegal fly-tipping of waste in the San Rocco riverbed in Naples.[28] Although the European Court of Justice (ECJ) did not think that this Article was of direct application to any given specific situation,[29] it did underline that the management (or, as in the San Rocco case, lack of management) of waste not in conformity with the environmental protection requirements laid down in Article 4, which actually worsens the environment over a protracted period of time, could run counter to the provisions of that Article. This is an important clarification of its 'legal power' and

---

[25] One could also argue that the landspreading of waste as a disposal operation is in practice prohibited, as any disposal of waste on land would be subject to the requirements of the Landfill Directive.

[26] Regulation (EEC) 259/93 on the supervision and control of shipments of waste within, into and out of the European Community, OJ 1993 L 30/1.

[27] Directive 94/62/EC on packaging and packaging waste, OJ 1994 L 365/10.

[28] Case C-365/97 *Commission* v. *Italy* [1999] ECR I-7773.

[29] See in particular para. 67-68 of the judgement.

enforceability. Clearly, it needs the willingness of the competent authorities in Member States and eventually of the Commission to exploit its potentialities.

In the case of landspreading of animal manure and slurry, the overloading of the soil with an excessive amount of nutrients where the soil is already saturated (for instance because of phosphorus) should in principle lead to stopping this practice, as it is not in line with Article 4 of Directive 75/442/EEC. Article 2(1)(b) of Directive 75/442/EEC excludes 'animal carcasses and the following agricultural waste: faecal matter and other natural, non-dangerous substances used in farming' from the scope of the Directive 'where they are already covered by other legislation'. In a preliminary ruling in the proceedings brought before the Finnish Supreme Administrative Court by *AvestaPolarit Chrome Oy*,[30] the ECJ has recently clarified that 'other legislation' in Article 2(1)(b) means Community *or* national legislation. However, in the latter case, the ECJ specifies that the national legislation must contain precise provisions organising the management of the waste in question within the meaning of Article 1(d) of Directive 75/442/EEC.[31] Moreover, such national legislation must pursue the same objectives of that Directive and result in a level of protection of the environment which is at least equivalent to that resulting from the measures taken in application of the Directive.[32]

This means that animal manure and slurry – that could potentially be outside the scope of Directive 75/442/EEC if there is appropriate national legislation in place – would nevertheless have at least to comply with the requirements laid down in Article 4 of the Directive, which are essential to the fulfilment of the environmental objectives of that Directive.

3.2 The Landfill Directive

Although the Community Strategy for waste management and its review call for waste avoidance and diminution of waste at source, the quantity of waste produced per capita in the Community is increasing. On average, 65% of municipal waste is still landfilled, despite this option being at the lowest ranking in the waste hierarchy.[33] In several Member States this percentage exceeds 80%. The Member States with the highest percentage of landfilling of household waste are Greece and Ireland (above 90%), the lowest percentage is found in the Netherlands and Denmark (about 15%). Of the approximately 200 million tonnes of municipal waste generated in the EU in 2000, around 30-40% was highly putrescible wastes such as food scraps, cuttings from parks

[30] Case C-114/01 *AvestaPolarit Chrome Oy* (not yet reported).

[31] Art. 1(d), Directive 75/442/EEC as amended: 'management' shall mean the collection, transport, recovery and disposal of waste, including the supervision of such operations and after-care of disposal sites.

[32] See in particular para. 59 of the judgment.

[33] The waste hierarchy is defined in Article 3 of Directive 75/442/EEC and sees at the first place waste avoidance, followed by waste minimisation, recycling, energy recovery, and at the bottom safe disposal.

and green waste from gardens, and another 25-30% was paper and cardboard waste. Thus, about two thirds of municipal waste can be classified as biodegradable waste.

There are big differences in the environmental standards of landfill sites in the EU. Uncontrolled or poorly engineered landfills can have long lasting negative effects on the environment. The most important include emissions of hazardous substances to soil and ground water, emissions of methane into the atmosphere, dust, noise, explosion risks as well as use and deterioration of land (including loss of natural areas). The mere space occupied by a landfill site is *per se* a pressure on the environment and on neighbouring dwellings. These motivations, among others, are the drive behind the Landfill Directive, which aims at ensuring that landfills are properly managed during their active lifetime and properly monitored when they are filled up.

One of the main innovations of the Directive refers to the introduction of a quantified reduction strategy for the landfilling of biodegradable municipal waste (Article 5). The quantity of this type of waste accepted for landfill shall be reduced to 75%, 50% and 35% of the tonnage produced in 1995, or the latest year before 1995 for which standardised Eurostat data is available, by 2006, 2009 and 2016 respectively.[34] This is one of the elements of the Directive that makes it a management tool for waste policy, as opposed to simply setting technical standards for the installation. It was originally introduced as a contribution to the fight against climate change.[35] This is also one of the elements most interesting from the point of view of the relationship with soil policy, because biodegradable waste is in principle a fairly 'easy' waste stream to treat and can lead to the production of a soil improver in the form of compost. But the Landfill Directive is also important because it gives much emphasis to the protection of soil and requires the operator to take appropriate measures to avoid that leachate generated within the body of the landfill pollutes aquifers and soil (point 3 in Annex I).

3.3 The Sewage Sludge Directive

Sludge originates from the treatment of waste water. Sludge is, however, rich in nutrients such as nitrogen and phosphorous and contains organic matter that is useful for soils which are depleted or subject to erosion. The organic matter and nutrients are the two main elements that make the spreading of this waste on land as fertiliser or organic soil improver suitable. However, due to the physical-chemical processes involved in the treatment, the sludge tends to concentrate heavy metals and poorly biodegradable trace organic

34 Member States which in 1995 landfilled more than 80% of their municipal waste are allowed to reach these targets four years later.

35 Biodegradable waste degrades anaerobically in a landfill environment giving origin to methane, which is 21 times more powerful than carbon dioxide in increasing the Earth's temperature.

compounds as well as potentially pathogenic organisms – viruses, bacteria etc. – present in waste waters.

The Sewage Sludge Directive establishes the principle that as a rule sewage sludge ought to be treated before its use. Treated sludge is defined as sludge which has undergone biological, chemical or heat treatment, long-term storage or any other appropriate process so as to significantly reduce its fermentability and the health hazards resulting from its use. Exception to this general rule may be allowed by Member States on condition that the untreated, raw sludge is injected or ploughed into the soil.

This Directive provides for maximum heavy metals concentrations in sewage sludge for re-use in agriculture as well as for maximum heavy metals concentrations in soil. The aim is to avoid that spreading of sludge on the same agricultural plot increases heavy metal concentrations to a level that could potentially cause adverse effects on the soil eco-system. However, it does not fix any limits for concentrations of organic pollutants, although some Member States do. Among those regulated are polychlorinated biphenyls (PCBs) in France, Austria, Germany and Sweden; dioxins and furanes (PCDD/Fs) in Austria and Germany; and polyaromatic hydrocarbons (PAHs) in France, Denmark and Sweden.

If we want to keep open the possibility of re-using sewage sludge on agricultural soil, it seems important that we reduce the overall pollution by heavy metals – and organic compounds – in waste water. This means that products and materials of everyday use along with industrial processes need to be progressively upgraded in order to reduce their load of polluting substances. Sludge is the typical waste for which the concrete application of the prevention principle of Article 174 EC would bring about considerable improvements. The saying 'garbage in, garbage out' reflects perfectly well the situation of sludge management. An improvement of sludge quality in terms of heavy metal concentrations and organic pollutants can only come by a serious policy of enforcement of discharge consent for industrial sources of pollution and product policy for diffuse pollution. The composition of detergents, cleaning products, cosmetics, paints, solvents, textiles, pharmaceuticals (the list could continue) are of crucial importance in determining a good sludge quality. In the long run the actions to be undertaken under the auspices of the Water Framework Directive (including the tracking down of pollutant sources and the phasing out of certain priority substances, including cadmium, lead and mercury) will help improve, albeit indirectly, sludge composition.

Directive 86/278/EEC was passed under the joint legal basis of old Articles 100 and 235 EEC Treaty, now Articles 94 and 308 EC respectively. It can be assumed that its provisions would have now to be assessed under the auspices of Article 175 EC, as the explicitly stated objective of the Directive (Article 1) is an environmental one. It is the only environmental Directive adopted so far by the Community that aims *expressis verbis* to the protection of soils.

An important question that is becoming more and more of political relevance given the current debate in a number of Member States is whether a Member State can prohibit altogether the use of sludge in agriculture regardless of its actual quality. On a first reading, it is arguable that the Directive is not designed to provide an exhaustive set of rules on the use of sewage sludge, as it only deals with the landspreading on agricultural land. The objective of the Directive is set out in Article 1, which states that the purpose of the Directive is to regulate the use of sewage sludge in agriculture. The word 'use' is important. It would seem to mean that the Directive sets out rules determining how the Member States should regulate the use of sewage sludge when they have decided to allow it to be applied, *i.e.* in setting rules on its quality. It does not appear to cover the situation where a Member State decides to ban its use totally. It could therefore be considered that the 'more stringent measures than those provided for in this Directive' referred to in Article 12 relate to situations where a Member State decides to insist on stricter quality control standards than those set out in the Directive.[36] As a matter of fact, the majority of Member States is actually applying stricter rules (on heavy metal concentrations, on allowed spreading periods, on type of agricultural land suitable for landspreading etc) than the minimum ones provided for in the Directive.[37]

However, it could be argued that with Directive 91/271/EEC[38] the Community legislature has further clarified the matter. Indeed, Article 14(1) of that Directive says that 'Sludge arising from waste water treatment shall be re-used whenever appropriate. Disposal routes shall minimise the adverse effects on the environment'. There is no definition of 're use' in Directive 91/271/EEC, although Directive 86/278/EEC defines 'use' as 'the spreading of sludge on the soil or any other application of sludge on and in the soil' (Article 2(d)). The eighth preamble to Directive 86/278/EEC states that 'sludge can have valuable agronomic properties and it is therefore justified to encourage its application in agriculture provided it is used correctly; whereas the use of sewage sludge must not impair the quality of the soil and of agricultural products'. The seventh preamble of Directive 91/271/EEC says 'the recycling of sludge arising from waste water treatment should be encouraged (...)'. It can be concluded that there is no obligation under Community law to use sludge in agriculture. Such an obligation would not make any sense because there are a number of conditions that have to be fulfilled before sludge can be safely used on agricultural land.

36 In any case, if the Directive is today to be assessed in light of Article 175 EC, Member States have always the possibility of invoking Article 176 EC, which states that 'The protective measures adopted pursuant to Article 175 shall not prevent any Member State from maintaining or introducing more stringent protective measures. Such measures must be compatible with this Treaty. They shall be notified to the Commission'.

37 For an update of applicable legislation in Member States see COM (2003) 250 final, 19.5.2003 (http://europa.eu.int/comm/environment/waste/reporting/index.htm).

38 Directive 91/271/EEC concerning urban waste-water treatment, OJ 1991 L 135/40.

Moreover, agricultural land is not always available near a waste water treatment plant nor is the owner of the land necessarily willing to use such a waste for fertilising purposes.

Still, in light of the above, it seems clear that the Community legislature has expressed the wish to see the use of sludge regulated (in order to prevent negative effects), but at the same time encouraged as a source of nutrients and organic matter. An outright ban of sludge landspreading would not be in line with the spirit of Community environmental policy if not with the letter of Community law. However, not everyone agrees. For instance, Ludwig Krämer has a different opinion on the matter.[39] Indeed, there are at least three Regions in the EU where a formal ban on sludge use in agriculture is already enacted: the Tyrol and Vienna *Länder* in Austria and the Flemish Region in Belgium. In the Netherlands, although there is no prohibition as such, the heavy metal limits in sludge are so strict that in practice sewage sludge from urban waste water treatment plants has not been used in agriculture since 1995. The Commission has not, at least so far, taken any action against these Member States on these grounds.

3.4 The common agricultural policy (CAP) and its 2003 reform[40]

Agriculture makes use of 41% of the EU-15 territory while its sister, forestry, accounts for a further 33%. Land use in agriculture varies enormously. The total utilised agricultural area (UAA) in 2002 was 130 million hectares and, of this, 28% was devoted to cereals, 4.5% to oilseeds, 3.6% to olives and 4.3% to green fodder. Grassland in its broad sense accounted for 53% of the UAA.[41]

Farmers are dependent on soil for their livelihoods and therefore have a vested interest in its care and protection. However, a series of factors including economic pressures, changing technology and sometimes ignorance, particularly of the long-term effects of certain agricultural practices, are combining to undermine the relationship between agriculture and soil. Farming can both cause several of the main problems currently associated with soil and be the unwilling recipient of problems resulting from other activities.

The key problems arising from farming can be summarised very briefly as:

- Physical degradation in the form of erosion, desertification, water logging and compaction. Land use practices including deforestation, overgrazing,

39 Krämer (2003a) 341.

40 In this section the author quotes extensively from Hamell (1999). For a detailed description of the past and present of the CAP, see Dhondt (2003) 199-290.

41 European Commission, Directorate-General for Agriculture, *Agriculture in the European Union. Statistical and economic information* (Brussels 2004)(http://europa.eu.int/comm/agriculture/agrista/2003/table_en/index.htm).

poor cultivation, removal of hedgerows or vegetative cover etc, can exacerbate these.

- Chemical degradation due to acidification, salinisation, contamination by pollutants such as heavy metals or overloading with nutrients. Eutrophication and diffuse contamination may result and the related agricultural practices are over-use of manure and mineral fertilisers, emissions of pollutants by intensive livestock production, the spreading of unsuitable waste on agricultural soils and the use of pesticides with unintended side effects.
- Biological degradation in the form of lowering the organic content or changing the soil bio-diversity due to inappropriate land use practices or pesticide use.

The fact that within the EU there has been a common agricultural policy for over 40 years[42] tends to suggest that it is within this policy that solutions to soils problems should be found. However, until 1992 this policy was driven largely by Member States expectations in relation to markets and farmers' incomes with the result that environmental problems, including those related to soil, were not seen as within the established scope of policy development.[43]

That situation changed with the 'MacSharry 1992' CAP reform, which introduced the integration of environmental concerns into its financial rules so as to ensure farming practices necessary to safeguard the environment and preserve the countryside. This can be clearly seen in Article 1 of Regulation (EEC) 2078/92,[44] which gave more emphasis to the environmental pillar of sustainable development within the CAP. Nevertheless, the CAP is still very concerned with markets and farmers' incomes as can be seen from the distribution of funding and it is against this background that soil/agriculture relationships need to be faced. The key CAP measures are based on the philosophy that farmers should observe a minimum level of environmental practice as part and parcel of the direct support schemes. However, society should pay for any additional environmental service, beyond the basic level of good agricultural practice and respect for environmental law, through agri-environment programmes.

A further step in the 'greening' of the CAP was Regulation 1259/99,[45] which introduced environmental protection requirements (agri-environment) in its

---

42 The Council adopted the first regulations on the common agricultural policy (CAP) on 14 January 1962 (http://europa.eu.int/abc/history/1962/index_en.htm).

43 As Ludwig Krämer wittily says 'If Community measures in the area of transport or agricultural policy were to be assessed under the principles that the environmental damage should be prevented, that the polluter should pay, or that damage should be rectified at source: not many measures would survive such a test' (Krämer (2002d) 163, footnote 27).

44 Regulation (EEC) 2078/92 on agricultural production methods compatible with the requirements of the protection of the environment and the maintenance of the countryside, OJ 1992 L 215/85.

45 Regulation (EC) 1259/1999 establishing common rules for direct support schemes under the common agricultural policy, OJ 1999 L 160/113.

Article 3, including support in return for agri-environmental commitments, general mandatory environmental requirements, and specific environmental requirements constituting a condition for direct payments. An important part of this approach is that Member States may shift any funding not paid to producers due to the implementation of this Article to their new rural development programmes. To the extent that CAP direct payments affect agricultural land, Member States now have a powerful tool at their disposal for environmental protection. Given that arable crops, most grazing livestock and the main Mediterranean crops attract direct payments for producers and that total 'market' spending in the period 2000-2006 is over €40 billion annually, it would be difficult to underestimate the strength of the tool. Member States will have to decide how much importance they attach to soil protection in deciding how to make use of this new power. One should note that what exactly these 'environmental measures' mentioned in Article 3 that are considered 'to be appropriate' are, is left to the discretion of the Member States. The Community defines the broad lines of the agri-environmental measures, but does not enter into the detail of what these measures should be.

Another element to the CAP that is of mounting importance is the Rural Development pillar.[46] It comprises a series of measures to be taken at national and/or regional level and within these are several of environmental interest including training and agri-environment. Among the concepts behind the agri-environmental measures to date has been the reducing of the polluting effects of agriculture. Within the various undertakings to achieve this and several environmentally desirable aims there are many of benefit to soil. These include reductions in pesticide, fertiliser and water use, stocking limits and grazing management techniques, cultivation measures, landscape conservation and the protection of field margins.

Further to that, the reform agreed in 2003 under the initiative of Commissioner Fischler (the 'Luxembourg compromise') has further strengthened an important element attempting to link the existing environmental regulatory instruments and the issue of financial support to farmers. This element is the cross-compliance mechanism laid down in Regulation (EC) 1782/2003.[47] Article 3 of that Regulation establishes a link between, on the one hand, the direct payments received by a farmer and, on the other, the statutory management requirements and good agricultural and environmental conditions to

46 Cf. in particular Articles 22-24 of Regulation (EC) 1257/1999 on support for rural development from the European Agricultural Guidance and Guarantee Fund (EAGGF) and amending and repealing certain Regulations, OJ 1999 L 160/80.

47 Regulation (EC) 1782/2003 establishing common rules for direct support schemes under the common agricultural policy and establishing certain support schemes for farmers and amending Regulations (EEC) 2019/93, (EC) 1452/2001, (EC) 1453/2001, (EC) 1454/2001, (EC) 1868/94, (EC) 1251/1999, (EC) 1254/1999, (EC) 1673/2000, (EEC) 2358/71 and (EC) 2529/2001, OJ 2003 L 270/1.

be respected. This Article, together with the provisions in Article 6, which requires the reduction or cancellation of the direct payment to farmers where the statutory management requirements or good agricultural and environmental conditions are not complied with, constitutes a powerful tool in the hands of Member States to ensure that environmental requirements are seriously taken into account.

Although the list in Annex III to the Regulation is unfortunately fairly short, as it consists of only five environmental Directives (six including rules on pesticides),[48] it is still a first step in the right direction. One could wonder whether it is wise to introduce such a stick-and-carrot approach, as Community legislation should be applied regardless of economic sanctions. It could be regarded as a bit of surrendering to the harsh reality of political willingness (or lack of) as opposed to strict adherence to the enforcement of legislation. The fact that we need the cross-compliance mechanism may be considered the symptom of the failure of Member States to implement and/or enforce Community legislation. From a more positive angle, the introduction of monetary sanctions in case of non-respect of environmental rules may in the end also result in increased awareness among farmers.

Moreover, Article 5 of Regulation (EC) 1782/2003 requires Member States to define, at national or regional level, minimum requirements for good agricultural and environmental conditions, taking into account the specific characteristics of the areas concerned, including soil and climatic condition, existing farming systems, land use, crop rotation, farming practices, and farm structures. Annex IV to the Regulation sets out the framework conditions that Member States have to consider in defining these minimum requirements. Some are very relevant for soil protection purposes, as they refer to soil erosion, soil organic matter (with a requirement to maintain soil organic matter levels through appropriate practices), soil structure, and protection of permanent pasture.

Another important aspect of the reform brokered by Commissioner Fischler (leaving aside, for want of space, the much debated decoupling of aid from production) is the 'communitarisation' of environmental measures, *i.e.* the fact that, for the first time, the definition of substantial measures for the protection of the environment is not left to Member States, but makes an explicit reference to EU legislation (albeit limited). Naturally, the possibility of this reform to contribute even more to soil protection depends on the existence of substantial EU legislation on this sector, which is not yet the case. The five environmental Directives concerned by the cross-compliance mechanism have a limited effect on soil protection. The Sewage Sludge Directive, the Habitat Directive and the

[48] Directive 79/409/EEC on the conservation of wild birds, OJ 1979 L 103/1; Directive 80/68/EEC on the protection of groundwater against pollution caused by certain dangerous substances, OJ 1980 L 20/43; the Sewage Sludge Directive (footnote 20 above); the Nitrate Directive (footnote 21 above); the Habitat Directive (footnote 7 above); Directive 91/414/EEC concerning the placing of plant protection products on the market, OJ 1991 L 230/1.

Nitrate Directive have provisions somewhat linked to the preservation of the soil ecosystem for future generations. However, the relevance of these instruments is limited by their scope, which is far from covering the majority of soils in the EU. Had the Community already adopted specific legislation on soil quality and standards there would have been the possibility of a linkage with the payments to farmers. This not being the case, the relevance of this reform for soil protection is somewhat limited.

4 Conclusion and forward outlook

Although the Community legislature has adopted an impressive number of pieces of legislation which relate indirectly to soil protection, soil protection *per se* has been regarded so far as a low-profile issue. There is no coherent frame for ensuring that the different sector policies brought forward by the Community take into account the needs of soils – especially the long-term effects which may not have an immediate impact on soil exploitation (for instance, the accumulation of heavy metals in topsoil is a slow business and may not be problematic for a long time but when the effects are there it could be too late to counteract).[49] There is room for a more comprehensive approach to soil policy that should look not only at the short-term effects. Soils – including soil biota, soil eco-systems and soil biomass – should be preserved for future generations and not just because they have an economic value.

From the point of view of the relationship between soil protection and waste management, the recycling of biodegradable wastes (biowastes) is particularly important. The products from which biowastes are eventually generated have their origin, one way or the other, from agricultural or forestry activities (except for marine resources like fish). The meat that we eat, the vegetables that garnish our dishes, the paper on which this book is written – all originate from the exploitation, either directly in the case of plant growth or indirectly in the case of animal husbandry, of agricultural land and forests. With the recycling of biowaste on soil, materials that otherwise may be placed into landfills or incinerated, thus presenting environmental pollution problems, can contribute to soil protection and possibly create potential markets. The aim should be to achieve an integrated organic matter management for different biowastes (separately collected, controlled, appropriately treated), leading to a high level of protection and conservation of soil organic matter in the different types of European soils. The development of a quality-orientated biowaste recycling in the whole of Europe would be a substantial contribution to sustainable development targets.

Animal manure and slurries, industrial residues (*e.g.* waste lime from cement manufacturing, slag from steel production, waste from food and drink

---

[49] Witter (1996).

preparations), dredging spoils etc are not subject to specific controls. True, the requirements of Directive 75/442/EEC apply (including the need for a permit pursuant to Article 9 or 10).[50] However, in practice Member States tend to turn a blind eye on these legal requirements especially in the case of the spreading on land of animal manure and slurry.

Insofar as modern agriculture is concerned, can the mechanisms now in place provide protection for soil in its relationship with practical farming? The answer probably lies in the commitment of Member States and Regions to use the mechanisms already in place and make effective use of the cross-compliance tool reinforced by the 2003 reform of the CAP. This would already be a step in the right direction. However, as mentioned earlier, the relevance of the cross-compliance mechanism for soil protection depends on the existence of meaningful legislation of a substantial nature in the soil field. And this is something that at the moment is sorely lacking at the EU level, but also in many Member States that do not have framework legislation for soil protection in place.

Specific actions on areas relating to industry can make an important contribution to soil protection. For instance, a careful watch should be maintained on the practical implementation of the IPPC Directive[51] and the work being carried out for the elaboration of Best Available Techniques Reference documents (BREFs). The positive effects expected from this Directive on soil crucially depend on taking into account soil concerns when elaborating the sector BREFs as well as the subsequent application of the BREFs in the permitting process. The strengthening of Article 3(f) of the Directive, which provides for returning the site of operation to a 'satisfactory state', could be envisaged, as it is not defined anywhere in the IPPC Directive what a satisfactory state is. This is particularly important in terms of soil quality, as the application of this provision by the competent authority may considerably differ from one Member State to the other.

Another important contribution of the IPPC Directive will surely be the European Pollutant Emission Register (EPER), soon to be complemented by the UN-ECE Pollutant Release and Transfer Registers (PRTRs)[52] that will include emissions to soils and increase the number of pollutants to be monitored and reported from 50 to 86, the number of activities from 56 to 65 and the reporting frequency from three years to one. Although these instruments do not directly deal with soil protection, their potential for improving knowledge about soil impacts is large. The fact that the European Institutions as well as the wider public will be able to know what kind of pollutants, in which concentrations and

---

50 With the possible exceptions mentioned in section 2.1, *i.e.* animal manure and slurry that could potentially be outside the scope of Directive 75/442/EEC if there is appropriate national legislation in place.

51 Directive 96/61/EC concerning integrated pollution prevention and control, OJ 1996 L 257/26.

52 UN-ECE, Protocol on Pollutant Release and Transfer Registers to the Aarhus Convention on Access to Information, Public Participation in Decision-Making and Access to Justice in Environmental Matters, Kiev, 21 May 2003.

from which installation have been emitted may have dramatic consequences on the improvement of pollutant abatement equipment in turn resulting in a diminution of direct and indirect pollutant emissions to soils.

As this paper has attempted to illustrate, the relevance of certain pieces of legislation to soil protection depends on an agreed concept at EU level, maybe in the form of a Soil Framework Directive. Such a Directive would need to contain more elements than just soil quality standards – in itself a mighty task to achieve given the differences in soil types across Europe. Management of urban sprawl, transport infrastructure, minimisation of pollutants entering the soil ecosystem from diffuse sources, and contribution to organic matter increase where needed are some of the issues that would need to be addressed. Judging from the insight gained in the development of the Water Framework Directive, it will be a long and probably politically painful process to bring to a successful end not least because the Council does not seem to be particularly excited by the idea.[53] The soil medium has specific features unlike water and air, e. g. generally it does not move, and the Council may have an easy ride in underlining that the large diversity of soil types in Europe would make a one size-fits-all policy impossible. However, just to make a few examples, agricultural products are freely traded within the Internal Market and soil characteristics are definitively an important parameter when it comes to a healthy crop production; the currently wide variety of definitions of a 'contaminated site' gives origin to a disparities of enforcement rules in the Member States raising potential competition problems for companies operating internationally; and soil may indeed move, *e.g.* because of erosion phenomena involving the transboundary transfer of contaminants.

The Community as a whole and the Member States should strive for increasing the degree of awareness for soil protection in policy-making bearing in mind that this very precious and non-renewable resource is as important as water and air for life on our planet.

---

[53] The Community is signatory and has ratified the Alpine Convention adopted in 1991 by Austria, France, Germany, Italy, Liechtenstein, Slovenia and Switzerland. In 1998 a Protocol on soil protection was adopted under the aegis of the Convention. This Protocol has never been signed nor ratified by the Community. This may be due to a lack of interest in an instrument that can be perceived as being of limited geographical importance. Or it could be a signal of the lack of interest among Member States in a Community intervention on soil matters.

CHAPTER 10

Developments in European Legislation on Noise Protection

Anna Karamat[1]

1 Introduction

Noise is defined as 'unwanted sound' or 'sound that is loud, unpleasant or unexpected'.[2] The effects of noise are difficult to quantify as people's tolerance to noise levels and different types of noise vary considerably. Noise levels above 40 dB L_{Aeq}[3] can influence wellbeing. Most people are moderately annoyed at 50 dB L_{Aeq} and seriously annoyed at 55 dB L_{Aeq}. Levels above 65 dB L_{Aeq} can be detrimental to health.[4]

Noise can have a number of effects on exposed people, such as disturbance of sleep, auditory and non-auditory effects (*e.g.* on blood pressure and the cardiovascular system), interference with communication and general annoyance. These health effects, in turn, can lead to social handicap, reduced productivity, decreased performance in learning, absenteeism in the workplace and school, and possibly increased drug use and accidents.[5]

According to the European Environment Agency a large proportion of the population is exposed to traffic noise levels which can be annoying or harmful to health. It is estimated that more than 30% of Europeans are exposed to road noise levels, and around 10% to rail noise levels above 55 L_{dn}[6] dB(A), the level at which most people are seriously annoyed. Data on noise nuisance by aircraft are the most uncertain, but 10% of the total EU population may be highly annoyed by air transport noise.[7]

Noise has impacts not only on humans but also on ecosystems. The negative effects of noise on wildlife populations are becoming more and more documented.

Nuisances caused by noise have grown with the increased industrial development and urbanisation of our society. The sources of noise are related to almost all human activities, in particular road traffic, rail traffic, air traffic, industry, civil engineering and building site activities, recreational activities and outdoor equipment. The numerous different sources of noise show the cross cutting nature of noise problems. Accordingly, as will be explained in this article, noise is addressed in a wide variety of political and legal instruments.

Noise pollution is considered to be an environmental problem. Still, it remains to be seen to what extent a coherent environmental noise policy has been developed.

---

1 European Commission, DG Environment. Opinions expressed are personal to the author.

2 European Green Paper on the Future Noise Policy, 4.11.1996, COM (96) 540.

3 L_{Aeq} is the energy equivalent sound pressure level in dB(A).

4 See Green Paper on Noise, footnote 2 above.

5 World Health Organisation, Guidelines for Community Noise, 1999, www.who.int.

6 L_{dn} is the Day–night level. It is a descriptor of noise level based on energy equivalent noise level (Leq) over the whole day with a penalty of 10 dB(A) for night time noise (22.00-7.00 hrs).

7 European Environment Agency Transport and Environment Reporting Mechanism (TERM) Report, 2001, www.eea.eu.int. There is no data available on the situation in the acceding countries.

2 Origin and development of community action on environmental noise: The policy framework

From the 1970s on, Community measures to address noise problems consisted almost exclusively of legislation fixing maximum sound levels for vehicles, aeroplanes and machines. These measures aimed principally to ensure the functioning of the single market and were not conceived as part of an overall noise abatement programme. Noise exposure was also taken into consideration in worker protection standards. No environmental dimension was envisaged.

Although the problem of noise was already addressed as a priority in the First Environment Action Programme of 1973[8] and restated in all the following environment action programmes, it was not before the mid nineties that an overall Community environmental noise policy started to evolve.

2.1 Fifth Environment Action Programme

In the 5th Environment Action Programme[9] the Commission considered the problem of noise mainly under the heading of urban environment. Noise was considered one of the most pressing problems in urban areas. The Commission set the general objective that no person should be exposed to noise levels which endanger health and quality of life and more specifically that the night-time exposure of population to noise levels in excess of 65 dB(A) should be phased out and at no point in time a level of 85 dB(A) should be exceeded. The Commission proposed a broad range of actions to remedy the problem of noise. These actions include the establishment of an inventory of exposure levels in the Community, setting up a noise abatement programme, further reductions of noise emissions through new Directives, standardisation of noise measurement and ratings, measures to influence behaviour and measures related to infrastructure and physical planning.

In the review of the 5th Environment Action Programme[10] these objectives and indicative actions were reconfirmed with particular emphasis on the development of the noise abatement programme, which should address common noise exposure indices and targets for noise quality and noise emissions of products.

---

[8] OJ 1973 C 112/1. The Action Programme provided that criteria for measuring noise level and nuisance indicators at various levels of intensity should be determined.

[9] OJ 1993 C 138/1.

[10] Decision 2179/98/EC of the European Parliament and of the Council of 24.9.1998 on the review of the European Community programme of policy and action in relation to the environment and sustainable development 'Towards sustainability', OJ 1998 L 275/1.

2.2 Green Paper on noise policy

In 1996 the Commission adopted the Green Paper 'Future Noise Policy'.[11] The Green Paper examined the sources and impacts of noise, analysed existing policies to reduce noise exposure and their application and set out the Commission's proposed new framework for noise policy.

This framework consists of the following future actions:

- harmonisation of methods of assessment of noise exposure
- measures to reduce road traffic noise (tyre noise, integration of noise costs into fiscal instruments, inclusion of noise in road-worthiness tests)
- research in the field of rail noise; investigation of feasibility of setting emission limit values
- more stringent emission limit values for air traffic, economic instruments to promote lower noise aircraft
- simplification of legislation on outdoor equipment

As a follow-up to the Green Paper the Noise Expert Network was established. This network consists of representatives from the Commission and the Noise Steering Group where all stakeholders are represented. Its mission is to assist the Commission in the development of its noise policy. Under the network several working groups have been set up that deal with research, roads, railways, airports, outdoor machinery, health and socio-economic aspects.[12]

2.3 Sixth Environment Action Programme

In the 6th Environment Action Programme noise is addressed under the chapter 'Environment and Health and Quality of Life'. The Programme provides that Thematic Strategies will be developed for key environmental issues that need a holistic approach because of their complexity, the diversity of actors concerned and the need to find multiple and innovative solutions. Thematic strategies are forseen for soil protection, protection and conservation of the marine environment, the sustainable use of pesticides, air pollution, urban environment, the sustainable use and management of resources and waste recycling. No Thematic Strategy is foreseen for noise. However, the future Thematic Strategy on Urban Environment could contain elements relating to noise reduction in urban areas.

With regard to the overall noise exposure of people the Commission's Communication on the 6th Environment Action Programme[13] set the objective to 'achieve a reduction in the number of people regularly affected by long term

---

[11] See footnote 2 above.

[12] More information on the Noise Expert Network can be found on DG Environment's noise policy website (http://europa.eu.int/comm/environment/noise/home.htm).

[13] COM (2001) 31 of 24.1.2001.

high levels of noise from an estimated 100 million people in the year 2000 by around 10% in the year 2010 and in the order of 20% by 2020'. The European Parliament and the Council, however, did not confirm this objective in their Decision, but limited themselves to the more general objective of a substantial reduction of the number of people regularly affected by long-term average levels of noise without laying down precise reduction targets.[14]

The main action proposed by the Commission in the 6th Environment Action Programme is the adoption and implementation of a Directive on Noise. The Council and Parliament Decision also mention the further development of measures on noise emissions from services and products and the development of instruments to mitigate traffic noise where appropriate.

3 Main community legislative instruments contributing to noise protection

3.1 Vehicles

The first harmonised noise requirements for road vehicles were introduced in 1970.[15] These consisted of type approval noise and emission limits for vehicles. A vehicle type that fulfils the harmonised requirements is approved by a Member State and may be marketed in all Member States. Individual vehicles can be controlled to check whether they conform to the approved type. The requirements of the Directive have been reviewed and tightened several times since then. The current allowable noise limits range from 74 dB(A) for motor cars and 80 dB(A) for high-powered goods vehicles. The Directive does not apply to trains, tractors and mobile machinery. Agricultural and forestry tractors are also subject to a type approval system.[16] Their maximum noise limits are set at 85 dB for tractors under 1,75 tonnes and 89 dB for tractors over 1,75 tonnes.[17]

In 1997 similar legislation was adopted for motor cycles[18] and in 2001 additional noise requirements were set out for tyres.[19]

---

14 Decision 1600/2002/EC of the European Parliament and the Council laying down the Sixth Community Environment Action Programme, OJ 2002 L 242/1.

15 Directive 70/157/EEC, OJ 1970 L 42/16 as last amended by Directive 99/101/EEC, OJ 1999 L 334/41.

16 Directive 74/150/EEC, OJ 1974 L 84/10.

17 Directive 74/151/EEC, OJ 1974 L 84/25.

18 Directive 97/24/EC, OJ 1997 L 226/42.

19 Directive 2001/43/EC, OJ 2001 L 211/25.

3.2 Pleasure boats

Directive 2003/44/EEC[20] amended existing harmonised provisions on the design and construction of recreational craft to include noise emissions from engines intended to be installed on recreational craft. The maximum sound pressure levels range from 67 to 75 dB depending on the engine power. The Commission had proposed this amendment in 2000[21] after several Member States expressed their intention to introduce noise limits for recreational craft and there were concerns that this could lead to obstacles to the internal market.

3.3 Aircraft

Community legislation on noise from aircraft is for the most part based on the international standards set in the Convention on international civil aviation adopted under the auspices of the International Civil Aviation Organisation (ICAO), to which all Member States are party. Annex 16, Volume I, Part II of the Convention contains the noise certification standards, which are regularly reviewed. The initial noise standards for jet aeroplanes were taken up under Chapter 2 of the Annex. Stricter standards were added in Chapter 3. The newest standards were included in Chapter 4, which will be applicable from 1 January 2006.[22] The Annex further gives guidance on land-use planning and management, noise abatement operational procedures, operating restrictions and noise charges.

Directive 80/51/EEC on the limitation of noise emissions from subsonic aircraft[23] introduced an obligatory noise certification for certain aeroplanes falling under Chapter 2 of the ICAO standards. Member States have to ensure that these aeroplanes may not be used in their territory unless they were granted noise certification on the basis of satisfactory evidence that the aeroplane complies with requirements that are 'at least equal to the applicable standards set by the Convention on international civil aviation'. The Court of Justice has interpreted this Directive as setting minimum requirements, allowing Member States to adopt more stringent measures, if those are compatible with the provisions of the Treaty.[24]

Directive 89/629/EEC[25] laid down stricter requirements for the limitation of noise emission from subsonic jet aeroplanes in accordance with the Chapter 3 standards. The Directive limits the addition to the civil air registers of Member

20 OJ 2003 L 214/18.

21 OJ 2001 C 62E/139.

22 www.icao.org.

23 OJ 1980 L 18/26 as amended by Directive 83/206/EEC, OJ 1983 L 117/15.

24 C-389/96 [1998] ECR I-4473; see Krämer (2002a) 275.

25 OJ 1989 L 363/27.

States of aeroplanes that comply only with the Chapter 2 standards. This was a first step to phasing out completely Chapter 2 aeroplanes.

Directive 92/14/EEC[26] went a step further and provided the gradual withdrawal of Chapter 2 aeroplanes from Member States' registers. By 1 April 2002 all civil subsonic aeroplanes operating in the Community had to comply with the chapter 3 standards. Exemptions were provided for certain aeroplanes from developing countries that had purchased European aeroplanes. The Directive was amended in 1998[27] mainly for clarification purposes but also granting further exemptions. With regard to this Directive, the Commission adopted a decision in 1998 stating that the noise limits of Directive 92/14/EEC are not minimum requirements but a total harmonisation and Member States are not allowed to set more stringent limits.[28]

In 1999 Regulation (EC) 925/1999[29], the so-called 'Hush kit Regulation' was adopted. Hush kitted aeroplanes are older types of aeroplanes that have been modified and recertificated in order to meet chapter 3 standards. These aeroplanes were considered to have a significantly worse noise performance than modern Chapter 3 aeroplanes. The Regulation thus banned the addition of these aeroplanes to Member States' registers as from 1 April 1999 and the operation of these aeroplanes at Community airports as from 1 April 2002. Exemptions were foreseen for aeroplanes operated in the Community before 1 April 1999.

This Regulation was heavily opposed by the United States, who would have been mainly affected by the ban and who saw this regulation as a discriminatory trade barrier that was not compatible with the Convention on international civil aviation. The Community postponed the entry into force of the Regulation by one year and finally decided to replace it by a new Directive.

Directive 2002/30/EC on operating restrictions at Community airports[30] repealed the Hush kit Regulation. Instead of banning the recertificated airplanes, the Directive introduces a more flexible approach to safeguard noise protection around airports. This approach is based on the 'balanced approach' to aircraft noise management endorsed by the ICAO Assembly in 2001. This consists of identifying the noise problem at an airport and then analysing the various measures available to reduce the noise. Such measures include the reduction of airplane noise at source, land-use planning and management measures, noise abatement operational procedures and operating restrictions. The goal is to achieve the maximum environmental benefit in the most cost-effective manner. The Directive lays down rules for the assessment and introduction of operating restrictions. Given the fierce competition between airports

---

[26] OJ 1992 L 76/21, as amended by Directive 98/20/EC, OJ 1998 L 107/4.

[27] Directive 98/20/EC, OJ 1998 L 107/4.

[28] Decision 98/523/EC, OJ 1998 L 233/25, see also Krämer (2003a) 100.

[29] OJ 1999 L 115/1.

[30] OJ 2002 L 85/40.

it remains to be seen how this Directive will be applied and whether it will really lead to an improvement of the noise problems at airports.

In 2001 the Commission presented a proposal for a Directive establishing a framework for noise classification of civil subsonic aircraft[31] for the purposes of calculating noise charges. The objective of this proposal is to set harmonised criteria for the calculation of noise charges by airports in order to safeguard the functioning of the internal market.

The exposure to noise near airports is a serious problem for the people affected and is also of relevance in the context of human rights. In the 'Hatton case'[32] residents living near Heathrow airport brought a case against the United Kingdom before the European Court of Human Rights. They considered that the decision to allow the extension of night flights at the airport constituted a breach of their right to respect for home and private life. In 2001 the European Court of Human Rights decided that with its decision to extend night flights at Heathrow airport the United Kingdom had breached the right to respect for private and family life of residents living near the airport. The Court held that the United Kingdom had not sufficiently analysed the economic value of night flights and their effect on the population. Upon appeal of the United Kingdom the Grand Chamber, however, decided in July 2003 that the United Kingdom government had not overstepped its margin of discretion and had thus not breached the right to respect for home and private life.[33] Although the Court in the end decided that there was no breach in this case, it still acknowledged that noise nuisances can in principle constitute a breach of the Human Rights Convention if the evaluation of competing interests is not properly carried out.

3.4 Household appliances

Concerning household appliances only the information on noise levels, the methods of measuring noise and the monitoring methods are harmonised.[34] There are no maximum noise limits and Member States are free to impose (or not) noise labelling for household appliances.

3.5 Noise from outdoor equipment

Since 1978 the Community adopted 9 Directives regarding noise from specific outdoor equipment (construction plant and equipment,[35]

---

31 OJ 2001 C 103/221.

32 See footnote 33 below.

33 European Court of Human Rights, Case of *Hatton and others* v. *United Kingdom*, Judgments of 2.10.2001 and 8.7.2003; www.echr.coe.int.

34 Directive 86/594/EEC, OJ 1986 L 344/24.

35 Directive 79/113/EEC, OJ 1979 L 033/15 and Directive 84/532/EEC, OJ 1984 L 300/111.

compressors,[36] tower cranes,[37] welding generators,[38] power generators,[39] powered hand-held concrete breakers and picks,[40] lawnmowers,[41] hydraulic excavators[42]). These Directives aimed to harmonise the requirements for the placing on the market of these products in order to ensure the functioning of the single market. The harmonised requirements included permissible noise levels, noise test codes, marking and conformity assessment procedures.

In 2000 a Directive was adopted to simplify this legislation and to create a framework for the reduction of noise emission by outdoor equipment.[43] All outdoor equipment must comply with the requirements of the Directive, bear the CE marking, which shows that it complies with the requirements, and be accompanied by a declaration of conformity. The Directive sets maximum noise levels for some equipment and for other equipment requires noise marking only. The Directive repealed the existing Directives as from 3 January 2002.

3.6 Directive on Environmental Noise

Directive 2002/49/EC relating to the assessment and management of environmental noise[44] was adopted as a follow-up to the Commission's Green Paper on Noise and constitutes the first general framework for an overall Community noise policy. It lays down common methods and indicators for the monitoring and assessment of noise levels to produce information that is comparable across Europe.

Competent authorities must draw up 'strategic noise maps' for major roads, railways, airports and agglomerations, using harmonised noise indicators. The strategic noise maps must be completed by 2007 for large agglomerations of more than 250.000 inhabitants, major roads with more than 6 million vehicles passages a year, railways with more than 60.000 passages per year and airports. For other agglomerations, major roads and railways the noise maps must be presented by 2012. These maps will be used to assess the number of people in Europe who are exposed to noise.

Competent authorities must also draw up action plans to reduce noise where necessary and maintain good environmental quality. However, the measures to be taken and the acceptable levels of noise are left to the discretion of the competent authorities. The noise action plans will be presented in 2008 and the action

---

36 Directive 84/533/EEC, OJ 1984 L 300/123.

37 Directive 84/534/EEC, OJ 1984 L 300/130.

38 Directive 84/535/EEC, OJ 1984 L 300/142.

39 Directive 84/536/EEC, OJ 1984 L 300/149.

40 Directive 84/537/EEC, OJ 1984 L 300/156.

41 Directive 84/538/EEC, OJ 1984 L 300/171.

42 Directive 86/662/EEC, OJ 1984 L 384/1986.

43 Directive 2000/14/EC, OJ 2000 L 162/1.

44 OJ 2002 L 189/12.

plans for the case that noise limits are exceeded in 2013. A further important element of the Directive is the obligation to inform and consult the public on noise levels.

Pursuant to Article 1(2) the Directive also aims at providing a basis for developing Community measures to reduce noise emitted by the major sources and calls on the Commission to submit the appropriate legislative proposals by 18 July 2006. The Commission made a declaration[45] to this article stating that the preparation of legislation relating to sources of noise would be considered where necessary.

3.7 Other legislation

Noise is also addressed in several other pieces of Community environmental legislation which do not specifically focus on noise reduction.

Installations falling under the IPPC Directive[46] have to apply best available techniques in order to prevent or reduce emissions to the environment. The concept of best available techniques aims to achieve a high level of environmental protection as a whole, while taking into account the technical, geographical and economic conditions of the individual installation. Emission limit values are to be included in the permit of an installation. If the exchange of information between the Member States shows that this is necessary, emission limit values will be set at Community level. Emissions are defined as 'the direct or indirect release of substances, vibrations, heat or noise from individual or diffuse sources in the installation into the air, water or land'. Noise is therefore covered by the definition of emissions. It is however not mentioned in Annex III, which lists the emissions for which limit values must be set. For noise other requirements than emission limit values have to be set in the permit. The best available techniques will be described for the sectors falling under the Directive in reference documents, which also take into account noise. To date reference documents for 17 sectors have been adopted.[47]

Directive 75/442/EEC on waste[48] lists noise as one of the nuisances of waste recovery or disposal operations that should be prevented by Member States.[49]

---

45 OJ 2002 L 189/26.

46 Directive 96/61/EC, OJ 1996 L 257/26.

47 See the article by A. Paquot in this book.

48 OJ 1975 L 194/39, as amended by Directive 91/156/EEC, OJ 1991 L 78/32.

49 Article 4 states: 'Member States shall take the necessary measures to ensure that waste is recovered or disposed of without endangering human health and without using processes or methods which could harm the environment, and in particular:

- without risk to water, air, soil and plants and animals,
- without causing a nuisance through noise or odours,

In practice this provision does not have much relevance, as no Community requirements on noise from waste treatment installations exist. It is thus for the Member States to decide on the level of acceptable noise emissions and the appropriate reduction measures. Some indications on the margin of discretion of Member States in applying Article 4 have been given by the European Court of Justice. In a case regarding the functioning of an illegal landfill the European Court of Justice stated that Article 4 sets the objective to be achieved and gives the Member States a margin of discretion in assessing the need for measures. The fact that a situation is not in conformity with these objectives is not automatically a breach of Article 4.

> *'However, if that situation persists and leads in particular to a significant deterioration in the environment over a protracted period without any action being taken by the competent authorities, it may be an indication that the Member States have exceeded the discretion conferred on them by that provision'.*[50]

It can be deduced from this that if a Member State tolerates a situation of evident noise nuisance over a prolonged period of time, this would be a breach of Article 4.

Another decision that sheds light on the obligations of governments with regard to effects from waste installations was taken by the European Court of Human Rights. In a case concerning a waste treatment plant the Court stated that the fact that the applicant had lived for years at 12 meters distance to the plant, which was causing odours, noise and air emissions, was a breach of her right to respect for home and private life.[51]

Directive 85/337/EEC on the assessment of the effects of certain public and private projects on the environment (EIA)[52] requires that projects likely to have significant effects on the environment are made subject to an assessment prior to granting the development consent. In this context the effects of the project with regard to noise would also need to be assessed before the project can be approved. The Directive lists the projects for which such an assessment is obligatory. This list includes the construction of airports, railway lines and certain roads, where the effects of noise will be of particular relevance. The Directive however only requires that an assessment of the effects of the project on the environment is carried out. It does not require that these effects should be taken into account.

- without adversely affecting the countryside or places of special interest.

Member States shall also take the necessary measures to prohibit the abandonment, dumping or uncontrolled disposal of waste.

50 Case C-365/97, [1999] ECR I-7773, paragraph 68.

51 European Court of Human Rights, Case *Lopez Ostra* v. *Spain*, Judgment of 9.12.1994; see also Krämer (1998) 353.

52 OJ 1985 L 175/40 as amended by Directive 97/11/EC, OJ 1997 L 73/5.

With Directive 2001/42/EC on the assessment of the effects of certain plans and programmes on the environment[53] plans and programmes which could have an impact on the environment will also have to be assessed. The Directive covers in particular plans and programmes prepared for agriculture, forestry, fisheries, energy, industry, transport, waste management, water management, telecommunications, tourism, town and country planning or land use and which set the framework for future development consent of projects listed in Annexes I and II to Directive 85/337/EEC. It constitutes an important step in integrating environmental aspects already at the planning stage. This Directive contains more detailed requirements than the EIA Directive on how to take into account environmental impacts. It requires an environmental report to be drawn up which identifies, describes and evaluates the likely significant environmental impacts of implementing the plan or programme and reasonable alternatives taking into account the objectives and geographical scope of the plan or programme. When they adopt the plan or programme the authorities have to make a statement outlining how environmental considerations were integrated and how the environmental report and the consultations were taken into account.

Pursuant to Regulation (EC) 761/2001[54] organisations[55] can participate on a voluntary basis in the Community eco-management and audit scheme for the evaluation and improvement of their environmental performance and the provision of information on their environmental performance to the public. In this scheme all environmental aspects of the organisation, including noise, must be considered.

Regulation (EC) 1980/2000[56] sets up a voluntary system with rules for the award of a Community Eco-label to products and services with reduced environmental impacts. Criteria for the award of the eco-label have been developed for several products. The reduction of noise to certain levels is required for instance for refrigerators, washing machines, computers and vacuum cleaners. For example the eco-label on a dishwasher would indicate noise emissions of less than 53 dB(A) for free standing models or less than 50 dB(A) for built-in models. On a computer it would indicate an idle operating emission of 48 dB(A) or less, and accessing of disk drive at 55 dB(A) or less.

Most of the legislation relevant to noise focuses on the effects of noise on humans. For the effects of noise on wild animals nature legislation is of particular relevance. Directive 92/43/EEC on the conservation of natural habitats and of wild fauna and flora[57] contains provisions for the development of a coherent European ecological network known as 'Natura 2000'. The network comprises

---

53 OJ 2001 L 197/30.

54 OJ 2001 L 114/1.

55 This terms covers private companies as well as public authorities and institutions (Art. 2s, Regulation (EC) 761/2001).

56 OJ 2000 L 237/1.

57 OJ 1992 L 206/7

'special areas of conservation' designated by Member States in accordance with the provisions of the Directive, and 'special protection areas' classified pursuant to Directive 79/409/EEC on the conservation of wild birds.[58] Member States must take measures for the conservation of the special areas of conservation as well as measures to avoid the deterioration of protected sites. Plans and projects likely to have an impact on a protected site must be subject to an assessment. Competent authorities may only agree to the plan or project if it will not adversely affect the integrity of the site concerned. If it does affect the site but there is no alternative solution, the plan or project can nevertheless be carried out if it is necessary for imperative reasons of overriding public interest. In this case compensatory measures must be taken.

4 Challenges for the future

4.1 Contribution of legislation to noise levels

According to the Commission's Green Paper of 1996 significant reductions of noise from individual sources have been achieved, thanks to the adopted legislation and technological progress. For example the noise from individual cars has been reduced by 85% since 1970 and the noise from lorries by 90%. An aircraft's noise impact around airports was reduced by a factor of 9 compared to an aircraft with 1970s technology. However, the exposure to noise, in particular to road traffic noise, has not significantly improved in the past 15 years. This problem is expected to worsen in future due to the growth in traffic.

The European Environment Agency states that noise levels around several large airports have dropped in recent years as a result of phasing out of noisier aircraft. However, this trend is expected to reverse, as the growth in aircraft movements is no longer compensated by the use of quieter aircraft.[59]

The potential effectiveness of the Directive on environmental noise in reducing noise problems in the EU has not been assessed yet, but it is expected that the harmonised data that will be derived from its implementation will allow for a better assessment of the potential benefits linked to further tightening of source legislation.

4.2 Internal market and trade

Member States have been adopting different measures at national, regional or local level to reduce noise exposure. Such measures include a whole range of solutions including the reduction of speed, the reduction of

---

58 OJ 1979 L 103/1

59 European Environment Agency, Transport and Environment Reporting Mechanism (TERM), Report 2001.

transport volume and use of equipment, the construction of sound barriers between the source and people affected and noise insulation of buildings. As far as national measures concern the placing on the market of products or the restriction of certain activities, they could lead to problems with the internal market. Extensive Community legislation has been enacted in order to prevent such internal market problems. From the lack of Court cases in this area it seems that there have not been major disturbances of the internal market due to noise reduction measures, which seems to indicate that Member States have not been particularly active in this field.

Even if product related measures are taken at Community level, there is still the risk that third countries could object to these measures on the grounds of restrictions of trade. This was the case for the European ban of hush kitted aeroplanes. The Community under pressure from the United States decided to repeal the Hush kit Regulation. Unfortunately no legal decision was ever taken under international trade rules (WTO or ICAO) on the permissibility of the ban. It will be important for the Community to continue its effort to further develop the noise standards set at international level.

4.3 Noise policy and the principle of subsidiarity

Article 5 of the EC treaty states that 'in areas which do not fall within its exclusive competence, the Community shall take action, in accordance with the principle of subsidiarity, only if and in so far as the objectives of the proposed action cannot be sufficiently achieved by the Member States and can therefore, by reason of the scale or effects of the proposed action, be better achieved by the Community.'

The principle of subsidiarity is of particular relevance in the field of noise policy and has often been used as an argument against the development of a Community noise policy. Noise is generally seen as a local problem with no transboundary effects. It is argued that, as the solutions to this problem depend on differing sensitivities, cultural and social backgrounds and lifestyles, they should preferably be sought at national or local level. It is perhaps for this reason that the actions at Community level against noise have so far been mainly focussed on measures necessary to ensure the functioning of the internal market.

However, one of the objectives of Community policy is to achieve a high level of health and environmental protection, including the protection against noise for the whole of the Community. The measures taken so far have not sufficiently achieved this objective. Thus, it has been recognised that a common approach at Community level is necessary and a general consensus on the maximum levels of noise to which the public should be exposed in order to protect health and quality of life is evolving.

5 Conclusions

According to the Eurobarometer[60] surveys noise is still one of the main environmental concerns mentioned by citizens. Despite this, Community actions on noise seem to have a much lower priority than actions in other areas such as water and air. Perhaps this is because the seriousness of the effects of noise is not so well known yet.

Community action has focussed on reducing the noise emissions from individual products and further noise reduction measures have been left to Member States.

In the Green Paper on Noise the Commission considered that a change in this approach was needed. As the Commission points out, there is a need to improve the coherence of the multitude of actions being undertaken and to ensure greater integration and coordination with Community policies in order to increase the effectiveness of noise policy.

One difficulty in defining a European noise policy was the different measuring systems in the Member States that made comparisons very difficult. In this respect the harmonised measuring system of the Directive on environmental noise is a very important step towards a Community noise policy. The effects of the Directive will, however, not become evident for quite a long time.

Reduction of noise at source is seen as the most effective solution to the noise problem. This will include further measures to reduce noise from products where necessary and possible. Community policy should however not be limited to such actions. Reducing noise emissions from cars or aeroplanes to a level where they do not cause annoyances to the population directly exposed to them will take a very long time, if possible at all. It will thus be necessary to increase the efforts to integrate noise aspects into other policies, in particular on transport and town and country planning. Taking into account the complexity of the issue a coordinated approach at Community level will have to be taken.

Noise is an important environmental issue and will become more and more so. It is an issue that has not been given high political priority. This is also reflected in the scarcity of academic debate on noise policy and the way forward. Although noise features in a large number of environmental Directives a coherent and coordinated noise policy has still not been developed and is also not on the agenda for the next years.

---

60 www.europa.eu.int/comm/public_opinion/index.htm/

CHAPTER 11

Community Action in the Fight Against Climate Change

Yvon Slingenberg[1]

1 Introduction

End 1980s, general awareness of global environmental problems was increasing. With international action to remedy the hole in the ozone layer, knowledge about the potentially devastating effects caused by emissions of certain gases increased. One started to suspect that the emissions of carbon-dioxide (CO_2), methane (CH_4), nitrous-oxide (N_2O), hydrofluorocarbons (HFCs), perfluorocarbons (PFCs) and sulphur-hexafluoride (SF_6), are not degraded but stay in the atmosphere and thus keep the heat of the sun 'trapped'. This could lead to an increase in global temperatures, melting of big ice-stacks such as glaciers and the ice at the North and South Pole, rising sea levels, more flooding as well as droughts, and generally more extreme weather events. Together these phenomena are referred to as 'climate change' and the gases that cause them as 'greenhouse gases' (GHG).

Such emissions are generated by most human activities, such as industry, agriculture, transport, energy use in houses and other buildings, waste, etc. The wide range of emission sources makes it more difficult to tackle than for example the ozone depleting substances. Furthermore, all countries produce these emissions with the countries that are the most industrialised are therefore also the 'biggest polluters'. In addition, with the expected further industrialisation of the developing countries, the emissions of these countries are expected to increase significantly.

But although all countries produce GHG emissions, of course different groups of countries have different priority interests. As such there are the richest industrialised countries that in principle have the technology to reduce emissions and can afford to take such action. There are the Central and Eastern European countries, including Russia, which have a great potential to reduce their emissions but need a lot of money to modernise their economy and installations. And there are the developing countries, which are very heterogeneous in them selves: some have quite advanced economies and are already OECD members, others belong to the group of Least Developed Countries (LDCs). Many developing countries are likely to be the worst affected by climate change. Some will see largely expanding deserts, others, in particular small island states, risk to disappear completely if the sea level rises. Cutting across these groups are the oil-producing countries.

Thus, in view of the gravity of the potential effects of climate change, there was a clear need to act. And the industrialised countries that have been at the origin of the problem ever since the industrial revolution bear the main responsibility to do so and show the developing countries a more sustainable track for their economic development.

---

[1] European Commission, Environment Directorate-General. With special thanks to Damien Meadows, as well as the other colleagues of the Climate Unit. The opinions contained in this article are personal to the author.

2 Climate action at international level

As a first step the Intergovernmental Panel on Climate Change (IPCC) was set up jointly by the World Meteorological Organisation (WMO) and the United Nations Environment Programme (UNEP) in 1998. This Panel comprises scientists from all over the world who together examine and research the perceived and potential climatic changes and what causes them. In 1990 the IPCC issued its First Assessment Report[2] and on the basis of its findings, it was decided that an international legal instrument was needed to address the situation and try to cut the emissions of greenhouse gases.

An international negotiating process was started under the auspices of the United Nations (UN), which culminated, at the Earth Summit in Rio de Janeiro in 1992, in the signature of the United Nations Framework Convention on Climate Change (UNFCCC).[3] The ultimate objective of the Convention is stabilisation of concentrations of the above-mentioned greenhouse gases in the atmosphere at a level that would prevent dangerous climate change (cf. Article 2 UNFCCC).

The Convention divides the participating countries in 'Annex I' and 'non-Annex I'. Annex I lists 41 industrialised countries, which have to take policies and measures to limit and reduce GHG. They have a specific aim to limit emissions at 1990 levels in the year 2000 (Article 4.2(a) and (b) UNFCCC). Most but not all countries listed in Annex I are also listed in Annex II[4] which implies supplementary efforts compared to the obligations for Annex I countries; Annex II countries are to promote technology transfer to and capacity building in developing countries, in particular to help these countries to adapt to the effects of a changing climate (Articles 4.4, 4.5, 4.8 and 4.9 UNFCCC).

While Annex I is flexible and countries can be added to it, many of the discussions in the Convention have centred around 'who acts first'. On the one hand, developing countries insist that industrialised countries have a 'historic responsibility' and must have made clear reductions in their emissions before the developing countries should be asked to take on similar commitments that – in their view – might limit their economic growth. On the other hand, industrialised countries maintain that whatever they do, the ultimate objective can never be achieved without action being taken *also* by the developing countries, notably the bigger ones such as Brazil, China and India.[5]

The first reasoning was actually accepted by many Annex I countries, which led to the thinking that in addition to the Convention something more was

---

[2] IPCC 1990: Climate Change. The IPCC Scientific Assessment (ed. by J.T. Houghton, G.J. Jenkins, J.J. Ephraums), Cambridge, Cambridge University Press.

[3] http:/unfccc.int; the full texts of the Convention, the Kyoto Protocol and all COP Decisions can be found here.

[4] The Central and Eastern European countries are not included in Annex II.

[5] Cf., for example, the 'Byrd-Hagel' resolution of the US Senate of 12.6.1997.

needed. At the first Conference of the Parties (COP1) in Berlin in 1995, the Parties agreed on the 'Berlin Mandate' under which further negotiations should focus on the goal of laying down quantified emission limitation and reduction objectives within specified time frames for Annex I countries, but without imposing new commitments on developing countries.[6]

As a result, at COP3 in December 1997, the Kyoto Protocol (KP) was adopted. The Protocol lays down binding emission targets for all Annex I countries, this time listed in Annex B, except Turkey and Belarus.[7] The European Community and each of its Member States individually have a target of an 8% reduction in GHG emissions compared to 1990 levels, to be achieved over a 5 year period between 2008 and 2012. However, the EU also obtained the possibility to achieve this target jointly (Article 4 KP), *i.e.* with some Member States reducing more than –8% and others less.

In addition to the novelty of specific, legally binding targets, the Protocol foresees innovative ways how the emission reductions can be achieved, known as the 'flexible mechanisms': Joint Implementation (JI), Clean Development Mechanism (CDM) and International Emission Trading (IET) (Articles 6, 12 and 17 KP). Parties can also take into account carbon uptake (or 'sequestration') in so-called 'carbon sinks' such as trees and the soil (Article 3.3 and 3.4 KP). Furthermore, there are extensive monitoring and reporting requirements that Annex B Parties have to comply with (Articles 5 and 7 KP).

Joint Implementation is a mechanism whereby an Annex I Party carries out projects in another Annex I Party aimed at reducing GHG emissions in the latter, for example through technological projects. The two countries involved share the emission reductions resulting from a project and are allowed to use these 'credits' for fulfilling their respective target. The Clean Development Mechanism is similar to JI in that it is also a project-based mechanism. However, CDM projects are carried out by Annex I Parties in non-Annex I Parties, with the first obtaining credits for the emissions reduced. Non-Annex I Parties do not have specific targets and therefore cannot use such credits for compliance purposes. Their main gain from such projects is the investment in their country. Furthermore, under IET Annex I Parties can trade their emission quota's derived from their targets in Annex B, *i.e.* not on the basis of any projects but rather close to simple selling. However, the Conference of the Parties has established strict implementing rules for each of these mechanisms, and Parties are to ensure that the use of the mechanisms is supplemental to domestic action ('supplementarity'), as required in the Protocol.

6 Decision 1/CP.1.

7 Australia +8%, Bulgaria –8%, Canada –6%, Croatia –5%, Czech Republic –8%, Estonia –8%, European Community and each of its Member States (EU15) –8%, Hungary –6%, Iceland +10%, Japan –6%, Latvia –8%, Liechtenstein –8%, Lithuania – 8%, Monaco –8%, New Zealand 0%, Norway +1%, Poland –6%, Romania –8%, Russian Federation 0%, Slovakia –8%, Slovenia –8%, Switzerland –8%, Ukraine 0%, United States of America –7%.

2.1 The Hague, Bonn, Marrakech

Since the adoption of the Kyoto Protocol, there were four years of negotiations and five conferences of the Parties on the implementing rules. At the first COP after Kyoto, COP4 in Buenos Aires, a two-year work programme was established with a view to completion at COP6 in The Hague in November 2000. However, the innovative aspects of the Protocol were so new that Parties had difficulties to come to grip with concepts such as the flexible mechanisms and sinks and how these could be used in practice in a way that would ensure their environmental effectiveness without becoming too burdensome in terms of procedures and administrative costs.

The EU and some other Annex I countries such as Switzerland, Iceland, Norway and New Zealand, as well as the developing countries considered the 'environmental integrity' of the Protocol, to be the overriding criterion. They insisted on strict procedures and sanctions in case of non-compliance with reporting requirements and ultimately with the targets. Other countries such as the US, Canada, Japan and Australia wanted first of all to safeguard the widest possible use of sinks and the flexible mechanisms, so as to have a maximum amount of emission reduction credits on the market and hence lower compliance costs.

The implementing rules could not be finished in The Hague and the COP was 'suspended', to resume in July 2001 in Bonn. In these few months, however, the political spectrum changed completely: in March 2001 the new US President George Bush declared that his country would not ratify the Kyoto Protocol which he referred to as 'fatally flawed'.[8] Australia supported the US and took the same position. Subsequently, the EU launched a full-fledged diplomatic attack to 'save' the Kyoto Protocol as the only available international framework to effectively fight climate change.

This resulted in a very different negotiating setting at COP6-bis in July 2001, where the US was present but, probably not least because of the political pressure exerted on them in the preceding months, declared that they would not stand in the way of other Parties reaching agreement. In this situation, compromises were finally struck on the main outstanding political issues, such as to which extent the flexible mechanisms and sinks could be used, what the sanctions for non-compliance would be and what kind of money would be made available for the developing countries for climate change activities through three new funds.

---

8 In this context, it is interesting to note that the US is a party to the UNFCCC, which was ratified by President George Bush Sr. and that, as a party to the Convention, the US is committed to limit and reduce greenhouse gas emissions.

At COP7 in October-November 2001 in Marrakech, the political agreements reached in Bonn were translated into legal decisions[9] which paved the way for Parties to – finally – proceed with ratification of the Kyoto Protocol.

Today,[10] almost two and a half years later, over 120 countries have ratified the Protocol, including the EU, Japan, Canada and important developing countries such as China, India, Brazil and South-Africa. Still, the Protocol has not yet entered into force since, although more than 55 Parties have ratified the Protocol, these do not cover 55% of Annex I countries' emissions in 1990.[11] Without the US, this second condition can only be met when Russia ratifies the Protocol. Russia has pledged to do so at several occasions, including at the World Summit on Sustainable Development in Johannesburg in September 2002. However, it has still not done so and, when pressed, keeps referring to the need for more analysis of the economic impact of ratification for Russia. Yet, the economic gains that Russia can get from selling surplus credits stemming from its over-generous target and from investments in JI projects are obvious and on this basis there is still hope that Russia will fulfil its commitment and ratify.

At the same time, there is no way back, at least not for the EU and other countries committed to fight climate change. Even without the Kyoto Protocol in force, these countries will do their utmost[12] to curb emission trends and get to the targets they accepted under the Protocol or the EU burden sharing.[13]

2.2 The role of the Commission in international negotiations

The European Community is a Party to the UNFCCC[14] and has ratified the Kyoto Protocol in May 2002.[15] Both the Convention and the Protocol are so-called mixed agreements,[16] which means that some of the issues dealt with come under EC competence and some come under the competence of individual Member States. The ratification instruments contain a declaration of competence, the purpose of which is to determine for which issues the Community is competent and for which competence remains with the Member

9 Some specific aspects notably as regards the use of sinks were agreed later, at COP8 in Delhi and COP9 in Milan, and some smaller issues are still under negotiation.

10 This article is based on developments up to 1.5.2004.

11 Article 25(1) KP.

12 For example, the EU's 6th Environmental Action Programme, adopted by Decision 1600/2002/EC explicitly states that the Community is committed to achieving an 8% reduction in emissions of greenhouse gases by 2008 to 2012 compared to 1990 levels, and that in the longer term global emissions of greenhouse gases will need to be reduced by approximately 70% compared to 1990 levels.

13 See *infra*.

14 Council Decision 94/69/EC, OJ 1994 L 33/11.

15 Council Decision 2002/358/EC, OJ 2002 L 130/1.

16 Cf. Rosas (1998).

States. Generally, for the parts falling under EC competence, negotiations are conducted by the Commission under a mandate from the Council.

The declaration of competence for the UNFCCC lists as measures of EC competence a number of measures taken at Community level with relevance for climate change, namely instruments in the area of energy, waste, agriculture, etc., while the declaration for the Kyoto Protocol is more generic, in line with more recent practice in the European Community.

Prior to the adoption of the UNFCCC, the Council had agreed that the Commission, in accordance with Article 300 EC,[17] participates in the negotiations on behalf of the EC concerning issues of Community competence.[18] For the negotiations on the Kyoto Protocol, there was the intention to ask the Council for a negotiating mandate. However, the Commission did not pursue this. The exact reasons for this are not documented but it is likely that the Commission anticipated difficulties with the Member States in accepting that the Commission negotiates on their behalf – and thus accepting Community competence – on issues that are not only of importance for the environment, but that could have major economic impact.

Since then, the Commission has often used Communications to set out its views and proposals for the international negotiations on climate change. These have constituted an input to the EU position, laid down by the Council in the form of Council conclusions adopted prior to or during COPs. Although the Commission could have contested this practice as incompatible with the Treaty and the jurisprudence of the Court of Justice, it rather opted for a pragmatic approach and accepted this way of operating. From this practice stems also the somewhat awkward situation that the Commission acts like a sixteenth member State when it comes to the formulation of EU positions. If Member States unanimously agree on a certain line to take, opposition by the Commission will not make any difference. However, as the general approach for reaching EU positions is consensus-based, this is not likely to happen very frequently and in practice the Commission has an important say in the establishment of EU positions.

This consensus-based approach has advantages and disadvantages. In a similar way as Community decisions taken by unanimity run the risk of representing the least common denominator, the need for consensus sometimes lowers the degree of ambition of EU positions. Furthermore, it makes the EU rather inflexible in the negotiations, where changes in position require lengthy debates and co-ordination meetings. This risks becoming even more difficult and time-consuming in an EU of 25 Member States.

On the positive side, finding consensus often also implies a reality check;

---

17 The Commission makes recommendations to the Council which authorises the Commission to participate in negotiations at international level for issues of EC competence and on the basis of specific negotiating directives. The Commission carries out the negotiations in continuous consultation with a special committee comprising of all the Member States.

18 Council doc. 4446/91 of 31.1.1991.

will everybody be able to actually implement later what they are signing up to now as a negotiating position? Another advantage is that once a position has been agreed, all Member States fully support it, thus ensuring that the EU can exercise its full political weight in the negotiations.

Once the negotiating positions have been agreed, the EU is represented in the negotiations by the so-called 'troika', consisting of the country that holds the Presidency, the country next in line to become EU President, and the Commission. Negotiating for the EU, including in the crucial final phases of the negotiations, the troika is in a key position to influence the process. With the Conferences of the Parties taking place once a year, the current troika system means that the Commission is the stable factor in the EU's representation at the international level. One of the tasks of the Commission is therefore to ensure continuity and consistency in EU positions.

3 Climate action at EU level

3.1 The EU Burden-Sharing Agreement

As mentioned before, under the Kyoto Protocol the EU[19] has the possibility to fulfil its commitments jointly. This means that the EU as a whole has a certain emission target, but that this can be divided up between the Member States in non-equal ways. Non-EU actors have labelled this the 'EU bubble'.

Already before COP3, the Member States established how the EU's proposed emission reduction target would be divided up between them.[20] The whole idea behind this was that some Member States still had to catch up economically and this should not be hampered by stringent emission limits. But of course allowing some Member States a generous target with an actual increase in emissions meant that other Member States would have to reduce their emissions even more than the common target. This has generally been referred to as 'burden sharing'.

The definitive burden sharing on the basis of the EU target of –8% that was agreed in Kyoto was established in June 1998.[21] It has been made legally binding in the ratification instrument[22] and notified to the Secretariat of the Convention. It should be noted that the Decision on the ratification of the Protocol and laying down the burden-sharing targets for the Member States is a self-stand-

[19] As well as any other Regional Economic Integration Organisation (REIO), Article 4 KP

[20] Council conclusions of 3 March 1997, Council Doc. CONS/ENV/97/1/Rev.1.

[21] Austria –13%, Belgium –7.5%, Denmark –21%, Germany –21%, Greece +25%, Finland 0%, France 0%, Ireland +13%, Italy –6.5%, Luxembourg –28%, Netherlands –6%, Portugal +27%, Spain +15%, Sweden +4%, United Kingdom –12.5%; cf. Council conclusions of 16-17 June 1998, Council Doc. 9702/98.

[22] Council Decision 2002/358/EC, see footnote 15 above.

ing act, applicable and binding on the Member States, irrespective of entry into force of the Protocol. Although Decision 2002/358/EC can of course be changed through the normal procedures, any changes to the burden-sharing would not have any effect in international law. Article 4 KP states that 'any such agreement shall remain in operation for the duration of the commitment period' and, since the EU burden-sharing agreement has been notified to the UNFCCC Secretariat, it is already applicable to the EC and its Member States.[23]

Although this 'burden-sharing' may seem quite convenient for the EU compared to other Parties, it should be remembered that in accordance with Article 4.6 KP the Community and the Member States are individually and jointly responsible when it comes to achieving the target. In practice this means that as long as the EU as a whole reaches a reduction of 8% of its emissions, it will not be checked under the Kyoto Protocol whether individual Member States complied with their respective targets under the burden sharing. However, if the -8% is not achieved, the European Community as well as the Member State(s) that failed to achieve its target can be held accountable and face sanctions.[24]

In this context, it is worth noting that the EU burden sharing or 'bubble' consist of the 15 Member States which the EU comprised in 1997 when the Kyoto Protocol was adopted. The countries of Central and Eastern Europe which have acceded to the EU per 1 May 2004 are not part of the EU bubble and, in accordance with Article 4.5 KP cannot become part of it during the first commitment period (2008-2012). Cyprus and Malta are special cases as, contrary to the other new Member States, they are not listed in Annex I UNFCCC and do not have any targets.

3.2 Community policies and measures

The Commission is responsible for preparing the transposition of what is agreed at international level into Community legislation. As already stated, the Community and the Member States have ratified the Kyoto Protocol in May 2002. Already before that, however, action was undertaken at EU level to reduce GHG emissions, which after all was an obligation already under the UNFCCC.

3.2.1 Monitoring

The first specific 'climate' measure was to set up rules and procedures for the adequate monitoring of emissions. Although under the UNFCCC there are no legally-binding targets to measure emissions against, it is still necessary to establish emission levels in order to find out whether emis-

[23] Cf. Article 24(4) of the 1969 Vienna Convention on the Law of Treaties.

[24] For details of the compliance regime under the Kyoto Protocol see Decision 24/CP7. See also Oberthür-Marr (2002) 81-89.

sions go down, are more or less stable over a certain period or increase. Thus, to measure progress towards the stabilisation of emissions at 1990 levels and towards the ultimate objective of the Convention, it had to be established how much each Annex I Party had emitted in 1990. Council Decision 93/389/EEC[25] (hereafter 'the Monitoring Decision') obliges Member States to put in place national programmes to tackle climate change, to make emission inventories and submit yearly reports.[26] The Commission receives these reports and makes one consolidated report for the Community. Both the Community report and the individual Member States reports are sent to the Secretariat of the UNFCCC, which publishes this information on its web site.[27] Furthermore, the Commission makes a so-called progress evaluation report, assessing whether Member States are making sufficient progress, based on already adopted as well as planned measures, towards their UNFCCC and Kyoto targets.

Under the 'Monitoring Decision', there is a committee consisting of Member States' representatives and chaired by the Commission which regularly takes stock of the situation. This mechanism is very useful: it provides transparency between Member States and creates a certain 'peer pressure' on Member States which inventories show that they are lagging behind in reducing or limiting their emissions.

In 2003, a proposal for a Decision on a Greenhouse Gas Monitoring Mechanism was adopted, repealing Decision 93/389/EC.[28] This Decision extends the scope of the Community Monitoring Mechanism and implements provisions of the Kyoto Protocol and the Marrakech Accords. It will also cover emissions at the level of individual installations, which is necessary in order to track emissions trading between companies. How exactly such emissions are to be reported is laid down in Commission Decision 2004/156/EC[29] on company-level emissions monitoring, adopted pursuant to the EU Emissions Trading Directive.[30] Also emission credits acquired through JI and CDM projects have to be accurately accounted for. It should be noted that under the Kyoto Protocol compliance with the monitoring and reporting rules is a pre-requisite for participation in the Kyoto mechanisms.

The revised Decision entered into force in March 2004.[31] As of then, Member States will be obliged to report every two years on their climate change programmes and emission forecasts. A Community registry is to be set up alongside Member State registries, as required for all Parties under the Marra-

---

25 OJ 1993 L 167/31; amended in 1999 by Decision 99/296/EC (OJ 1999 L 117/35), which extended the scope to the non-CO2 GHG.

26 For emissions of year N-1, *i.e.* report in 2000 on emissions in 1999 (cf. Article 3(2)).

27 http://unfccc.int/program/mis/ghg/index.html.

28 COM (2003) 51 of 5.2.2003, OJ C 234/51.

29 OJ 2004 L 59/1.

30 See Emissions Trading Directive explained below.

31 Decision 280/2004/EC, OJ L 49/1.

kech Accords, and provisions on the purchase and use of JI and CDM credits held in the Community registry should be elaborated further through co-decision procedure (Article 251 EC). As an additional measure to promote compliance with emission targets, Member States are committed to 'retire', on an annual basis, sufficient credits to cover their annual emissions once these have been finally determined. In addition, a review is foreseen for 2006 that will consider whether further compliance measures are necessary, and whether all commitments under the Kyoto Protocol are being respected, including supplementarity.

3.2.2 'Policies and measures' and the European Climate Change Programme

The term 'policies and measures' is used in the UNFCCC and the Kyoto Protocol to describe policy decisions taken by the public authorities of a State that lead to a reduction or limitation of GHG emissions. Some policies and measures are specific 'climate measures' in the sense that they have been elaborated with as their main objective to reduce/limit emissions. However, other policies and measures target other objectives but also have positive effects on emissions. A good example of the latter is the landfill Directive,[32] the primary objective of which was to regulate the disposal of waste in landfill sites. It also sets limits on the amount of biodegradable waste that can be disposed in landfills, and this has an important effect on the generation of methane in these landfills. Other measures in this category one can think of are agricultural measures leading to enhanced vegetation and hence uptake of carbon, as well as certain energy and transport related measures, *e.g.* speed limits (normally taken for safety reasons).

The Commission thought it was a good idea to 'bundle' the activities that would have a bearing on GHG emissions to get an overview of the orientations in the different policy areas and in particular of the scope for emission reductions. To this effect, in 1999 it set up the so-called European Climate Change Programme (ECCP).[33] The programme consists of a number of working groups that look at options for policies and measures in different policy areas: energy, transport, agriculture, industry. It includes the active involvement of the responsible Commission services, under the general management of DG Environment. The fact that the main stakeholders (Member States, NGOs, industry) are represented in each working group should ensure considerable support for the measures proposed by the respective working group.

The focus of the working groups has been to identify possible measures and their emission reduction potential (quantified in tonnes per year) and on this basis to take the most cost-effective ones and elaborate these further into

[32] Directive 99/31/EC, OJ 1999 L 182/1.

[33] COM (2000) 88 of 8.3.2000.

specific proposals. These proposals are subsequently taken up by the Commission and translated into draft legislation or other measures (*e.g.* voluntary agreements). As an illustration, the second progress report on the ECCP of May 2003[34] identified policies and measures amounting to a total emission reduction potential of 578-696 Mt, almost twice the EU's target under Kyoto!

Since the start of the ECCP, already a large number of measures has been proposed and quite a few have also been adopted at Community level, such as a Directive on the promotion of electricity from renewable energy sources,[35] a Directive on the energy performance of buildings,[36] a Directive on the taxation of energy products,[37] a Directive on the promotion of cogeneration (combined heat and power generation)[38] and a Directive on the measurement of CO2 emissions from light commercial vehicles.[39]

3.2.3 Emission trading and project-based mechanisms

Apart from the more 'traditional' policies and measures in the sectors of energy, transport etc., the Commission also took up the challenge of introducing the 'flexible mechanisms' of the Kyoto Protocol (which have been explained above) into Community law.

The concept of emissions trading (ET) and how it could work within the European Community was first set out in a Green Paper,[40] subject to a wide consultation of stakeholders. Taking into account the reactions to the Green Paper and the recommendations of the ECCP working group which had concluded that ET between individual companies could substantially reduce the costs of compliance with the Kyoto target by the EU, the Commission proceeded in 2001 with a proposal for a Directive.[41] After almost two years of negotiations in Council and the European Parliament, the Directive was adopted in July 2003.[42] For the time being, the Directive covers CO2 emissions from power stations and the main energy consuming installations, accounting in total for almost half of total CO2 emissions in the EU. However, the scope can be broadened: the Commission can propose to include additional sectors such as chemicals, aluminium and transport, and as of 2008 Member States can individually include other greenhouse gases in the scheme.

34 www.europa.eu.int/comm/environment/climat/eccp.htm.

35 Directive 2001/77/EC, OJ 2001 L 283/33.

36 Directive 2002/91/EC, OJ 2003 L 1/65.

37 Directive 2003/96/EC, OJ 2003 L 283/51.

38 Directive 2004/8/EC, OJ 2004 L 52/50.

39 Cf. ECCP Communications and Reports on www.europa.eu.int/comm/environment/climat/eccp.htm.

40 COM (2000) 87 of 8.3.2000.

41 COM (2001) 581, OJ 2002 C 75 E/33.

42 Directive 2003/87/EC, OJ 2003 L 275/32.

Thus, trading of emission quotas between companies will become a reality in the Community as of 1 January 2005. This will allow the EU to gain experience with this instrument for three years, and will enable a head start when International Emissions Trading can take off under the Kyoto Protocol at the start of the first commitment period in 2008. Furthermore, it will, for the first time, give a monetary value to greenhouse gas emissions and as emission quotas – or allocations – will inevitably be limited, this scarcity will lead us to a new society conscious of its contribution to climate change, a so-called 'carbon economy'. Exactly how limited the emission quotas will be, will become known once the national allocation plans, covering over 10.000 industrial installations, will have been adopted by Member States and accepted by the Commission. Member States were to submit such plans to the Commission by 31 March 2004 in which they set out the quantity of emission quotas that will be allocated to each installation covered by the Directive and the methodology for doing so. The Commission has to assess whether the plan is reasonable and justified in relation to the target of the respective Member State under the burden-sharing agreement and other criteria set out in the Directive.[43]

Although they are not part of the EU 'bubble', the new Member States will participate in the EU Emissions Trading scheme, consistent with their targets inscribed in the Kyoto Protocol (for all new Member States except Cyprus and Malta) and with the other criteria set out in the Directive. These countries have until 1 May 2004 to prepare their allocation plans.

In July 2003, the Commission also lived up to its promise to come forward with a proposal how credits gained through Joint Implementation and the Clean Development Mechanism could be used in the EU and fed into the EU emission trading scheme.[44] It goes beyond the requirements of the Kyoto Protocol by allowing the use by companies of credits gained through projects that reduce or limit emissions in other developed (JI) or developing (CDM) countries towards their commitments in EC law. These credits would then be used by Annex I countries to cover the corresponding emissions by companies, in order to ensure compliance with their Kyoto targets. However, in order not to undo the new scarcity of emission quotas by bringing unlimited JI/CDM credits into the system, the Directive foresees that such credits can be used up to a certain limit, to be decided by individual Member States in their National Allocation Plans in the form of a percentage of the allocations to each installation. This is of course essential in order to ensure that the overall system maintains the desired effect in terms of actual emission reductions. Nuclear projects are excluded, at least until 2012, in accordance with the Marrakech Accords. Also, in line with the long-standing negotiating position of the EU at international level, the Directive does not allow companies to use credits sinks projects, subject to review in 2006. The European Parliament voted in favour of the proposal in April 2004

[43] Cf. Article 9 and Annex III.

[44] COM (03) 403.

and final adoption by the Council is expected in May 2004. After entry into force upon publication, Member States have 12 months to transpose the Directive into national law.

Other proposals in the pipeline[45] concern Kyoto's fluorinated gases (HFCs, PFCs and SF6),[46] a framework for the eco-design of energy using products, rules for the public procurement of energy efficient and clean vehicles, energy end-use efficiency and services,[47] the promotion of biofuels[48] and an integrated strategy for a sustainable hydrogen economy.

4 Outlook and role of the Commission

4.1 Achieving the target

The start of the first commitment period under the Kyoto Protocol (2008-2012) is approaching rapidly; in less than 10 years EU emissions will have to be reduced by 8% compared to 1990 levels. Taking into consideration that according to the latest figures in 2001 emissions were at –2.3% and that without additional measures EU emissions will be at –0.5% in 2010, it will require a major effort for the EU to achieve its target.[49]

It is widely known that there are important uncertainties whether the Kyoto Protocol will enter into force. For this to happen, Russia needs to ratify, and although it has stated that it will do so 'in the near future', there are also recurring statements that ratifying Kyoto would not be in the interest of Russia and that 'further economic analysis' is needed. Again, this leaves the future rather uncertain, with Russia lingering in its role of decisive actor.

However, climate change is happening and action to stop it needs to continue, whether the Kyoto Protocol comes into effect or not. This was already recognised by EU Heads of State and Government at their Summit in Göteborg in June 2001, where they stated that 'the Community and the Member States are determined to meet their commitments under the Kyoto Protocol' and reaffirmed their 'commitment to delivering on the Kyoto targets'.[50] Therefore, irrespective of regular calls by some parts of industry to re-negotiate Kyoto or at least the EU burden sharing, the EU is committed to achieving its target of –8%. In this context, the self-standing measures the EU has taken such as the emissions trading Directive are of major importance.

---

45 www.europa.eu.int/comm/environment/climat/eccp.htm.

46 COM (2003) 492 .

47 COM (2003) 739.

48 COM (2001) 5 47, OJ 2001 C 103/205.

49 Fourth Progress Report under Council Decision 93/389/EC, COM (2003) 735 of 28.11.2003.

50 Conclusions of the European Council of 15-16 June 2001.

The revised Monitoring and Implementing Decision is the tool to track progress, for individual Member States as well as for the EU as a whole. The role of the Commission should be to keep a neutral eye on Member States actions and the (lack of) progress they make. The open exchange of experience with other Member States in the Climate Change committee[51] should allow identifying 'best practices' and – where need be – possible corrective measures. Ultimately, the Commission has of course the possibility to start a procedure before the European Court of Justice against a Member States that has not achieved its target. But these are very long procedures and in the meantime it does not help the climate. The obligation for Member States to withdraw each year an amount of credits equivalent to their annual emissions should help prevent non-compliance, and in the context of the review foreseen for 2006 the Commission should come forward with further measures if appropriate.

Once the Protocol is in force, sanctions would apply in international law in case of non-compliance, one of them being that the EU would have to reduce its emissions even more in order to 'make up' for the lost time. Thus, also at international level, it would be best to prevent non-compliance. Of course it would be particularly ironic if the EU failed to reach –8%, while certain Member States had actually over-complied, but sold their over-compliance credits to other, non-EU Parties. In that case, an extended form of 'EU solidarity', for example giving non complying Member States a preferential right to buy such extra credits, would seem highly recommendable. Another option would be to create a sort of common pot or 'compliance reserve' of any credits that Member States hold in surplus which could be drawn upon if the EU as a whole was in danger of non-compliance. An alternative to fill such a reserve could be for the Commission to also actively seek emission credits by participating in JI and CDM projects. The Community registry established under the Monitoring and Implementing Decision could be used to hold such credits. After all, the Commission is already in charge of spending vast amounts of the EU budget in projects in second and third world countries that could qualify as JI or CDM projects, and is actively involved in capacity-building work for JI and the CDM, for example, through the COOPENER programme.[52]

Already at the time of ratification of the Kyoto Protocol, there were reflections along these lines, but Member States did not find the time ripe for concrete proposals or decisions how to deal with such a situation. Member States and the Commission did, however, recognise the desirability of further Community legislation to address certain aspects of the implementation of the burden-sharing agreement, including 'arrangements (...) to ensure that the Community complies with its commitments under Article 4 KP'.[53] Some of these issues

[51] Renamed from the 'Monitoring Mechanism Committee' by Article 9 of the 2003 Monitoring and Implementing Decision, in recognition of its wider role.

[52] Decision 1230/2003/EC, OJ 2003 L 176/29.

[53] Annex II of Council doc. 6871/02 of 11.3.2002.

have been taken forward by the Monitoring and Implementing Decision, while further steps could be taken pursuant to the review foreseen for 2006.

4.2 Future commitments

Another important role of the Commission is to prepare, together with the Member States, for future commitments. It is generally acknowledged that the targets laid down in the Kyoto Protocol are only a first step. Much deeper emission cuts are needed to come closer to the ultimate objective of the UNFCCC, namely to prevent dangerous climate change.

It is often said that climate change is a global problem, which requires a global solution. This should not be interpreted in the way of the Bush administration that industrialised countries should not do anything until the developing countries do their part. It means rather that after 2012, those countries that already have emission limitation or reduction targets will need to take on even more ambitious ones, and others that currently do not have targets will have to consider taking them on.

It is not imperative that each and every country gets an emission limitation or reduction target. For example, it would certainly seem to go too far to formulate such targets for Least Developed Countries, where the primary concern of the people is survival. But there are countries, such as Mexico, South-Korea, South-Africa, Brazil and China, that are rapidly developing and for which it would seem appropriate to try to limit the impact of this development on the global climate. Targets do not necessarily need to be defined in absolute terms as in the Kyoto Protocol. However, a specific target, 'tailor-made' on the basis of its specific situation, can be useful to guide such countries in their economic development.

Ultimately, it will of course be very important that the biggest emitters of greenhouse gases, not only the EU, but also the US and Russia, take their responsibility and do their share of emission limitation. This may entail costs, but there will certainly also be win-win solutions, for example avoided costs and damages. Generally, an economy that generates less GHG emissions will in the long run often be the more healthy and competitive one (*e.g.* lower energy costs due to higher energy efficiency).

The EU Member States and the Commission should continue to emphasise this in their relations with other countries. This would best be done not by delivering it as a 'climate' message – environment not being high on the agenda of most countries these days -, but as a structural and consistent part of the EU's trade relations or specific dialogues in areas such as energy, transport, development cooperation, health, etc.

Also, the EU should become more self-confident: as the biggest economic block in the world, it should dare to demand commitment from those countries it has close economic cooperation with on issues that it considers of vital importance, such as climate change. Conditionality is practised by many countries these days; the EU should consider whether it isn't time to make this 'fist' for the fight against climate change.

Furthermore, to be a credible messenger, the EU should of course stay in the lead when it comes to emission reducing actions. The ECCP should and will continue, but it will inevitably (if only for resource reasons) be limited in scope. Therefore, in order for the EU to strengthen its policies and measures, the impact on GHG emissions should become a structural factor to take into account in the development of any EU policy, be it energy, transport, agriculture, industrial or fiscal policy, competition, and – last but certainly not least – research.

5 Conclusion

The EU has developed a leadership role in the international negotiations on climate change. It is also in the lead as regards implementing action producing real emission reductions, which reinforces its credibility at international level.

With the enlargement of the EU from 15 to 25 Member States in May 2004, the voice of the EU should become even stronger. The new Member States will represent showcases of economic development without a linear increase in GHG emissions. Of course there are Member States that are more proactive than others, or that have had circumstances which have helped them reduce emissions more than others. But the Community framework allows precisely for Member States to learn from each other and helps them identify best practices and most cost-effective options.

Having learnt from each other and continuing ever closer cooperation, is the basis for the EU's strong position also internationally. If individual Member States would negotiate, they would inevitably take less balanced positions and would be more likely to ferociously defend their own interests. In doing so, the bigger Member States would probably be more successful than the smaller ones. However, by the time the EU has come to a position in the international climate negotiations, the issue will already have been looked at from many different angles by different Member States and taken account of concerns which may also be voiced by other Parties. The clear added value of the EU is therefore that it can speak with a strong and convincing single voice.

The Commission also has a clear added value. The smaller Member States may not have the resources to develop detailed measures covering all policy sectors themselves. Also, their competitive position is more vulnerable when they take individual measures. The Commission embodies the mechanism that can help these Member States by putting forward proposals for Community-wide measures. It can also analyse certain issues and propose solutions which are fair to everyone (for example, as regards the burden-sharing of the

EU target). And it can table questions that no Member State would pose out of a certain inter-Member State solidarity, *e.g.* concerning the efficacy of a Member State's national climate change programme. This role has got its clearest dimension sofar in the context of the national allocation plans under the Emissions Trading Directive, where the Commission can reject a plan if it esteems it contains over-allocation not consistent with achieving the target under the burden-sharing of the respective Member State.

The Commission has taken the lead in climate action, not only internationally, by speaking up for and basically 'saving' the Kyoto Protocol when the Bush administration rejected it, but also within the EU by making proposals for ground-breaking measures such as the Directive on emissions trading and important measures to promote energy efficiency, renewable energy sources, etc.

Extremely motivated and highly competent persons have worked hard to take these measures forward and thus enabled progress in emission reductions in the EU. One of these persons is Ludwig Krämer who, as Head of the Unit in charge of Waste Policy, pushed relentlessly until a very important piece of legislation for the reduction of methane emissions, the Landfill Directive, was adopted. Other initiatives taken or pursued under his guidance in the waste area, aiming at enhanced re-use and waste recycling, will also contribute significantly to lower GHG emissions in the EU.

Bibliography

ALLKEMPER (1995)
L. Allkemper, *Der Rechtschutz des Einzelnen nach dem EG-Vertrag* (Baden-Baden 1995).
ARNULL (2001)
Arnull, *Private Applicants and the Action for Anullment since Cordoniu* (1/2001) *CMLRev.* 7-49.
BADER (2000)
P. Bader, *Europäische Treibhauspolitik mit handelbaren Emissionsrechten* (Berlin 2000).
BAIL, MARR & OBERTHÜR (2003)
C. Bail, S. Marr, S. Oberthür, *Klimaschutz und Recht* (2003/2) *Handbuch zum Europäichen und deutschen Umweltrecht* 254-304.
BÄR & ALBIN (2000)
S. Bär, S. Albin, *The 'Environmental Guarantee' on the rise? The Amended Article 95 after the Revision Through the Treaty of Amsterdam* (1/ 2000) *EJLR* 119-134.
BÄR & KRAEMER
S. Bär, A. Kraemer, *European Environmental Policy After Amsterdam* (2/1998) *JEL* 315-330.
BENARDI (2002)
A. Benardi, *Europe sans frontières et droit pénal,* (1-3/2002) *Revue de science criminelle et de droit pénal comparé,* 3.
BERKHOUT & SMITH (2003)
F. Berkhout, A. Smith, *Carbon Flows between the EU and Eastern Europe: Baselines, Scenarios and Policy Options* (2003/3) *IEA* 199-219.
BIRNIE & BOYLE (2002)
P. W. Birnie, A. E. Boyle, *International Law and the Environment.* Second Edition (Oxford UP 2002).
BLUME, SCHMIDT & ZIESCHE (2001)
J-F. Blume, A. Schmidt, M. Zschiesche, *Verbandsklagen im Umwelt- und Naturschutz in Deutschland 1997-1999 – eine empirische Untersuchung,* Hrsg. Unabhängiges Institut für Umweltfragen e.V. (UFU) Berlin/Halle (Berlin 2001).
BRADY (1998)
K. Brady, *New Convention on Access to Information and Public Participation in Environmental Matters* (28/2-1998) *EPL* 69-75.
BURUMA & SOMSEN (2001)
Y. Buruma and J. Somsen, *Een strafwetgever te Brussel inzake milieubescherming?* 17/2001 *NJB* 795-797.
BUWAL 2000
BUWAL – Environmental Protection Agency of Switzerland: *Wie wirkt das Beschwerderecht der Umweltschutzorganisationen* (Bern 2000).
COOK, ROBERTS & LOWTHER (2002)
D. Cook, M. Roberts, J. Lowther *The International Wildlife Trade*

and Organised Crime – A review of the evidence and the role of the UK, Regional Research Institute, University of Wolverhampton (Wolverhampton 2002).

CORINO (2001)
C. Corino, *The Kyoto Protocol: Tradable mission credits and compensatory solutions under the Bonn Resolutions* (10/2001) *EELR* 294-298.

DEIMAN-DYSSLI (1995)
S. Deimann and B. Dyssli (eds.), *Environmental Rights – Law, Litigation and Access to Justice* (London 1995).

DE SADELEER (2003)
N. De Sadeleer, *Procedures for derogations from the principle of approximation of laws under Article 95 EC* (40/2003) CMLRev 889-915.

DE SADELEER, ROLLER & DROSS (2003)
N. de Sadeleer, G. Roller, M. Dross, *Access to Justice in Environmental Matters – Final Report* (Brussels 2003).

DHONDT (2003)
N. Dhondt, *Integration of Environmental Protection into other EC Policies* (Groningen 2003).

DOPPELHAMMER (2000)
M. Doppelhammer, *More Difficult than Finding The Way round Chinatown? The IPPC Directive and its implementation* (2000/7 & 2000/8-9) *EELR* 199-206 & 246-252.

DROSS (2004)
M. Dross, *Access to Justice in Environmental Matters* – Article to be published in (4/2004) *Tilburg Foreign Law Review.*

EBBESSON (2002)
J. Ebbesson (ed.), *Access to Justice in Environmental Matters in the EU* (London 2002).

EPINEY (1999)
A. Epiney, *Gemeinschaftsrecht und Verbandsklage* (1999) NVwZ 485-495.

EPINEY (2003)
A. Epiney, *Zu den Anforderungen der Aarhus-Konvention an das europäische Gemeinschaftsrecht*, Additional edition (2003) ZUR 176-183.

EPINEY & SOLLBERGER (2002)
A. Epiney, K. Sollberger, *Zugang zu Gerichten und gerichtliche Kontrolle im Umweltrecht, Umweltbundesamt* – Forschungsbericht 1/02 (Berlin 2002).

FAIRLEY ET AL. (2002)
R. Fairley *et al.*, *Riding the New Wave of European Water Law. How Member States are Tackling the Water Framework Directive* (2002/8-9) *EELR* 232-238.

FITZMAURICE (1992)
M. Fitzmaurice, *International Legal Problems of the Environmental Protection of the Baltic Sea* (London 1992).
FITZPATRICK (1992)
B. Fitzpatrick, *Local Protection of the Environment and European Commubity Harmonization Directives: the London Lorries Case* (1/1992) *JEL* 121-137.
FÜHR, ORMOND, GEBERS & ROLLER (1992)
M. Führ, T. Ormond, B. Gebers, G. Roller, *Access to Justice – study carried out by Öko-Institut in cooperation with Field* (Darmstadt 1992).
GALE (1997)
L. Gale, *Access to Environmental Justice before the ECJ* (May-June 1997) *EBLR* 132-136.
GILLESPIE (2002)
A. Gillespie, *International Environmental Law, Policy and Ethics* (Cambridge UP 2002).
GLINSKI & ROTT (2000)
C. Glinski, P. Rott, *Waste incineration – legal protection in European Environmental Law* (2000) *JEL* 129-154.
GLOWKA (1994)
L. Glowka, et al, *A Guide to the Convention on Biological Diversity*, IUCN, (Gland and Cambridge 1994).
GODT (2000A)
C. Godt, *Enforcement of Environmental Law by Individuals and Interest Groups: Reconceptualizing Standing* (23/2000) *JCP* 79 -105.
GODT (2000B)
C. Godt, *EG-rechtlicher Rahmen der Stoffstromsteuerung durch Produktregulierung*, in M. Führ (ed), *Stoffstromsteuerung durch Produktregulierung* (Baden Baden 2000) 41-55.
GONZALEZ-LEBRERO (2000)
R. A. Gonzalez-Lebrero, *The Damage to the Environment Caused by the Noise from Aircraft* (2000/35) *ETR* 161-174.
GRAICHEN & HARDERS (2002)
P. Graichen, E. Harders, *Die Ausgestaltung des Internbationalen Emissionshandels nach dem Kyoto-Protokoll und seine nationalen Umsetzungsvoraussetzungen* (2002/2) *ZUR* 73-81.
GRIMEAUD (2001)
D. Grimeaud, *Reforming EU Water Law: Towards Sustainability?* (2001/2, 3 & 4) *EELR* 41-51, 88-97 & 125-135.
HAIGH (1994)
N. Haigh, *Manual of Environmental Policy: the E.C. and Britain* (London 1994).

HAMELL (1999)
M. Hamell, *Soil and Agriculture*, speech delivered at the European Soil Forum 24-26 November 1999 (Bonn 1999), *pro manuscripto*.

HANF (2003)
D. Hanf, *Talking with the 'pouvoir costituant' in Times of Constitutional Reform: The ECJ on Private Applicant's Access to Justice* (3/2003) *Maastricht Journal of European and Comparative Law* 265-290.

HATTAN (2003)
E. Hattan, The Implementation of EU Environmental Law (3/2003) *JEL* 273-288.

HAYMAN & BRACK (2002)
G. Hayman & D. Brack, *International Environmental Crime – The nature and control of environmental black markets*, Workshop supported by the European Commission. Report, Royal Institute of International Affairs, 2002.

HEDEMANN-ROBINSON (2003A)
M. Hedemann-Robinson, *The EU Directives on Waste Electrical and Electronic Equipment and on the Restriction of Use of Certain Hazardous Substances in Electrical and Electronic Equipment: adoption achieved* (2/2003) *EELR* 52-60.

HEDEMANN-ROBINSON (2003B)
M. Hedemann-Robinson, *EU waste management law and the marine environment* (3/2003) *EL* 89-104.

JACKSON (2000)
C. Jackson, *Playing by the Green Rules: the adoption and neglect of EU environmental laws* (2000 London)

JANS (2000)
J. H. Jans, *European Environmental Law* (Groningen 2000).

JANS (2003)
J.H. Jans (ed.), *The European Convention and the Future of European Environmental Law*, proceedings of the Avosetta Group of European Environmental Lawyers (Groningen 2003).

JENDROSKA (2002)
J. Jendroska, *Citizens' access to court and enforcement in Poland*, paper presented for the Avosetta Meeting on January 12/13, 2002 in Copenhagen (http://www-user.uni-bremen.de/~avosetta/access2002.html).

JENDROSKA (2003)
J. Jendroska, *The UN ECE Protocol on Strategic Environmental Assessment, Do We Need It?* in L. Krämer (ed.), *Recht und Um-Welt, Essays in Honour of Prof. Dr. Gerd Winter* (Groningen 2003) 281-293.

KISS & SHELTON (1995)
A. Kiss, D. Shelton, *Traité de droit européen de l'environnement* (Paris 1995).

KÖNGETER (2003)
M. Köngeter, *Die Ambivalenz effektiven Rechtschutzes Einzelner gegen EG-Verordnungen* (4/2003), *Zeitschrift für Rechtsvergleichung,* Internationales Privatrecht und Europarecht 123-132.

KRÄMER (1991)
L. Krämer, *Participation of Environmental Organisations in the Activities of the EEC,* in M. Führ and G. Roller (eds.) *Participation and Litigation Rights of Environmental Associations in Europe* (Frankfurt am Main 1991) 129-140.

KRÄMER (1992)
L. Krämer, *Focus on European Environmental Law* (London 1992).

KRÄMER (1995)
L. Krämer, *Rights of Complaint and Access to Information at the Commission of the EC,* in S. Deimann and Bernard Dyssli (eds.) Environmental Rights – Law, Litigation and Access to Justice (London 1995) 53-70.

KRÄMER (1996A)
L. Krämer, *Public interest litigation in environmental matters before European Courts* (1/1996) *JEL* 1 -18.

KRÄMER (1996B)
L. Krämer, *L'apport de la Communauté européenne au droit de l'environnement,* in *Quel avenir pour le droit de l'environnement?* Faculté Universitaires Saint-Louis (Bruxelles 1996) 451-460.

KRÄMER (1996C)
L. Krämer, *Community waste management and consumer rights – theory and practice* In n. Boucquey (ed.) European Consumer Law and Waste Management (Louvain-la-Neuve 1999) 31-56.

KRÄMER (1996D)
L. Krämer, *Environmental Protection and Trade – the Contribution of the European Union,* in R. Wolfrum (ed.) *Enforcing Environmental Standards: Economic Mechanism as Viable Means?* (Heidelberg 1996) 413-450.

KRÄMER (1997A)
L. Krämer, *Focus on European Environmental Law* (London 1997).

KRÄMER (1997B)
L. Krämer, *Vom Rechte das mit uns geboren – der Einzelne im gemeinschaftlichen Umweltrecht* in L. Krämer, H.-W. Micklitz, K. Tonner (eds.) Law and diffuse interests in the European legal order (Baden-Baden 1997) 741-754.

KRÄMER (1998)
L. Krämer, *Droit à l'environnement et installations de déchets,* in *Mankind and the Environment, en hommage à Alexandre Kiss* (Paris 1998) 353-365.

KRÄMER (1999A)
L. Krämer, *El accidente de Aznalcóllar y el Derecho Comunitario Ambiental* (May 1999) *Revista Mensual de Gestión Ambiental* 13-24.
KRÄMER (1999B)
L. Krämer, *The Citizen in the Environment – Access to Justice* (3/1999) *RMJ* 1-20.
KRÄMER (2000A)
L. Krämer, *E.C. Treaty and Environmental Law*. Fourt Edition (London 2000).
KRÄMER (2000B)
L. Krämer, *Die Rechtsprechung der EG-Gerichte zum Umweltrecht 1998 und 1999* (9-10/2000) *EuGRZ* 265-280.
KRÄMER (2000C)
L. Krämer, *Introduction into the European chemicals regulation: Basic structures and performance*, in G. Winter (ed), *Risk Assessment and Risk Management of Toxic Chemicals in the European Community, Experiences and Reform* (Baden Baden 2000) 14-32.
KRÄMER (2000D)
L. Krämer, *Perspektiven eines EG-Stoffstromrechts: Vom Gefahrstoff- und Abfallrecht zu einer umweltorientierten Produkt-regelung auf Gemeinschaftsebene*, in M. Führ (ed), *Stoffstromsteuerung durch Produktregulierung* (Baden Baden 2000) 225-245.
KRÄMER (2001)
L. Krämer, *The Distinction between Waste and Product in Community Law*, in *Waste in Europe at the Beginning of the 21st Century* (Madrid 2001) 15-35.
KRÄMER (2002A)
L. Krämer, *Casebook on EU Environmental Law* (Oxford 2002).
KRÄMER (2002B)
L. Krämer, *Die Rechtsprechung der EG-Gerichte zum Umweltrecht 2000 und 2001* (10/2002) *EuGRZ* 483-498.
KRÄMER (2002C)
L. Krämer, *Altlasten und gemeinschaftliches Umweltrecht* in V. Franzius, H.-P. Lühr and G. Bachmann (eds), *Boden und Altlasten Symposium 2001* (Berlin 2002) 49-72.
KRÄMER (2002D)
L. Krämer, *Thirty years of EC Environmental Law: Perspectives and Prospectives* (2002) *YEEL* 155-182.
KRÄMER (2002E)
L. Krämer, *Umweltmediation und Umweltpolitik in der Europäischen Union* (2002) *NuR* 257-264.
KRÄMER (2002F)
L. Krämer, *Europäisches Umweltrecht in der Rechtsprechung des EuGH* (Wien 2002).

KRÄMER (2002G)

L. Krämer, *Precaution, the protection of health and the environment, and the free circulation of goods within the European Union*, in E. Freytag *et al* (eds.) *The role of Precaution in Chemicals Policy*, Conference proceedings 15-16 November 2001 (Wien 2001) 42-54.

KRÄMER (2003A)

L. Krämer, *E.C. Treaty and Environmental Law*. Fifth Edition (London 2003).

KRÄMER (2003B)

L. Krämer, *Überlegungen zu Ressourceneffizienz und Recycling*, in *Aktuelle Entwicklungen des europäischen und deutschen Abfallrechts* (Berlin 2003) 119-156.

KRÄMER (2003C)

L. Krämer, *Dispute Resolution in Environmental Law – Can the European Union be a model?* in A. Kiss, D. Shelton, K. Ishibashi (eds.) Economic Globalization and Compliance with International Environmental Agreements (London 2003) 271-282.

KRÄMER (2004)

L. Krämer, *The Roots of Divergence: A European Perspective*, in N. J. Vig & M. Faure (eds.), *Green Giants? Environmental Policies of the United States and the European Union* (Cambridge MA 2004) 53-72.

KROISS (2001)

F. Kroiss, *Die Verbandsbeschwerde im Umweltrecht – neue Impulse für Österreich durch die Aarhus Konvention* (3/2001) *RU* 87-95.

KUIK (2003)

O. Kuik, *Climate Change Policies, Energy Security and Carbon Dependency: Trade-offs for the European Union in the Longer Term* (3/2003) *IEA* 221-242.

KUNZLIK (1997)

P. Kunzlik, *The Enforcement of EU Environmental Law: Article 169, the Ombudsman and the Parliament* (2/1997) *EELR* 46-52.

LACASTA, DESSAI & POWROSLO (2002)

N.S. Lacasta, S. Dessai, E. Powroslo, *Consensus among many voices: articulating the European Union's position on climate change* (2002/32) *Golden Gate University Law Review*, 351-414.

LEE-ABBOT (2003)

M. Lee and C. Abbot , *The Usual Suspects? Public Participation under the Aarhus Convention* (1/2003) *The Modern Law Review* 80-108.

LEAL ARCAS (2001)

R. Leal Arcas, *Kyoto Protocol: an Adequate Agreement?* (10/2001) *EELR* 282-293.

LEPRINCE (2001)

S. Leprince, *La nouvelle directive 2000/60CE instituant un cadre pour l'action communautaire dans le domaine de l'eau: coordination et efficacité?* (2001) *Actualités du Droit* 833-875.

LONG & MEREU (1999)

A. Long, C. Mereu, *Integrated Pollution Prevention and Control: the Implementation of Directive 96/61/EC* (6/1999) *EELR* 180-184.

LÜBBE-WOLFF (1996)

G. Lübbe-Wolff, *Der Vollzug des europäischen Umweltrechts* (Berlin 1996).

MACRORY (1992)

R. Macrory, *The Enforcement of Community Environmental Laws: Some Critical Issues* (29/1992) *CMLRev.* 347-369.

MARGUÉNAUD (2002)

J.P. Marguénaud, *Vol de nuit et droit européen des droits de l'homme* (2002/2) *RJE* 171-181.

MARTIN-RETORTILLO BAQUER (2003)

L. Martín-Retortillo Baquer, *El Ruido: una pesadilla del justicia* (2003/58) *Revista interdisciplinar de gestión ambiental.*

MATHIESEN (2003)

S. Mathiesen, *Public Participation in Decision-making and Access to Justice in EC Environmental law: the Case of certain Plans and Programmes* (2/2003) *EELR* 36-52.

MONTINI (2001)

M. Montini, *La necessità ambientale nel diritto internazionale e comunitario* (Padova 2001).

MUÑOZ (2003)

R. Muñoz, *Le Contrôle de L'application du Droit Communautaire: Plus Qu'une Amélioration, Une Reforme Nécessaire* (6/2003) *Europe Juris Classeur* 3-7.

NEWELL & GRANT (2000)

P. Newell & W. Grant, *Environmental NGOs and EU Environmental Law* (2000) *YEEL* 225-252.

NICOLAZO & KACZMAREK (1996)

J.L. Nicolazo, B. Kaczmarek, *L'Europe de l'eau, de Bruxelles à Paris* (Paris, 1996).

OBERTHÜR & MARR (2002)

S. Oberthür, S. Marr, *Das System der Erfullungskontrolle des Kyoto-Protokolls: Ein Schritt zur Wirksamen Durchsetzung im Umweltvölkerrecht* (2002/2) *ZUR* 81-89.

OBERTHÜR & OTT (1999)

S. Oberthür, H.E. Ott, *The Kyoto Protocol: International Climate Policy for the 21st Century* (Berlin 1999).

ÖKO-INSTITUT (1994)

Öko-Institut *Final report on access to Justice – Legal standing for environmental associations in the European Community* (4/1994) *RECIEL* 261-267.

ONIDA (2000)

M. Onida, *Challenges and Opportunities in EC Waste Management: Perspectives on the Problem of End of Life Vehicles* (2000) *YEEL* 253-289.

ONIDA (2003)

M. Onida, *The Determination of EC Environmental Technical Rules, with specific regard to the Implementation Procedures of the Commission*, in A. Biondi et al. (eds) *Scientific evidence in European Environmental Rule-Making* (London 2003) 187-208.

ONIDA (2004)

M. Onida, *The practical application of Article 95(4) and 95(5) EC Treaty: what lessons can we learn?* in M. Pallemaerts (ed.), *Greening production and consumption or creating barriers to trade?* VUB University Press, Brussels (to be published in Fall 2004).

PAQUE (2003)

G. Paque, *EU environmental noise policy: an integrated approach* Euronoise (Naples 2003).

PEEL (2001)

J. Peel, *Giving the Public a Voice in the Protection of the Global Environment* (2001) *Colorado Journal of International Environmental Law and Policy* 1 -25.

POCKLINGTON (2002)

D. Pocklington, *European emissions trading – the business perspective* (7/2002) *EELR* 209-218.

POPPE (2003)

Final Report : Organised Crime in the EU Member States, study for the Commission by Betreuungsgesellschaft für Umweltfragen Dr Poppe MbH Umweltgutachtorganisation in cooperation with Max-Planck Institute for Foreign and International Criminal Law (Freiburg 2003).

POUSSENKOVA (2003)

N. Poussenkova, *Russia: A Country with an Unpredictable Past* (2003/3) *IEA* 243-267.

PRIEUR (1998)

M. Prieur, *Complaints and Appeals in the Area of Environment in the Member States of the European Union* Study commissioned by DG XI European Commission (Funchal 1998).

RAGNEMALM (2000)

H. Ragnemalm, *The Community Courts and Openness within the European Union* (1999) *Cambridge Yearbook of European Legal Studies* (Oxford 2000) 19-30.

RAGOLLE (2003)

F. Ragolle (2003), *Access to justice for private applicants in the Community legal order: recent (r)evolutions* (1/2003) *EELR* 90-101.

REHBINDER & LOPERENA (2001)
E. Rehbinder, D. Loperena, *Legal Protection of environmental rights* (31/6-2001) *EPL* 282-293.

ROLLER (2001)
G. Roller, *La Comitologie – entre efficacité et légitimité démocratique* CEDRE Facultés Universitaires St. Louis (Brussels 2001).

ROSAS (1998)
A. Rosas, *Mixed Agreements in* M. Koskenniemi (ed.) *International Law aspects of the European Union: Symposium on the International Law aspects of the Common Foreign and Security Policy of the European Union and of the Union's External relations* University of Helsinki and University of Cambridge (The Hague 1998).

RYALL (2002)
A. Ryall, *The EIA Directive and the Irish Planning Participation Fee* (2002/3) *JEL* 317-329.

SACH & REESE (2002)
K. Sach, M. Reese, *Das Kyoto Protocoll nach Bonn und Marrakesch* (2002/2) *ZUR* 65-73.

SAETWIK (1988)
S. Saetevik, *Environmental Co-operation between the North Sea States* (Belhaven 1988).

SANCY (1998)
M. Sancy, *La nouvelle directive IPPC : le recours au concept de meilleure technique disponible – quelques réflexions*, in *Les Hommes et l'Environnement – Etudes en hommage à Alexandre Kiss* (Paris 1998) 381-387.

SANDS (2003)
P. Sands, *Principles of International Environmental Law*. Second Edition (Cambridge 2003).

SELIN (2001)
C. Selin, *Your Money or Your Life: a Look at the Convention on the Protection of the Environment through Criminal Law* (10/2001) *RECIEL* 106-114.

SEVENSTER (2000)
H. Sevenster, *The Environmental Guarantee After Amsterdam: does the Emperor Have New Clothes?* (2000) *YEEL* 291-310.

SCHEUING (1999)
D.-H. Scheuing, *Instrumente zur Durchführung des europäischen Umweltrechts* (1999) *NVwZ* 475-485.

SCHRADER (2001)
C. Schrader, *Europa bald mit Umweltstrafrecht?* (5-6/2001) *Umweltmagazin* 16-17.

SCHIKHOF (1998)
S. Schikhof, *Direct and Individual Concern in Environmental Cases: The Barriers to Prospective Litigants* (10/1998) *EELR* 279 -281.
SCHWARZE (2002)
J. Schwarze, *Der Rechtsschutz Privater vor dem Europäischen Gerichtshof* (19/2002) *DVBl* 1297-1315.
SHEATE (2003)
W. R. Sheate, *The EC Directive on Strategic Environmental Assessment: A Much-Needed Boost for Environmental Integration* (12/2003) *EELR* 331-347.
SIMILÄ (2002)
J. Similä, *Pollution Regulation and its effects on technological innovations* (2002) *JEL* 143-160.
SOMSEN (2000)
H. Somsen, *The Private Enforcement of Member State Compliance with EC Environmental Law: an Unfulfilled Promise?* (2000) *YEEL* 311-360.
SOMSEN (2003)
H. Somsen, *Current Issues of Implementation, Compliance and Enforcement of EC Environmental Law* in L. Krämer (ed.), *Recht und Umwelt – Essays in Honour of Prof. Dr. Gerd Winter* (Groningen 2003) 416-428.
STANNERS & BOURDEAU (1995)
D. Stanners and P. Bourdeau (eds), *Europe's Environment: The Dobris Assessment* (Copenhagen 1995).
STOLZENBERG & AHLERS (2003)
H.C. Stolzenberg-J. Ahlers, *Substitution of Hazardous Substances; Links to Precaution, Innovation, Regulation*, in L. Krämer (ed.), *Recht und Um-Welt, Essays in Honour of Prof. Dr. Gerd Winter* (Groningen 2003).
STOOKES (2003)
P. Stookes, *Getting to the Real EIA* (2003/2) *JEL* 141-151.
STOTZ (2003)
R. Stotz in H.-W. Rengeling (ed.) *Handbuch zum Europäischen und deutschen Umweltrecht* (München 2003).
THIEFFRY (1998)
P. Thieffry, *Droit Européen de l'Environnement* (Paris 1998).
THIEFFRY (2001)
P. Thieffry, *Le nouveau cadre de la politique communautaire de l'eau* (2/2001) *Juris-Classeur Europe* 4, quoted by Leprince (2001) 834.
THOMAS & GUITART (2003)
V. Thomas, R. Guitart, *Lead Pollution from Shooting and Angling and a Common Regulative Approach* (3-4/2003) *EPL* 143-149.
THOMAS & OWEN (1996)
V. Thomas, M. Owen, *Preventing lead toxicosis of European waterfowl*

by regulatory and non-regulatory means (23-4/1996) *Environmental Conservation* 358-364.

TREBILCOCK & HOWSE (1995)
M. Trebilcock, R. Howse, *The Regulation of International Trade.* Second Edition (London and New York 1995)

USHER (2003)
J.A. Usher, *Direct and individual concern – an effective remedy or a conventional solution* (5/2003) *EELR* 575-600.

VERSCHUUREN (2000)
J. Verschuuren *et al.*, *Complaint procedures and access to justice in the field of the environment within the EU* IMPEL-Report (Tilburg 2000).

VAN CALSTER (1977)
G. Van Calster, *EC Noise Legislation and Policy* (6/1997) *EELR* 174-181.

VAN RIJSWICK (2003)
M. van Rijswick, *EC Water Law in Transition: the challenge of integration* (2003) *YEEL* 249-304.

VERHEYEN (2000A)
R. Verheyen, *Article 95 EC Treaty in practice: the Europeam Commission decisions on creosote, sulphite, nitrates and nitrites – Case Note* (9(1)2000) *RECIEL* 71-75.

VERHEYEN (2000B)
R. Verheyen, *The Environmental Guarantee in practice – a Critique* (9(2)2000) *RECIEL* 178-187.

WANG & WISER (2002)
X. Wang, G. Wiser, *The Implementation and Compliance Regimes under the Climate Change Convention and its Kyoto Protocol* (2002/11/2) *RECIEL* 181-199.

WANNERÅS (2003)
P. Wennerås, *Fog and Acid Rain Drifting from Luxembourg over Art. 95(4) EC* (6/2003) *EELR* 169-178.

WEGENER (1998)
B. Wegener, *Die Rechte des Einzelnen* (Baden-Baden 1998).

WIERS (2002)
J. Wiers, *Trade and Environment in the EC and the WTO* (Groningen 2002).

WILLIAMS (1995)
R. Williams, *The European Commission and the Enforcement of Environmental Law: An Invidious Position* (1995) *YEL* 351-399.

WILLIAMS (2002)
R. Williams, *Enforcing European Environmental Law: Can the European Commission be Held to Account?* (2002) *YEEL* 271-294.

WINKELMANN (2002)
C. Winkelmann, *Die Verbandsklage im Umweltschutz im internationalen Vergleich Umweltbundesamt* (Berlin 1992).

WINTER (2000)

G. Winter (ed), *Risk Assessment and Risk Management of Toxic Chemicals in the European Community, Experiences and Reform* (Baden Baden 2000).

WITTER (1996)

E. Witter, *Towards zero accumulation of heavy metals in soils* (43/1996) *Fertilizer Research* 225-233.

ZSCHIESCHE (2002)

M. Zschiesche, *The Aarhus Convention – More Citizens participation by setting out environmental standards?* (2002/1) *ELNI Review* 21-29.

Abbreviations

CEN	European Commitee for Standardisation
CMLRev.	Common Market Law Review
DVBl	Deutsches Verwaltungsblatt
EC	European Community (Treaty)
EBLR	Environmental Business Law Review
EELR	European Environmental Law Review
EJLR	European Journal of Law Reform
EL	Environmental liability
ELNI	Environmental Law Network International
EPL	Environmental Policy and Law
ETR	European Transport Law
EU	(Treaty on) European Union
EuGRZ	Europäische Grundrechte Zeitschrift
IEA	International Environmental Agreements Politics, Law and Economics
IMO	International Maritime Organization
JCP	Journal of Consumer Policy
JEL	Journal of Environmental Law
NJB	Nederlands Juristenblad
NuR	Natur und Recht
NVwZ	Neue Zeitschrift für Verwaltungsrecht
POPs	Persistent Organic Pollutants
RECIEL	Review of European Community and International Environmental Law
RJE	Revue juridique de l'environnement
RMJ	Resource Management Journal
RU	Recht der Umwelt
TOA	Treaty of Amsterdam
YEEL	Yearbook of European Environmental Law
YEL	Yearbook of European Law
ZUR	Zeitschrift für Umweltrecht

Table of Cases

European Court of Justice and Court of First Instance

Table of Legislation

Directives

Council Directive 67/548/EC on the classification, packaging and labelling of dangerous substances, OJ 1967 196/1

Council Directive 70/156/EEC relating to the type-approval of motor vehicles and their trailers, OJ 1970 L 42/1

Council Directive 70/157/EEC relating to the permissible sound level and the exhaust system of motor vehicles, OJ 1970 L 42/16 as last amended by Directive 99/101/EC, OJ 1999 L 334/41

Council Directive 70/220/EEC relating to measures to be taken against air pollution by gases from positive-ignition engines of motor vehicles, OJ 1970 L 76/1

Council Directive 71/320/EEC relating to the braking devices of certain categories of motor vehicles and of their trailers, OJ 1971 L 202/37 as amended by Directive 98/12/EEC, OJ 1998 L 81/1

Council Directive 72/306/EEC relating to the measures to be taken against the emission of pollutants from diesel engines for use in vehicles, OJ 1972 L 190/1

Council Directive 73/404/EEC relating to detergents, OJ 1973 L 347/51

Council Directive 74/150/EEC relating to the type approval of wheeled agricultural or forestry tractors, OJ 1974 L 84/10

Council Directive 74/151/EEC relating to certain parts and characteristics of wheeled agricultural or forestry tractors, OJ 1974 L 84/25

Council Directive 75/439/EEC on waste oils, OJ 1975 L 194/23

Council Directive 75/440/EEC on the quality required of surface water intended for abstraction of drinking water in the Member States, OJ 1975 L 194/26

Council Directive 75/442/EEC on waste, OJ 1975 L 194/39 as amended by Directive 91/156/EEC, OJ 1991 L 78/ 32

Council Directive 75/716/EEC relating to the sulphur content of certain liquid fuels, OJ 1975 L 307/22

Council Directive 76/160/EEC concerning the quality of bathing water, OJ 1976 L 31/1

Council Directive 76/403/EEC on the disposal of PCB and PCT, OJ 1976 L 108/41. Replaced as from 16/9/1996 by Council Directive 96/59/EC, OJ 1996 L 243/31

Council Directive 76/464/EEC on pollution caused by certain dangerous substances discharged into the aquatic environment of the Community, OJ 1976 L 129/23

Council Directive 76/769/EEC on the restriction on marketing and use of chemicals, OJ 1976 L 262/201

Council Directive 78/170/EEC on the performance of heat generators for space heating and the production of hot water in new or existing non- industrial buildings and on the insulation of heat and domestic hot-water distribution in new non-industrial buildings, OJ 1978 L 52/32

Council Directive 78/176/EEC on waste from the titanium dioxide industry, OJ 1978 L 54 /19

Council Directive 78/659/EEC on the quality of fresh waters needing protection or improvement in order to support fish life, OJ 1978 L 222/1

Council Directive 78/319/EEC on toxic and dangerous waste, OJ 1978 L 84/43

Council Directive 79/113/EEC relating to the determination of the noise emission of construction plant and equipment, OJ 1979 L 33/15

Council Directive 79/409/EEC on the conservation of wild birds, OJ 1979 L 103/1

Council Directive 79/869/EEC concerning the methods of measurements and frequencies of sampling and analysis of surface water intended for the abstraction of drinking water in the Member States, OJ 1979 L 271/44

Council Directive 79/923/EEC on the quality required of shellfish waters, OJ 1979 L 281/47

Council Directive 80/51/EEC on the limitation of noise emissions from subsonic aircraft, OJ 1980 L 18/26 as amended by Directive 83/206/EEC, OJ 1983 L 117/15

Council Directive 80/68/EEC on the protection of groundwater against pollution caused by certain dangerous substances, OJ 1980 L229/11 as last amended by Directive 98/83/EC, OJ 1998 L 330/32

Council Directive 80/777/EEC relating to the exploitation and marketing of natural mineral waters, OJ 1980 L 229/1

Council Directive 80/778/EEC relating to the quality of water intended for human consumption, OJ 1980 L 229/11

Council Directive 80/779/EEC on air quality limit values and guide values for sulphur dioxide and suspended particulates, OJ 1980 L 229/30

Council Directive 80/1268/EEC relating to the fuel consumption of motor vehicles, OJ 1980 L 375/36

Council Directive 82/176/EEC on limit values and quality objectives for mercury discharges by the chlor-alkali electrolysis industry, OJ 1982 L 81/29

Council Directive 83/513/EEC on limit values and quality objectives for cadmium discharges, OJ 1983 L 291/1.

Council Directive 84/156/EEC on limit values and quality objectives for mercury discharges by sectors other than the chlor-alkali electrolysis industry, OJ 1984 L 74/ 49

Council Directive 84/360/EEC on the combating of air pollution from industrial plants, OJ 1984 L 188/20

Council Directive 84/491/EEC on limit values and quality objectives for discharges of hexachlorocyclohexane, OJ 1984 L 274/11

Council Directive 84/532/EEC relating to common provisions for construction plant and equipment, OJ 1984 L 300/111

Council Directive 84/533/EEC relating to the permissible sound power level of compressors, OJ 1984 L 300/123
Council Directive 84/534/EEC relating to the permissible sound power level of tower cranes, OJ 1984 L 300/130
Council Directive 84/535/EEC relating to the permissible sound power level of welding generators, OJ 1984 L 300/142
Council Directive 84/536/EEC relating to the permissible sound power level of power generators, OJ 1984 L 300/149.
Council Directive 84/537/EEC relating to the permissible sound power level of powered hand- held concrete-breakers and picks, OJ 1984 L 300/156
Council Directive 84/538/EEC relating to the permissible sound power level of lawnmowers, OJ 1984 L 300/171
Council Directive 84/631/EEC on the supervision and control within the European Community of the transfontier shipment of hazardous waste, OJ 1984 L 326/31
Council Directive 85/337/EEC on the assessment of the effects of certain public and private projects on the environment, OJ 1985 L 175/40 as amended by Council Directive 97/11/EC, OJ 1997 L 73/5
Council Directive 85/339/EEC on containers of liquids for human consumption, OJ 1985 L 176/18
Council Directive 86/278/EEC on the protection of the environment, and in particular of the soil, when sewage sludge is used in agriculture, OJ 1986 L 181/6
Council Directive 86/280/EEC on limit values and quality objectives for discharges of certain dangerous substances included in List I of the Annex to the Directive 76/464/EEC, OJ 1986 L 181/16
Council Directive 86/594/EEC on airborne noise emitted by household appliances, OJ 1986 L 344/24
Council Directive 86/662/EEC on the limitation of noise emitted by hydraulic excavators, rope-operated excavators, dozers, loaders and excavator- loaders, OJ 1984 L 384/1
Council Directive 88/609/EEC on the limitation of emissions of certain pollutants into the air from large combustion plants, OJ 1988 L 336/1
Council Directive 89/106/EEC relating to construction products, OJ 1989 L 40/12
Council Directive 89/369/EEC on the prevention of air pollution from new municipal waste incineration plants, OJ 1989 L 163/32
Council Directive 89/429/EEC on the reduction of air pollution from existing municipal waste-incineration plants, OJ 1989 L 203/50
Council Directive 89/629/EEC on the limitation of noise emission from civil subsonic jet aeroplanes, OJ 1989 L 363/27

Council Directive 90/313/EEC on the freedom of access to environmental information, OJ 1990 L 158/56; will be replaced with effect from 14.2.2005 by Directive 2003/4/EC on public access to environmental information, OJ 2003 L 41/26

Council Directive 90/394/EEC on the protection of workers from the risks related to exposure to carcinogens at work, OJ 1990 L 196/1

Council Directive 91/157/EEC on batteries and accumulators, OJ 1991 L 78/38, as amended by Commission Directive 98/101/EEC, OJ 1999 L 1/1

Council Directive 91/271/EEC concerning urban waste water treatment, OJ 1991 L 135/ 40

Council Directive 91/414/EEC concerning the placing of plant protection products on the market, OJ 1991 L 230/1

Council Directive 91/676/EEC concerning the protection of waters against pollution caused by nitrates from agricultural sources, OJ 1991 L375/1

Council Directive 91/689/EEC on hazardous waste, OJ 1991 L 377/20

Council Directive 92/14/EEC on the limitation of the operation of aeroplanes covered by Part II, Chapter 2, Volume 1 of Annex 16 to the Convention on International Civil Aviation, second edition (1988), OJ 1992 L 076/21, as amended by Directive 98/20/EC, OJ 1998 L 107/4

Council Directive 92/43/EEC on the conservation of natural habitats and of wild fauna and flora, OJ 1992 L 206/7

Council Directive 92/75/EEC on the indication by labelling and standard product information of the consumption of energy and other resources by household appliances, OJ 1992 L 297/16

Council Directive 93/76/EEC to limit carbon dioxide emissions by improving energy efficiency (SAVE), OJ 1993 L 237/28

European Parliament and Council Directive 94/12/EC relating to measures to be taken against air pollution by emissions from motor vehicles and amending Directive 70/220/EEC, OJ 1994 L 100/42

European Parliament and Council Directive 94/62/EC on packaging and packaging waste, OJ 1994 L 365/10

European Parliament and Council Directive 94/63/EC on the control of volatile organic compound emissions resulting from the storage of petrol and its distribution from terminals to service stations, OJ 1994 L 365/24

Council Directive 94/66/EC amending Directive 88/609/EEC on the limitation of emissions of certain pollutants into the air from large combustion plants, OJ 1994 L 337/83

Council Directive 94/67/EC on the incineration of hazardous waste, OJ 1994 L 365/34

Council Directive 95/21/EC concerning the enforcement, in respect of shipping using Community ports and sailing in the waters under the jurisdiction of the Member States, of international standards for ship safety, pollution prevention and shipboard living and working conditions (port State control), OJ 1995 L 157/1

European Parliament and Council Directive 96/57/EC on energy efficiency requirements for household electric refrigerators, freezers and combinations, OJ 1996 L 236/36

Council Directive 96/61/EC concerning integrated pollution prevention and control, OJ 1996 L 257/26

Council Directive 96/62/EC on ambient air quality assessment and management, OJ 1996 L 296/55

Council Directive 96/82/EC on the control of major-accident hazards involving dangerous substances, OJ 1997 L 10/13

European Parliament and Council Directive 97/24/EC on certain components and characteristics of two or three-wheel motor vehicles, OJ 1997 L 226/42

European Parliament and Council Directive 98/8/EC concerning the placing of biocidal products on the market, OJ 1998 L 123/1

European Parliament and Council Directive 98/34/EC laying down a procedure for the provision of information in the field of technical standards and regulations, OJ 1998 L 204/37

European Parliament and Council Directive 98/69/EC relating to measures to be taken against air pollution by emissions from motor vehicles and amending Council Directive 70/220/EEC, OJ 1998 L 350/1

European Parliament and Council Directive 98/70/EC relating to the quality of petrol and diesel fuels and amending Council Directive 93/12/EEC, OJ 1998 L 350/58

Council Directive 98/83/EC on the quality of water intended for human consumption, OJ 1998 L 330/32

Council Directive 1999/13/EC on the limitation of emissions of volatile organic compounds due to the use of organic solvents in certain activities and installations, OJ 1999 L 85/1

Council Directive 1999/31/EC on the landfill of waste, OJ 1999 L 182/1

European Parliament and Council Directive 1999/94/EC relating to the availability of consumer information on fuel economy and CO2 emissions in respect of the marketing of new passenger cars, OJ 2000 L 12/16

European Parliament and Council Directive 2000/14/EC relating to the noise emission in the environment by equipment for use outdoors, OJ 2000 L 162/1

European Parliament and Council Directive 2000/53/EC on end of life vehicles, OJ 2000 L 269/34

European Parliament and Council Directive 2000/60/EC establishing a framework for Community action in the field of water policy, OJ 2000 L 327/1

European Parliament and Council Directive 2000/76/EC on the incineration of waste, OJ 2000 L 332/91

European Parliament and Council Directive 2000/84/EC on summer-time arrangements, OJ 2001 L 31/21
European Parliament and Council Directive 2001/18/EEC on the deliberate release into the environment of genetically modified organisms and repealing Council Directive 90/220/EEC, OJ 2001 L 106/1
European Parliament and Council Directive 2001/42/EC on the assessment of the effects of certain plans and programmes on the environment, OJ 2001 L 197/30
European Parliament and Council Directive 2001/43/EEC amending Council Directive 92/23/EEC relating to tyres for motor vehicles and their trailers and to their fitting, OJ 2001 L 211/25
European Parliament and Council Directive 2001/77/EC on the promotion of electricity produced from renewable energy sources in the internal electricity market, OJ 2001 L 283/33
European Parliament and Council Directive 2001/80/EC on the limitation of emissions of certain pollutants into the air from large combustion plants, OJ 2001 L 309/1
European Parliament and Council Directive 2001/81/EC on national emission ceilings for certain atmospheric pollutants, OJ 2001 L 309/22
European Parliament and Council Directive 2002/30/EC on the establishment of rules and procedures with regard to the introduction of noise-related operating restrictions at Community airports, OJ 2002 L 85/40
European Parliament and Council Directive 2002/32/EC on undesirable substances in animal feed, OJ 2002 L 140/10
European Parliament and Council Directive 2002/49/EC relating to the assessment and management of environmental noise, OJ 2002 L 189/12
European Parliament and Council Directive 2002/91/EC on the energy performance of buildings, OJ 2003 L 1/65
European Parliament and Council Directive 2002/95/EC on the restriction of the use of certain hazardous substances in electrical and electronic equipment, OJ 2002 L 37/19
European Parliament and Council Directive 2002/96/EC on waste electrical and electronic equipment (WEEE), OJ 2002 L 37/24
European Parliament and Council Directive 2003/17/EC amending Directive 98/70/EC relating to the quality of petrol and diesel fuels, OJ 2003 L 76/10
European Parliament and Council Directive 2003/35/EC providing for public participation in respect of the drawing-up of certain plans and programmes relating to the environment and amending with regard to public participation and access to justice Council Directives 85/337/EEC and 96/61/EC, OJ 2003 L 156/17
European Parliament and Council Directive 2003/44/EEC amending Directive 94/25/EC relating to recreational craft, OJ 2003 L 214/18

European Parliament and Council Directive 2003/87/EC establishing a scheme for greenhouse gas emission allowance trading within the Community and amending Council Directive 96/61/EC, OJ 2003 L 275/32

Council Directive 2003/96/EC restructuring the Community framework for the taxation of energy products and electricity, OJ 2003 L 283/51

European Parliament and Council Directive 2004/8/EC on the promotion of cogeneration based on a useful heat demand in the internal energy market and amending Directive 92/42/EEC, OJ 2004 L 52/50

Regulations

Council Regulation (EEC) 2078/92 on agricultural production methods compatible with the requirements of the protection of the environment and the maintenance of the countryside, OJ 1992 L 215/85

Council Regulation (EEC) 3280/92 amending Regulation (EEC) No 1576/89 laying down general rules on the definition, description and presentation of spirit drinks, OJ 1992 L 327/3

Council Regulation (EEC) 259/93 on the supervision and control of shipments of waste within, into and out of the European Community, OJ 1993 L 30/1

Council Regulation (EEC) 793/93 on the evaluation and control of the risks of existing substances, OJ 1993 L 84/1

Council Regulation (EEC) 2847/93 establishing a control system applicable to the common fisheries policy, OJ 1993 L 261/1

Council Regulation (EC) 1164/1994 establishing a Cohesion Fund, OJ L 130/1 as amended by Council Regulation (EC) 1264/1999, OJ L 161/57

Council Regulation (EC) 925/1999 on the registration and operation within the Community of certain types of civil subsonic jet aeroplanes which have been modified and recertificated as meeting the standards of volume I, Part II, Chapter 3 of Annex 16 to the Convention on International Civil Aviation, third edition (July 1993), OJ 1999 L 115/1

Council Regulation (EC) 1257/1999 on support for rural development from the European Agricultural Guidance and Guarantee Fund (EAGGF) and amending and repealing certain Regulations, OJ 1999 L 160/80

Council Regulation (EC) 1259/1999 establishing common rules for direct support schemes under the common agricultural policy, OJ 1999 L 160/113

European Parliament and Council Regulation (EC) 1980/2000 on a revised Community eco-label award scheme, OJ 2000 L 237/1

European Parliament and Council Regulation (EC) 2037/2000 on substances that deplete the ozone layer, OJ 2000 L 244/1

European Parliament and Council Regulation (EC) 761/2001 allowing voluntary participation by organisation in a Community eco-management and audit scheme (EMAS), OJ 2001 L 114/1

European Parliament and Council Regulation (EC) 1049/2001 regarding public access to European Parliament, Council and Commission documents, OJ 2001 L 145/43
European Parliament and Council Regulation (EC) 782/2003 on the prohibition of organotin compounds on ships, OJ 2003 L 115/1
Council Regulation (EC) 1782/2003 establishing common rules for direct support schemes under the common agricultural policy and establishing certain support schemes for farmers and amending Regulations (EEC) 2019/93, (EC) 1452/2001, (EC) 1453/2001, (EC) 1454/2001, (EC) 1868/94, (EC) 1251/1999, (EC) 1254/1999, (EC) 1673/2000, (EEC) 2358/71 and (EC) 2529/2001, OJ 2003 L 270/1
European Parliament and Council Regulation (EC) 648/2004 on detergents, OJ 2004 L 104/1

Decisions

Council Decision 77/795/EEC establishing a common procedure for the exchange of information on the quality of surface fresh water in the Community, OJ 1977 L 334/29
Council Decision 81/462/EEC on the conclusion of the Convention on long-range transboundary air pollution, OJ 1981 L 171/11
Council Decision 93/389/EEC for a monitoring mechanism of Community CO2 and other greenhouse gas emissions, OJ 1993 L 167/31
Council Decision 94/69/EC concerning the conclusion of the United Nations Framework Convention on Climate Change, OJ 1994 L 33/11
Commission Decision 98/523 on a procedure relating to the application of Council Regulation (EEC) 2408/92 (Case VII/AMA/10/97 – Access to Karlstad airport), OJ 1998 L 233/25
Council Decision 1999/296/EC amending Decision 93/389/EEC for a monitoring mechanism of Community CO2 and other greenhouse gas emissions, OJ 1999 L 117/35
Commission Decision 1999/830/EC on the national provisions notified by the Kingdom of Denmark concerning the use of sulphites, nitrites and nitrates in foodstuffs, OJ 1999 L 329/1
Commission Decision 1999/836/EC on the national provisions concerning mineral wool notified by Germany derogating from Directive 76/769/EC adapting to technical progress for the 23rd time Council Directive 67/548/EEC on the approximation of the laws, regulations and administrative provisions relating to the classification, packaging and labelling of dangerous substances, OJ 1999 L 329/100
Commission Decision 2000/479/EC on the implementation of a European pollutant emission register (EPER) according to Article 15 of Council Directive 96/61/EC concerning integrated pollution prevention and control (IPPC), OJ 2000 L 192/36

Commission Decision 2000/509/EC concerning the draft national provisions notified by the Kingdom of Belgium concerning the limitations of the marketing and use of organostannic compounds, OJ 2000 L 205/7

Commission Decision 2000/532 replacing Decision 94/3/EC establishing a list of wastes pursuant to Article 1(a) of Council Directive 75/442/EEC on waste and Council Decision 94/904/EC establishing a list of hazardous waste pursuant to Article 1(4) of Council Directive 91/689/EEC on hazardous waste, OJ 2000 L 226/3

Commission Decision 2001/524/EEC relating to the publication of references for standards EN 13428:2000, EN 13429:2000, EN 13430:2000, EN 13431:2000 and EN 13432:2000 in the Official Journal of the European Communities in connection with Directive 94/62/EC on packaging and packaging waste, OJ 2001 L 190/21

Commission Decision 2001/570/EC on draft national provisions notified by the Federal Republic of Germany on limitations on the marketing and use of organostannic compounds, OJ 2001 L 202/37

Council Decision 2001/792/EC, Euratom establishing a Community mechanism to facilitate reinforced cooperation in civil protection assistance interventions, OJ 2001 L 297/7

European Parliament and Council Decision 2455/2001/EC establishing the list of priority substances in the field of water policy and amending Directive 2000/60/EC, OJ 2001 L 331/1

Commission Decision 2002/59/EC concerning draft national provisions notified by the Kingdom of the Netherlands under Article 95(5) of the EC Treaty on limitations on the marketing and use of creosote-treated wood, OJ 2002 L 23/37

Commission Decision 2002/231/EC establishing revised ecological criteria for the award of the Community eco-label to footwear and amending Decision 1999/179/EC, OJ 2002 L 77/50

Council Decision 2002/358/EC concerning the approval, on behalf of the European Community, of the Kyoto Protocol to the United Nations Framework Convention on Climate Change and the joint fulfilment of commitments thereunder, OJ 2002 L 130/1

Commission Decision 2002/366/EC on the national provisions notified by the Republic of Austria under Article 95(4) of the EC Treaty concerning the maximum admissible content of cadmium in fertilizers, OJ 2002 L 132/65

Commission Decision 2002/398/EC on the national provisions notified by the Republic of Finland under Article 95(4) of the EC Treaty concerning the maximum admissible content of cadmium in fertilisers, OJ 2002 L 138/15

Commission Decision 2002/399/EC on the national provisions notified by the by the Kingdom of Sweden under Article 95(4) of the EC Treaty concerning the maximum admissible content of cadmium in fertilisers, OJ 2002 L 138/24

Commission Decision 2002/884/EC concerning national provisions on restrictions on the marketing and use of creosote-treated wood notified by the Netherlands under Article 95(4) and (5) of the EC Treaty, OJ 2002 308/30

European Parliament and Council Decision 1600/2002/EC laying down the Sixth Community Environment Action Programme, OJ 2002 L 242/1

Commission Decision 2003/1/EC relating to national provisions on limiting the importation and placement on the market of certain NK fertilisers of high nitrogen content and containing chlorine notified by France pursuant to Article 95(5) of the EC Treaty, OJ 2001 L 1/72

Commission Decision 2003/653/EC relating to national provisions on banning the use of genetically modified organisms in the region of Upper Austria notified by the Republic of Austria pursuant to Article 95(5) of the EC Treaty, OJ 2003 L 230/74

Commission Decision 2003/829/EC concerning national provisions on the use of azodyes notified by Germany under Article 95(4) of the EC Treaty, OJ 2003 L 311/46

European Parliament and Council Decision 1230/2003/EC adopting a multiannual programme for action in the field of energy: 'Intelligent Energy – Europe' (2003 – 2006), OJ 2003 L 176/29

Commission Decision 2004/1/EC concerning national provisions on the use of short-chain chlorinated paraffins notified by the Kingdom of the Netherlands under Article 95(4) of the EC Treaty, OJ 2004 L 1/20

Commission Decision 2004/156/EC establishing guidelines for the monitoring and reporting of greenhouse gas emissions pursuant to Directive 2003/87/EC of the European Parliament and of the Council, OJ 2004 L 59/1

Commission Decision 2004/279/EEC concerning guidance for implementation of Directive 2002/3/EC of the European Parliament and of the Council relating to ozone in ambient air, OJ 2004 L 87/50

European Parliament and Council Decision 280/2004/EC concerning a mechanism for monitoring Community greenhouse gas emissions and for implementing the Kyoto Protocol, OJ 2004 L 49/1.

Other

Commission Recommendation 1999/125/EC on the reduction of CO2 emissions from passenger cars (ACEA), OJ 1999 L 40/49

Commission Recommendation 2000/303/EC on the reduction of CO_2 emissions from passenger cars (KAMA), OJ 2000 L 100/55

Commission Recommendation 2000/304/EC on the reduction of CO_2 emissions from passenger cars (JAMA), OJ 2000 L 100/57

European Parliament and Council Recommendation 2001/331/EC providing for minimum criteria for environmental inspections in the Member States, OJ 2001 L 118/41

Council Framework Decision 2003/80/JHA on the protection of the environment through criminal law, OJ 2003 L 29/55

Publications Ludwig Krämer

I Books – Handbooks – Commentaries

18) (ed.): Recht und Um-Welt. Essays in honour of Gerd Winter, Groningen: Europa Law Publishing, 2003.
17) (ed.) European Environmental Law, Dartmouth: Ashgate, 2003.
16) - Casebook on EU Environmental Law, Oxford: Hart, 2002.
- Europäisches Umweltrecht in der Rechtsprechung des EuGH; dargestellt anhand von 50 Urteilen, Wien: Verlag Österreich, 2002.
15) (ed. with Marco Onida): Codice dell'ambiente, Milano: 2001.
14) (with Florian Ermacora): Die Umsetzung des europäischen Umweltrechts in Österreich, Wien: Verlag Österreich, 2000.
13) EC Environmental Law, 4th ed. London: Sweet & Maxwell, 2000, 5th ed. London: Sweet & Maxwell, 2003.
12) - Umweltpolitische Aktionsprogramme mit Leitlinien und Regelungsansätzen – Direkte und indirekte Verhaltenssteuerung – Rechtsakte und Handlungsformen. In: H.W. Rengeling (ed.) Handbuch zum europäischen und deutschen Umweltrecht , Köln-Berlin-Bonn-München: Heymanns, 1st ed. 1998; 2nd ed. 2002.
11) (ed. with H.-W. Micklitz and K. Tonner): Law and diffuse interests in the European legal order – Liber amicorum Norbert Reich, Baden-Baden: Nomos 1997.
10) Focus on European Environmental Law. Vol.II, London: Sweet & Maxwell 1997.
9) (ed.with L. Parejo Alonso): Derecho medioambiental de la Unión Europea, Madrid: 1996.
8) European Environmental Law Casebook, London: Sweet & Maxwell, 1993.
7) (with N. Paelologou): I sinthiki EOK kai i prostasia tou periballontos, Athens: 1992.
6) Focus on European Environmental Law, Vol.I, London: Sweet & Maxwell 1992.
5) Umweltpolitik, in: M. Röttinger – C. Weyringer (eds): Handbuch der Europäischen Integration, Wien: 1st. ed. 1991; 2nd ed. 1996.
4) Umweltrecht der EU.Textsammlung, Baden-Baden: Nomos. 1st ed. 1991; 2nd ed. 1995; 3rd ed. 1998; 4th ed. 2001.
3) Droit Communautaire de l'environnement, Fascicule 1900. Paris: Juris Classeur 1990, Fascicule 120. Paris: Juris Classeur 1992.
2) EC Treaty and environmental law, London: Sweet & Maxwell. 1st ed. 1991; 2nd ed. 1995; 3rd ed. 1998.
- Derecho Ambiental y Tratado de la Comunidad Europea, Madrid: 1999.
- Manuale del diritto per l'ambiente, Milano: Giuffré 2002.

1) Umweltpolitik (Articles 6, 174-176 EG-Vertrag), in: v.d. Groeben-J. Thiesing-C.D. Ehlermann (eds): Kommentar zum EG/EU-Vertrag, Baden-Baden: Nomos. 3rd ed. 1983; 4th ed. 1991; 5th ed. 1999, 6th ed. 2003/2004.

II Articles

140) The Roots of Divergence: A European Perspective, in N.J. Vig and M. Faure (eds.): Green Giants? Environmental Policies of the United States and the European Union. The MIT Press, Cambridge MA 2004, p. 53-72.

139) Überlegungen zu Ressourceneffizienz und Recycling. In: Aktuelle Entwicklungen des europäischen und deutschen Abfallrechts, Dokumemtation zur Sondertag der Gesellschaft für Umweltrecht e.V.Berlin, Erich Schmidt Verlag, 2003, p. 119-156.

138) Environment in the "governance" process, in: L. Meulemans-I. Niestroy-C. Hey (eds): Environmental Governance in Europe, Utrecht: Lemma 2003, p. 69-77.

137) Summaries of EC Commission communications and reports 1.1.2000-31.12.2001, in: The Yearbook of European Environmental Law. 3(2003), p. 823-843.

136) Das sechste Umweltprogramm der EU. Zeitschrift für Europäisches Planungs- und Umweltrecht 2002, p. 1.

135) Trente ans de droit communautaire: ébauche d'un bilan. Lusíada, Revista de Ciencia e Cultura (Porto) 1-2/2003, p. 481.

134) Dispute resolution in environmental law – can the European Union be a model? In: A. Kiss-D. Shelton-K. Ishibashi (eds): Economic globalization and compliance with international environmental agreements. The Hague – London – New York: Kluwer, 2003, p. 271.

133) Liability for damage to the environment and the European Union. In: Institute for Environmental Policy, Prag (ed): Approximation: the never ending story. Prague:2002, p. 33.

132) On integration of scientific and technical evidence into EU environmental rule-making. In: A. Biondi and others (eds): Scientific evidence in European environmental rule-making. The Hague-London-New York: Kluwer, 2003, p. 209.

131) (Book review) J. Wiers: Trade and environment in the EC and WTO: a legal analysis. Common Market Law Review 2003, p. 783.

130) - Vertraulichkeit und Öffentlichkeit: Europäisches Vorverfahren und Zugang zu Informationen. In: L. Krämer (ed.): Recht und Um-Welt. Essays in honour of Gerd Winter Groningen: Europa Law Publishing, 2003, p. 153.

- Access to letters of formal notice and reasoned opinions in environmental law matters. European Environmental Law Review 2003, p. 197-203.

129) The future role of the ECJ in the development of European environmental law. In: J. Jans (ed.) The European Convention and the Future of European Environmental Law. Groningen: Europa Law Publishing, 2003, p. 85.

128) (in Chinese language) The EC, environmental protection and trade. Global Law Review (China) 2002, p. 421.

127) Die Rechtsprechung der EG-Gerichte zum Umweltrecht 2000 und 2001. Europäische Grundrechte Zeitschrift 2002, p. 483.

126) (in Hungarian language) The role of the European Commission in monitoring the environmental transposition of EC law. Európai Jog 2003, no. 3, p. 3.

125) Europäischer Umweltschutz und deutscher Föderalismus aus der Sicht der Praxis. In: M. Kloepfer (ed.): Umweltföderalismus. Berlin 2002, p. 143.

124) Umweltmediation und Umweltpolitik der Europäischen Union. Natur und Recht 2002, p. 257-264

123) (Book review) Jan Jans, European Environmental Law. 2000, Common Market Law Review 2002, 188.

122) Thirty years of EC environmental law: perspectives and prospectives. The Yearbook of European Environmental Law 2(2002) p. 155.

121) Precaution, the protection of health and the environment and the free circulation of goods within the EU in: E. Freytag-T. Jakl-G. Loibl-M. Wittmann (eds): The role of precaution in chemicals policy. Vienna 2002, p. 42.

120) Le sixième programme communautaire d'action environnementale. Lusíada. Revista de ciencia e cultura (Porto) 1-2/2000, p. 551.

119) Rechtsfragen betreffend den Emissionshandel mit Treibhausgasen der Europäischen Gemeinschaft. In: H.W. Rengeling (ed.): Klimaschutz durch Emissionshandel. Köln usw. 2001, p. 1.

118) Umweltvereinbarungen und Gemeinschaftsrecht. In: H.W. Rengeling (ed.): Instrumente des Umweltschutzes im Wirkungsverbund. Baden-Baden: Nomos 2001, p. 80.

117) Altlasten und gemeinschaftliches Umweltrecht in: V.Franzius-H.P. Lühr-G. Bachmann (eds): Boden und Altlasten. Berlin 2002, p. 49.

116) Zur Übernehme des EG-Umweltrechts durch die Beitrittsländer. Jahrbuch des Umwelt- und Technikrechts 2001, p. 455.

115) Dimensionen integrierter Gewässerpolitik. In: T. Bruha-H. Koch (eds): Integrierte Gewässerpolitik in Europa. Baden-Baden: Nomos 2001, p. 41.

114) Integración de los requisitos medioambientales en las demás politicas de la Comunidad Europea in: Centro de Documentación Europea (ed.): Curso de derecho europeo del medio amibente. Sevilla 2000, p. 243

113) The distinction between waste and product in Community law. (a) In: European Waste Club (ed.): Waste in Europe at the beginning of the 21st century. Madrid 2001, p. 15; (b) in: W. Klett-G. Schmitt-Glaeser-H. Schnurer (eds): Abfall ohne Ende? oder: Ende der Abfalleigenschaft durch Umwandlung zu Rohstoff. Köln 2001, p. 253.

112) (Book review) C.W. Backes: Duurzame groei? Milieu en Recht 2000, p. 314.

111) Entwicklungsperspektiven der Europäischen Abfallverwertungspolitik. In:G. Lübbe-Wolff (ed.): Umweltverträgliche Abfallverwertung. Baden-Baden: Nomos, 2001, p. 73.

110) Perspektiven eines EG-Stoffstromrechts. Vom Gefahrstoff- und Abfallrecht zu einer umweltorientierten Produktregelung auf Gemeinschaftsebene. In: M. Führ (ed.): Stoffstromsteuerung durch Produktregelung. Baden-Baden: Nomos, 2000, p. 225.

109) The European dimension of Dutch environmental policy. The relationship between The Hague and Brussels. In: H. Sevenster (ed.): Nederlandse milieurecht: de Europese dimensie. Alphen 2000, p. 1.

108) (Book review): S.Albin: Die Vollzugskontrolle des europäischen Umweltrechts Zeitschirft ür Umweltrecht 2000, p. 348.

107) Die Rechtsprechung der EG-Gerichte zum Umweltschutz 1998 und 1999. Europäische Grundrechte Zeitschrift 2000, p. 265.

106) Bilanz und Perspektiven der europäischen Umweltpolitik, unter besonderer Berücksichtigung der Erweiterung. (a) In: Walter-Hallstein-Institut Berlin (ed.): Verfassungsrechtliche Reformen zur Erweiterung der Europäischen Union. Baden-Baden: Nomos 2000, p. 69 (b) (in Russian language): Environmental Policy of the EU. In: Ekologitscheskoge prabo 2/2002, p. 45.

105) Differentiation in EU environmental policy. (a) European Environmental Law Review 2000, p. 133; (b) in: B. de Witte-D. Hanf-E. Vos (eds): The many faces of differentiation in EU law. Antwerpen-Oxford-New York 2001, p. 83.

104) Environmental law in the European Union. In: F. Morrison-R. Wolfrum (eds): International, regional and national environmental law. the Hague-London-Boston, 2000 p. 455.

103) (Book review) D. Geradin: Trade and the environment. A comparative study of EC and US law. The Yearbook of European Environmental Law 1(2000), p. 543.

102) European Community eco-labelling in transition. The Yearbook of European Environmental Law 1(2000), p. 123.

101) Towards an EU compost strategy in: Federal Ministry for the Environment, Youth and Family Affairs (ed.): Compost – quality approach in the European Union. Vienna 1998, p. 6.

100) General principles of Community environmental law and their translation into secondary law. Law and European Affairs 1999, p. 355.

99) Introduction into the European chemicals regulation: basic structures and performance in: G. Winter (ed.): Risk assessment and risk management of toxic chemicals in the European Community. Baden-Baden: Nomos 2000, p. 14-34.

98) The citizen and the environment – access to justice. (a) Resource Management Journal (NZ) 1999, Nov. p. 1-20; (b) Environmental Liability 2000, p. 127.

97) Community waste management and consumer rights – theory and practice. In: N.Boucquey (ed.): European consumer law and waste management. Louvain-la-Neuve 1999, p. 31-56.

96) The jurisdiction of the European Courts in environmental matters between 1 July 1997 and 30 June 1998. Anuário de direito do ambiente 1998, p. 209-231.

95) El accidente de Aznalcóllar y el derecho comunitario ambiental. Revista mensual de gestión ambiental 5/1999, p. 13-25.

94) La normativa comunitaria in materia di rifiuti e lo stato di attuazione in Italia. In: Rifiuti nel XXI secolo; il caso Italia tra Europa e Mediterraneo. Milano 1999, p. 9-31.

93) EU-rechtliche Rahmenbedingungen in der Abfallwirtschaft. In: B. Gallenkemper-W. Bidlingmaier-H. Doldens.R. Stegmann (eds): 6. Münsteraner Abfalltage. Münster 1999, p. 33-38.

92) (Book review): C. London-M. Llamas: EC law on the protection of the environment and the free movement of goods. International and Comparative Law Quarterly 1998, p. 486.

91) (Book review): C. Zacker: Abfall im gemeinschaftlichen Umweltrecht. Common Market Law Review 1998, p. 1222-1223.

90) Die Europäische Union und der Export von Abfällen in die Dritte Welt. Kritische Justiz 1998, p. 345-357.

89) Die Rechtsprechung der EG-Gerichte zum Umweltrecht 1995-1997. Europäische Grundrechte Zeitschrift 1998, p .309-320.

88) The jurisdiction of the European Courts in environmental matters between 1 January 1995 and 30 June 1997. Anuário de direito do ambiente 1997, p. 147-172.

87) Perspektiven des europäischen Umweltrechts. In: Umweltrecht zwischen Gemeinschaftsrecht und Deregulierung. Österreichische

Umweltrechtstage 1997. Vienna 1998, Schriftenreihe des Österreichischen Wasser- und Abfallwirtschaftsverbandes, Heft 1169, p. 19-38 .

86) Europäisches Umweltrecht. Chronik vom 1.4.95 bis 31.12.97. Zeitschrift für Umweltrecht 1998, p. 70-76.

85) Das „hohe Schutzniveau“ für die Umwelt im EG-Vertrag – industrielle Norm oder politische Vorgabe? Zeitschrift für Umweltrecht 1997, p. 303-308.

84) Droit à l'environnement et installations de déchets. In: M. Prieur-C. Lambrechts (eds): Les hommes et l'environnement. Etudes en hommages à Alexandre Kiss. Paris 1998, p. 353-365.

83) O direito comunitario do ambiente e o papel do avocado. In: Ambiforum (ed.): O Jurista e o ambiente. Lisboa 1997, p. 7-28.

82) Grundlagen(Grundfragen) der EU-Umweltverfassung. Ziele, Kompetenzen, Durchführung. In: N. Reich-R. Heine-Mernik (eds): Umweltverfassung und nachhaltige Entwicklung in der Europäischen Union. Baden-Baden: Nomos 1997, p. 11-32.

81) Vom Rechte, das mit uns geboren – der Einzelne im gemeinschaftlichen Umweltrecht. In: L. Krämer-H.W. Micklitz-K. Tonner (eds): Liber amicorum N. Reich. Baden-Baden: Nomos 1997, p. 741-754.

80) (Book review): M. Dubrulle (ed.): Future European Policy and Subsidiarity. M. Ruffert: Subjektive Rechte im Umweltrecht der Europäischen Gemeinschaft. Common Market Law Review 1997, p. 1083-1087.

79) Recent developments in EC environmental law.** In: J. Holder (ed.): The impact of EC environmental law in the United Kingdom. Chichester 1997, p. 9-26.

78) La responsabilité civile dans le domaine de l'environnement, sujet de la réglementation communautaire. Lusiada, revista de ciencia e cultura. Numero especial 1996, p. 119-133.

77) Direct effect of EC environmental law.** In: H. Somsen (ed.): Protecting the European environment: enforcing EC law. London 1996, p. 99-134.

76) Contribution of the European Union. In: S. Nespor (ed.): Rapporto monidale sul diritto dell'ambiente. Milano 1996, p. 69-79.

75) L'apport de la Communauté européenne au droit de l'environnement. In: F. Ost-S. Gutwirth (eds): Quel avenir pour le droit de l'environnement? Bruxelles 1996, p. 451-460.

74) Environmental protection and trade – the contribution of the European Union.** In: R. Wolfrum (ed.): Enforcing environmental standards: economic mechanisms as viable means? Berlin-Heidelberg: 1996, p. 413-450.

73) Meeresumweltschutz im Recht der Europäischen Gemeinschaften.** (a) In: H. Koch-R. Lagoni (eds) Meeresumweltschutz für Nord- und Ostsee. Baden-Baden: Nomos 1996, p. 129-179; (b) A protecção ambiental do meio marinho no direito das Comunidades Europeias. Anuário de Direito do Ambiente 1996, p. 87-128.

72) Public interest litigation in environmental matters before European courts.** (a) Journal of Environmental Law 1996, p. 1-18 (b) in: H. Micklitz-N. Reich (eds): Public interest litigation before European courts. Baden-Baden: Nomos 1996, p. 297-318.

71) Defizite im Vollzug des EG-Umweltrechts und ihre Ursachen.** (a) In: G. Lübbe-Wolff (ed.): Der Vollzug des europäischen Umweltrechts. Berlin 1996, p. 7-35 (b) Deficits in application of EC environmental law and its causes, in: M. Campins i Eritja-I. Pont i Castejón (eds): Perspectives de dret Comunitari ambientali. Barcelona: Bellaterra 1997, p. 471-495.

70) Der Richtlinienvorschlag über die integrierte Vermeidung und Verminderung der Umweltverschmutzung.** In: H.W. Rengeling (ed.): Integrierter und betrieblicher Umweltschutz. Köln-Berlin-Bonn-München 1996, p. 51-78.

69) Die Richtlinie 85/337 über die UVP bei öffentlichen und privaten Projekten und der Änderungsvorschlag der Europäischen Kommission KOM(93(575).** In: Euregio (ed.) Konferenz der Euregion Maas-Rhein zur grenzüberschreitenden Umweltverträglich keitsprüfung in der Europäischen Union. Aachen 1996, p. 16.

68) Adaptations to EC environmental rules: options for Central and Eastern European States. In: G. Winter (ed.): European Environmental Law. Brookfield-Singapore-Sydney 1995, p. 423-436.

67) (Book review): J. Jans, Europees Milieurecht in Nederland. Milieu en Recht 1995, p. 169-171.

66) Rights of complaint and access to information at the Commission of the EC. (a) In: S. Deimann-B. Dyssli (eds): Environmental rights. Law, litigation and access to Justice. London 1995, p. 53-70; (b) Diritto a ricorrere e accesso all'informazione presso la Commissione della Comunità Europea. Rivista Giuridica dell'Ambiente 1995, p. 597.

65) (with P. Kromarek) The Seveso Directive: an example of the interface between Community law and national implementation rules. In: Ullmann's encyclopedia of industrial chemistry 5th ed. col. B.7. Weinheim 1995.

64) European Community legislation affecting chemicals. In: Ullmann's encyclopedia of industrial chemistry. 5th ed. vol. B.7. Weinheim 1995.

63) Tendances actuelles dans le droit européen de l'environnement. In: Actes du colloque des 17 et 18 novembre 1994. Bruxelles 1995, p. 62.

62) Community environmental law under the Maastricht Treaty on European Union and the fifth environmental action programme. In: F. Abraham-K. Deketelaere-J. Stuyck (eds): Recent economic and legal developments in European environmental policy. Leuven 1995, p. 75-106.

61) Europäische Umwelt, Schutz der Umwelt und Recht. Vorträge, Reden und Berichte aus dem Europa-Institut der Universität des Saarlandes, Nr. 267. Saarbrücken 1994.

60) Actions de l'Union européenne pour la protection de l'environnement marin de la Méditerranée. Revue de l'Indemer 3/1995 p. 142-163.

59) Le contrôle et la mise en oeuvre de la législation communautaire en matière de l'environnement. Aménagement-Environnement 1995, p. 8-17.

58) Monitoring environmental implementation at Community level. In: R. Raum-Degrève-F. de Hemptinne (eds): Le droit communautaire de l'environnement. Problèmes de mise en oeuvre nationale. Luxembourg 1995, p. 13-26.

57) L'Union européenne et la responsabilité civile dans le domaine de l'environnement. In: P. Renaudière-P. van Pelt (eds): Développements récents du droit communautaire de l'environnement. Diegem 1995, p. 139-151.**

56) LIFE – un instrument financier pour l'environnement.** In: P. Renaudière-P. van Pelt (eds): Développements récents du droit communautaire de l'environnement. Diegem 1995, p. 19-28.

55) Développements récents du contrôle de l'application du droit communautaire de l'environnement. In: P. Renaudière-P. van Pelt (eds): Développements récents du droit communautaire de l'environnement. Diegem 1995, p. 3-18.

54) El dret del medi ambient a la Comunitat Europea. In: Departement de Medi Ambient(Catalunya) (ed.): Estudis de dret ambiental. Barcelona 1995, p. 27-57

53) (with P. Kromarek) Europäisches Umweltrecht.Chronik vom 1.10.91-31.3.95 Zeitschrift für Umweltrecht. Beilage 3/1995, p. 1-16.

52) Le règlement communautaires des litiges environnementaux et les particuliers. In: C. Kye (ed.): Les politiques communautaires de protection des consommateurs et de l'environnement: convergences et divergences. Diegem 1995, p. 259-276.

51) Die Rechtsprechung des Gerichtshofs der Europäischen Gemeinschaft zum Umweltrecht 1992 bis 1994. Europäische Grundrechte Zeitschrift 1995, p. 45-53.

50) European Community Environmental Law. In: Danish Association of Environmental Law (ed.): First Nordic conference on EU environmental law. Copenhagen 1994, p. 21-43.

49) Schetika me to kinotiko kai to elliniko dikeo perivallontos. In: G. Papadimitrios (ed.): i diesthisi tou koinotikou dikeou perivallontos stin Ellada. Athina 1994, p. 43.

48) (with P. Kromarek) Droit communautaire de l'environnement; chronique du 1.10.1991 au 31.12.1993 Revue Juridique de l'Environnement 1994, p. 209-248.

47) Observations sur le droit communautaire de l'environnement. L'Actualité Juridique – droit administratif 1995, p. 588-594

46) Um eine Umweltpolitik von innen bittend. Das Europäische Parlament und der Umweltschutz. Zeitschrift für Umweltrecht 1994, p. 172-177.

45) Economic, fiscal and other financial measures to contribute to waste prevention. In: L. Wiggers-Rust and others (eds): Waste prevention in the EEC. Zwolle 1994, p. 163-173.

44) (Book review) T. Schröer, Kompetenzverteilung zwischen EWG und ihren Mitgliedstaaten auf dem Gebiet des Umweltschutzes. Common Market Law Review 1993, p. 1076.

43) On the interrelation between consumer and environmental policies in the European Community.** (a) Journal of Consumer Policy 1993, p. 455 (b) (in Greek language) Nomos kai phisi 1994, p. 13.

42) - Freshwater and Community law – The European Community and atmospheric pollution in: A. Kiss-D. Shelton (eds): Manual of Environmental Law. Cambridge 1993, p. 247-252 and 351-355.

41) Die Integrierung umweltpolitischer Erfordernisse in die gemeisnchaftliche Wettbewerbspolitik. In: H.W. Rengeling (ed.): Umweltschutz und andere Politiken der Europäischen Gemeinschaft. Köln-Berlin-Bonn-München 1993, p. 47-83.

40) The interdependency of Community and Member State activity on nature protection within the european Community. Ecological Law Quarterly 1993, p. 25.

39) L'environnnement et le marché unique européen. Revue du Marché unique européen 1993, p. 45-70.

38) The function of the law in the development of sustainable products.** In: J. Niewenhuis and others (eds): De rol van het recht bij een duurzame ontwikkeling. Zwolle 1993, p. 31.

37) Environmental protection and Article 30 EEC Treaty.** Common Market Law Review 1993, p. 111-143.

36) Community environmental law – towards a systematic approach.** Oxford Yearbook of European Law 11(1991), p. 151-185.

35) Ziele und Instrumente der Umweltpolitik der Europäischen Gemeinschaften. In: Bundesverband der deutschen Gas- und Wasserwirtschaft (ed.): EG-Umweltpolitik und Umweltschutz in den neuen Bundesländern. Bonn 1992, p. 22-31.

34) The implementation of environmental laws by the European Economic Communities German Yearbook of International Law 34(1991), p. 9-53.
33) Arbeit und Konzeption der EG-Kommission in der Umweltpolitik. In: C. Calliess-B. Wegener (eds): Europäisches Umweltrecht als Chance. Taunusstein 1992, p. 33-46.
32) UVP und Abfälle; zur Umsetzung der UVP-Richtlinie in Belgien, in den Niederlanden und in der Bundesrepublik Deutschland. In: F. Antwerpes-M. Jaeger (eds): Milieueffectrapportage in Nederland, Belgie en Duitsland. Bonn 1991, p. 69-82.
31) (with P. Kromarek) Droit communautaire del'environnement; chronique du 1.1.1990 au 30.9.1991. Revue Juridique de l'Environnement 1991, p. 473.
30) La directive 90/313 sur l'accès à l'information en matière d'environnement. * (a) In: M. Pallemaerts (ed.): Le droit à l'information en matière d'environnement. Bruxelles 1991, p. 17-39; (b) Revue du Marché Commun 1991, p. 866-876.
29) Participation of environmental organisations in the activities of the EEC.* In: M. Führ-G. Roller (eds): Participation and litigation rights of environmental associations in Europe. Frankfurt-Bern-New York-Paris 1991, p. 129-139.
28) Regulation – legislation(waste) in: A. Bradshaw-R. Southwood-F. Warner (eds): The treatment and handling of wastes. London etc. 1991, p. 41-49.
27) The European Communauties and environmental policies: the system of legislation. In: P. Eilander and others (eds): Milieu als wetgevingsvraagstuk. Zwolle 1991, p. 39-88.
26) Europe: laws and enforcement. In: Environment Strategy, Europe 1991. London 1991, p. 48-49
25) Grenzen der Subsidiarität. EG-magazin 5/1991, p. 11.
24) L'application des directives en matière d'environnement. Les enjeux de l'Europe 1990, p. 41.
23) Inquinamenti da rifiuti: CEE. (a) Docter (ed) Annuario Europeo dell'Ambiente 1990, Milano 1990, p. 384; (b) Pollution-waste: EEC. Docter (ed.): European Environmental Yearbook. London 1991, p. 357.
22) Direito comunitário em materia de ambiente. Revista da Ordem dos Advogados 1989, p. 1029
21) EWG-Umweltrecht und einzelstaatliche Alleingänge.* Jahrbuch für Umwelt- und Technikrecht 1990, p. 467.
20) Environmental legal systems and their institutional and administrative law contexts: The European Economic Community. In: T. Smith-P. Kromarek (eds): Understanding US and European Environmental Law. London-Dordrecht-Boston 1989, p. 4.

19) (a) Zur innerstaatlichen Wirkung von EG-Umweltrichtlininen – Wirtschaft und Verwaltung 1990, p. 81 – Anwaltsblatt 1991, p. 368; (b) Effet national des directives communautaires de l'environnement Revue Juridique de l'Environnement 1990, p. 325 (c) The implementation of Community environmental directives within Member States: some implications of the direct effect doctrine. * Journal of Environmental Law 1991, p. 39 (d) Sobre el efecto directo de las directivas comunitarias de medio ambiente Revista de Derecho Ambiental 1991, p. 2.

18) (with P. Kromarek) Droit communautaire de l'environnement; chronique du 1.5.1988 au 31.12.1989.

17) Gegenwärtiger Stand und Entwicklungschancen der inhaltlichen Harmonisierung des Umweltrechts der EG. In: K. Korinek-H. Rill (eds): Österreichisches Wirtschaftsrecht und das Recht der EG. Vienna 1990, p. 295.

16) (a) Das Verursacherprinzip im Gemeinschaftsrecht. Zur Auslegung von Artikel 130r EWG-Vertrag.* Europäische Grundrechte Zeitschrift 1989, p. 353 (b) Le principe du pollueur-payeur en droit communautaire. Interprétation de l'article 130R du Traité CEE. Aménagement-Environnement 1991, p. 3.

15) Stand der Harmonisierungsbestrebungen beim Luft- und Gewässerschutz in der EG. In: Internationale Handelskammer, Deutsche Gruppe (ed.): Umweltschutz zwischen Harmonisierung und Wettbewerbsverzerrung – Luft- und Gewässerschutz im europäischen Vergleich. Köln 1989, p. 16.

14) The open society, its lawyers and its environment.* Journal of Environmental Law 1989, p. 1.

13) Enkele opmerkingen over de tenuitvoerlegging van de milieurichtlijnen. Asser Instituut (ed.): Europees milieurecht; praktische problemen bij de totstandkoming en uitvoering. s' Gravenhage 1989, p. 109.

12) Regelingen van de Europese Gemeenschap inzake het milieu. Asser Instituut (ed.): Europees milieurecht; praktische problemen bij de totstandkoming en uitvoering. s' Gravenhage 1989, p. 93.

11) Enforcement of Community legislation on the environment.* RSA Journal 1989, p. 243.

10) La réparation des dommages catastrophiques et le droit communautaire.* Université Catholique de Louvain (ed.): Les risques technologiques majeures en droit international et en droit communautaire. Bruxelles 1990, p. 399.

9) (with P. Kromarek) Droit communautaire de l'environnement; chronique du 1.11.1986 au 30.4.1988. Revue Juridique de l'Environnement 1988, p. 307

8) La CEE, l'environnement et la politique régionale.* (a) Revue du Marché Commun 1988, p. 539; (b) in: M. Prieur (ed.): Europe des régions et environnement. Limoges-Paris 1989, p. 153.

7) (a) Grundrecht auf Umwelt und Gemeinschaftsrecht.* Europäische Grundrechte Zeitschrift 1988, p. 328; (b) Le droit á l'environnement et le droit communautaire in: Société portugaise pour le droit de l'environnement (ed.): La garantie du droit à l'environnement. Lisboa 1989, p. 216.

6) Le déversement des déchets en mer et le droit communautaire. (a) Revue du Marche Commun 1988, p. 328; (b) in: Société francaise pour le droit de l'environnement (ed.): Droit de l'environnement marin. Développements récents. Paris 1988, p. 133.

5) Aufgabenverflechtung zwischen Europäischer Gemeinschaft, Bund und Ländern, dargestellt am Beispiel des Umweltschutzes. In: S. Magiera-D. Merten (eds): Bundesländer und Europäische Gemeinschaft Berlin 1988, p. 191.

4) Zur Umweltbeschwerde des Einzelnen nach EWG-Recht.* In: Deutscher Naturschutzring (ed.): Von der Wirtschafts- zur Umweltgemeinschaft. Bonn 1988, p. 29.

3) Keine Absichtserklärungen, sondern durchsetzbares Recht: die Kontrolle der Anwendung von EWG-Umweltrichtlinien. (a) In: L. Gündling-B. Weber (eds): Dicke Luft in Europa. Aufgaben und Probleme der Europäische Umweltpolitik. Heidelberg 1988, p. 201; (b) Du contrôle de l'application des directives communautaires en matière de l'environnement – Fiscalité européenne 4/1988, p. 45 Revue du Marché Commun 1988, p. 22 – Integració Europea 4/1990 p. 14; (c) De controle op de toepassing van de EEG-milieurichtlijnen. Asser Instituut (ed.) Europees milieurecht; praktische problemen bij de totstandkoming en uitvoering. s'Gravenhage 1988, p. 8.

2) (a) Einheitliche Europäische Akte und Umwelt; Überlegungen zu einigen neuen Bestimmungen im Gemeinschaftsrecht. In: H.W. Rengeling (ed.): Europäisches Umweltrecht und Europäische Umweltpolitik. Köln-Berlin-Bonn-München 1988, p. 137; (b) The Single European Act and environmental protection; reflections on several new provisions in Community law.* Common Market Law Review 1987, p. 659; (c) L'Acte Unique Européen et la protection de l'environnement. Revue Juridique de l'environnement 1987, p. 449.

1) (with P. Kromarek) Droit communautaire de l'environnement; chronique du 1.1.1985 au 31.10.1986. Revue Juridique de l'environnement.

* English chapters of 'Focus on European Environmental Law 1992'

** English chapters of 'Focus on European Environmental Law 1997'.

ow or

a
he